Edward C. Moody

Handbook History
of the
Town of York

◆M◆A◆I◆N◆E◆

from
Early Times
to the
Present

Edward C. Moody

HERITAGE BOOKS
2015

HERITAGE BOOKS
AN IMPRINT OF HERITAGE BOOKS, INC.

Books, CDs, and more—Worldwide

For our listing of thousands of titles see our website
at
www.HeritageBooks.com

A Facsimile Reprint
Published 2015 by
HERITAGE BOOKS, INC.
Publishing Division
5810 Ruatan Street
Berwyn Heights, Md. 20740

Originally published 1914

International Standard Book Numbers
Paperbound: 978-0-7884-1455-8
Clothbound: 978-0-7884-6142-2

DEDICATED
TO THOSE
WHO SHALL AFTER LIVE

FOREWORD

THE HISTORIAN of low or high degree of attainment is liable to the charge of plagiarism. He can only record facts and describe events and scenes which he gathers from public documents, and from the description of others, save in the matter of contemporary affairs of which he was a witness and perhaps an incident. There are but few facts or incidents told in the pages of this book which may not be found elsewhere; and it is impossible to narrate events already penned by able writers, and to avoid likeness of expression, especially when one has not the advantage of a classically polished education. Using in part a quotation of Hon. J. C. Stewart—"To rescue from oblivion the memory of former incidents, and to render a just tribute of renown to the many great and wonderful actions both of Greeks and Barbarians, Herodotus of Halicarnassus produces this Historical Essay," is the modest introduction to the great work written two thousand three hundred and forty years ago by the "Father of History."

Eighteen hundred and twenty years ago, Josephus in his preface to his renowned work, "Antiquities of the Jews," used these words: "Those who undertake to write histories do not, I perceive, take that trouble on one and the same account, but for many reasons, and those are very different one from another, for some of them apply themselves to this part of learning to show their skill in composition, and that they may therein acquire a reputation for speaking finely; others of them there are who write histories in order to gratify those that happen to be concerned in them, and on that account have spared no pains, but rather gone beyond their own abilities in performance; but others there are who of necessity and by force are driven to write history, because they were concerned in the facts."

York is the native town of the writer of this volume, born within the sight and sound of the roaring sea; and I hope to present a biographical sketch of its birth, growth and maturity, that will be of interest and value. I wish to give, as far as within me lies, a faithful record of our wonderful past and present growth, and it has been for me a work of love — dimmed with the realization of my inadequacy to rightly perform it.

"Our Grand Old Town, with honest pride,
From sea-girt shore to forest wide,
    We would proclaim thy glory.
Ye men of York with purpose strong,
The Wheel of Progress roll along,
    And neither pause nor falter;
But freely each his offering bring,
The best he has of everything,
    To lay upon the Altar."

Edward C. Moody.

Feb. 14th, 1914.
    York Village, Maine.

CONTENTS

PAGE

Dedication ....

Foreword 3

Contents 5

Charter 7

Early General History.

Part I 16

Part II 21

Part III 32

Part IV 35

Early Families 40

Early Prominent Men 41

York in Colonial War—Louisburg.................... 58

York in the Revolution............................ 64

York in the War of 1812.......................... 72

York in the Civil War............................ 74

The Olde Gaol 79

First Parish Meeting House........................ 90

Court House, Now Town Hall....................... 96

York in the Constitutional Convention............. 101

Civil List 104

Passing of the Customs District of York........... 107

York Harbor and Beach Railroad,—Almshouse and
New Home,—York Hospital,—Electric Plant,—York
County National Bank,—York Realty Company.—
Newspaper,—Water Company,—Schools 110

The New Bridge 131

Proposed Division of the Town.................... 144

Commemoration of the Two Hundred and Fiftieth Anniversary 165

The Beginning of York as a Summer Resort.......... 174

Cotton and Woolen Mills 179

Facts, Legends, Traditions.

Witchcraft,—Cochranism,—The Norridgewock Expedition,—St. Aspinquid,—Story of Boon Island,—

The Devil's Invention,—Tea Party,—Hull A'Malew,
—Story of Seymour's Hanging,—Copies of Early
Land Grants,—The Earliest Authentic Record in
Handwriting of Town Clerk,—Tommy Disco,—
Wreath on Samuel Moody's Grave,—The Last Revo-
lutionary Survivor 183
Shipbuilding, Shipping, and Sea Captains............. 213
First Parish, First Church of Christ................. 216
Second Parish 224
Methodist 231
Episcopal 236
Non-Sectarian 237
Union Congregational 238
Baptist 239
Christian 242
Roman Catholic 246
Physicians and Surgeons 248
Country Club 250

CHARTER

TO ALL TO WHOME THESE PRESENTS shall come, I Sr Ferdinando Gorges, Knight Lord of ye Province of Mayne within ye Territories of New England in America send Greeting   Whereas our Soverig^e Lord the Kings Majestie that now is by his Highness letter Patente under the Great Seal of England bearing Date at Westminister the third Day of April in ye fifteenth year of his Majesty Reigne of England &c: hath created me ye said Sr Ferdinando Gorges, absolute Lord of the said Province of Mayne and thereby hath given unto me and my Heirs absolute power and authoritie over the said Province & of all ye Lands within ye Precincts & bounds of ye same & over all ye Inhabitants & people that from time to time shall be resident & abiding within ye limits and precints of ye said Province for ye welfare & good Government of all his Maj^{esty} loving subjects that shall have recourse unto ye same AND WHEREAS his said Maj^{est} by ye same Letters Patente hath further given & granted unto me my Heirs & Assigns full power leave licence & authorite to errect build & raise from time to time in ye Province Territories & coasts aforesaid & every or any of them such and so many Forts fortresses platforms, Castles, Cities, Towns & Villages & all Fortifications whatsoever & ye same & every of them to Fortifie & furnishe wth Men ordinances powder shot armo^e: & all other weapons ammunition and habiltiments of warr both for Defense & Offense whatsoever as to me my Heirs & Assigns or any of them shall seem meete & Convenient and Likewise to Commit from time to time ye Government Custodie and Defence thereof unto such person

& persons as to me my Heirs and Assigns shall seem meet
AND to ye several Cities Burroughs and Towns to grant
Letters or shires of Incorporations wth all Liberties and
things belonging to the same and in ye said several Cities
Burroughs & Towns to constitute such & so many Markets,
Marts and faires and to grant such meete tolles, Customs
Duties and Previlidges to or with ye same as by me my
Heirs & Assigns shall be thought fitt as in & by ye said
Letters Patente amongst Diverse & Sundrey other privi-
lidges liberties freedoms & Jurisdictions therein Contained
more plainly & at large it doth or may appear.   NOW
KNOW ye that I the said Sr Ferdinando Gorges having
allready through God's assistance settled the said Province
& Inhabitants thereof in a hopefull way of Goverment and
being desirous by all good ways and means to further and
advance ye same have thought fitt & resolved on to create
a citie or Town within ye said Province & to Incorporit y^e
same and to appoint thereunto such officers & Courts of
Justice and such liberties previlidges & Jurisdictions as are
hereafter in theirs (space)   particularised set forth and
declared AND DO THEREFORE for me my Heirs &
Assigns Grant ordaine & Establish that ye Circuite of ye
said Incorporation within ye Province aforesaid shall extend
from ye Beginning of ye Intrance in of ye River commonly
called & known by ye name of Agamenticus ∕ Agamenticus
& so up ye said River seven Inglish Miles and all along ye
East and North East side of ye seashore Three English
miles in Breadth from the Entrance of ye said River & up
into ye Mayne Land seven Miles Butting with ye seven
Miles from ye sea side up ye said River ye Breadth of three
Miles opposite thereunto AND that the said Citie or Town
shall be errected & Built in such place of the said Lymitts
as shall be thought most convenient by ye Assent of ye

Deputie of the said Province the Steward General there of
& ye Mayor and Justices of ye said Citie or Town for ye
time being And to ye end that ye said Citie or Town &
Bounds or Lymitts of ye Incorporation before set forth and
Discribed may for Ever hereafter be more particularlie known
& Distinguished, My will is that ye same from henceforth
be noiated formed and Called by ye name of Gorgeanna And
by that name of Gorgeanna, ye said Circuite Precinct Lymitt
and place aforesaid I do by these presents for me my Heirs
& Assigns name call erect found & Establish and by that
name to have continuance for Ever And for ye Better Governing of the said Citie or Town & Lymitt before men-
tinoned I do Constitute Assigne Lymitte & Appoint that
from henceforth for Ever hereafter there shall be one Body
politique and Corporate which shall have perpetual succession and shall consist of a Maio^r twelve Aldermen and four
and Twenty to be of ye Common Counsell there, and of ye
Rest of ye Coialtie of ye said corporation, and that the Maio^r
shall be yearly chosen by ye Common Counsel   Burgos-
sess of ye said Corporation or ye Greater part of them upon
every Five and Twentieth Day of March for Ever and that
ye Deputies Governor of the said Province shall appoint
Assigne & Notifie the first Maio^r for ye year to come who
shall enter into his office upon ye five and Twentieth Day of
March next ensuing ye date hereof and that the said Deputy
Governor shall likewise for this year appoint ye persons that
shall be Aldermen & that the Major part of the freeholders
shall elect & notifie such as shall be of ye Common Counsell
there, from time to time forever.   And I do appoint that
two fo ye said Aldermen shall be Justices written ye said
Corporation who shall be chosen fro this year alsoe by my
said Deputy Governor.   And that the said Maio^r Justices,
Aldermen, Common Council and Inhabitants of the Lymitts

& Precincts aforesaid & their Successors shall be in & by
those presents incorporated to have a perpetual succession
for Ever in Deed facte & name   And shall be And be oud
Body Corporate and Politique.   AND FURTHERMORE
I do by these presents for me and my Heirs Grant unto the
said Maio^r & Couialtie & Tehie successors that they and
their successors shall be and shall con^tinue persons able and
capable in Law from time to time as our Body and shall
have full power and authority and Lawfull Capacitie &
Abilitie to purchse take hold receive enjoy & to have to them
& their successors for Ever any Mann's Land Tenements,
Rents, Royalties, Previlidges Immunities revertions Annui-
ties Hereditaments Goods and Chattles whatsoever within
ye said Province of Mayne of & from me my Heirs &
Assigns and the same or any part thereof to Alein sell away
and to do execute ordayne & perform all other matters &
things whatsoever belonging or appertaining to a corporation.   And I do further constitute ordayne and appoint that
there shall be forever hereafter within the said corporation
a Recorded & a Town Clark which shall be from time to
time elected and chosen by the May^or Aldermen Common
Council & Coialtie of ye said Corporation or the Greater
part of them whereof the Maio^r for the time being to be
chief in the election & to have a Double voice   And I do
further by these presents ordaine & Create within ye said
Citie or town and Corporation a Court Leete or Law day
to be held for ever twice every year within a moneth of the
Feast of Easther & Michelmass for the good Government
&f weale publique of the said Corporation & for the the
punishing of all Offenders the same to be kept by the Recorder for this time being and the fines paynes & Amez-
tialts (?) from time to time to be to the use of the maio^r
of the said Town for the time being for Ever.   AND I do

also by these presents create and Establish with in the said
corporation a Court of Justice for the hearing and deter-
mining of all actions & differences between parties & parties
within the said Corporation) Noe action of Debt exceeding
ten pounds and the power of the said Court not extending
to the taking away of life or member nor to any title of
lands the same Court to be according or as neere as may be
to the Court of his Maj^{est} Court of Chancery at Westminister wherein the Maio^r for ye time being to sit as Judge with
the Recorder & Aldermen or so many of the said Aldermen
as shall be there & the Town Clark to be the Clark and minister of the said Court & in all Judgements and decrees it
shall be lawfull for ye partie against whome any decree or
Judgement shall passe to make an appeal to me or my Deputy
so as ye same be done within fourty days after such Judgement or decree made & not after nor otherwise AND I do
further create & appoint two or four serjants to attend on
ye said Maio^r who shall be called forever Serjants of ye
White Rod & shall serve & return all processes & precepts
Issuing out of ye said Court from time to time and shall be
Elected & Chosen by the Maio^r & Aldermen of the said Citie
or Town or the greater part of them whereof ye maio^r to
have a double voice & upon any misdemeanor of such serjant
of serjants ye Maio^r for ye time being & ye Aldermen or ye
greater part of them shall have power to put them out &
remove them from the said service & Imployments.   And
further I do grant by these / these presents for me and my
Heirs unto the said Maio^r & Coailtie and their successors
that they and their successors shall have and enjoy for ever
a common seal to be engraven according to their own discretion whereby the said Incorporation may or shall seal
any manner of Instrument touching ye same corporation &
such Maio^r's Lands Tenements, rents, Revertions, Ammuni-

ties, Hereditaments, goods, chattels, affairs & any other
things belonging unto or in any wise appertaining to the
same or any of them. And I do Further for me & my
Heirs for ye Considerations aforesaid & for divers other
good causes and considerations me moving by these presents
absolutely give grant and confirm unto the said Maio^r &
Coailtie of Gorgeana aforesaid & their successors for Ever
All such & so much of the aforesaid Lands, Lymitts, places,
& precincts hereby before perticularie Bounded out & Expressed as are not formerly granted & thereupon seized on
& possessed by any other person or Persons & ane called by
the name of Gorgeana aforesaid. Together alsoe with all
the Haven, Ports, Creeks, Rivers, Waters Fishings & all &
singular other profets commodities Jurisdictions previlidges
ffranchisses & preheminences within or belonging to the said
precincts & Lymitts called Gorgeana aforesaid or to any of
them. TO HAVE HOLD POSSE & enjoy all & singular
ye aforesaid Lymitts, precincts & places called Gorgeana &
all & singular other the said Grants premises with all &
singular their appurtenances to the said Maio^r & coailtie &
their successors & Assigns for Ever To the only use &
behoof of the said Maio^r & Coailtie their successors &
assigns for Ever. TO BEE Holden of ye Kings Maj^{est}
his Heirs & Successors of his Mamo* of Caste of Grrenwich
in the County of Kent in free & Common Cotage & note in
Capite nor by Knights service as the said Province of Mayne
is now held Yeilding & Paicinge therefore yearly to me the
said Ferdinando Gorges, my Heirs & Assigns on Quarter
of Wheat at Michalmas yearlie & every year for Ever And
in Regard that due Alleigance to his Maj^{est}, His Heirs and
Successors my Ever be rendered as in the said Province so
in & within the said Incorporation I do by these presents
order, ordayne & appoint that before any Maio^r now or here-

after to be named of the said Town shall execute his office
he shall first take ye oath of Alleigance towards his Maj^{est}
which shall be administered by the Governor or Chancellors
of the said Province & likewise that the said Justices &
Common Council & the Recorder Town Clerk and Serjants
& all other officers, their shall take the like oath to be administered by the Maio^r for the time being & alsoe that the
Governor of Chancellor of the said Province shall admin-
ister such formal oaths to the Maio^r as he and the Greater
part of the Council of the said Province & the Greater part
of the Incorporation shall devise & think meet for the due
administerinf of Justice within ye said Incorporation & for
the well Governing of the same to the ╱ the best good of the
said Incorporation and that the said Justices shall take an
oath to the like purpose to be administered by the Maio^r &
that the Recorder Town Clark and oters shall take such
oaths as are proper to the due execution of their office, places
and to such other intents as to the Maio^r and Justices shall
seem most fitt for the best good of ye said Incorporation and
the same oaths shall be administered alsoe by the said Maio^r
in the sight of the said Justices or any of them. AND I
do further for me and my Heirs by these presents give and
grant unto the said Maio^r and Coailtie full power, leave,
license and authority from time to time to make wharfs and
Keeife for Lading and Unlading goods and Merchandize.
And to erect, rayse and Build in & within the Lymitts and
precincts of the said Incorporation such and so many Forts,
fortresses, platforms and other fortifications whatsoever and
the same & every of them to fortifie with men and all manner
ammunition for the safety of the said Incorporation and for
the better safety &   need be of
the said whole Provicne as to the said Maio^r & Coailtie or
the greater part of them shall seem meet. And in Further

consideration of the tender regard I have and care to the
further good & advancement of the happiness and weale
publique of the said City or Town, and Incorporation & of
the said Province & that Trading Commerce may be the
more readilie advancte I do by these presents create, oor-
dayne appoint & establish a market to be kept upon Wednesday in every week for Ever within the said Town and that
their shall be two fairs held and kept there every year for
Ever hereafter viz. upon the Feast day of St. James and
St. Paul and that all the Benefit of ye Toll & other Customs
incident and belonging to fairs & markets shall forever re-
down to the use & advantage of the said Maio^r for ye time
being. AND I DO further by these presents for me and
my Heirs license and authorize the said Maio^r Aldermen
Council and Coailtie for the time being and the greater part
of them to make all such good & wholesome Laws for the
better for the better ordering and Governing of ye said Corporation as to them shall seem meete the same not being
repugnant but agreeable as neere as may be to the Laws of
this Kingdom of England nor repugnant or contrarie to the
Laws of this said Province now or hereafter to be established
there. AND I Do further by these presents for me and my
Heirs give and grant unto the said Maio^r & Coailtie and
Incorporation such and so many previlidges abortions &
freedons as far as in me lieth, as the City of Bristol holdeth
by their Charter of Incorporation. And I Do Further for
me and my Heirs Covenant my successors by these presents
that they and their successors shall at any time make any
Doubt of the validity in Law of this present Charter or be
desirous to have ye same revinell with ammendments of such
Imperfection as shall appear fitt ————— to be reformed
that then upon the suite and entreatie of the said Maio^r and
Coailtie and their successors for the time being I and my

Heirs shall forthwith pass a new Grantee and Cahrter to the said Maio^r and Coailtie with such further & better ————— promises as by the Council on the behalf of me and my Heirs anf od the said Maio^r and Coailtie and their successors shall be reasonably devised or advised   AND FURTHER that all doubts or questions that may arise touching this present charter or Coailtie & their successors or thing herein contained shall be constructed and expounded to be enbre and is hereby declared to be and enbre to the most benefit & and advantage of the said Incorporations and of every member thereof.   AND LASTLY I do for me and my Heirs and Assignes and command my Deputy Governor and all my Council and Freeholders of ye said Province to take notice of this present charter and to be ayding and assisting to the said Maio^r and Coailtie their successors and assgns in all things touching the same.

In witness whereof I the said Sr Ferdinando Gorges have hereunto sett my hand and seal the first day of March in the seventeenth year of the Reigne of our Soverigne Lord, Charles by the Grace of God of England, Scotland, France and Ireland King Defender of the Faith &c. 1641.

YORK

EARLY GENERAL HISTORY

PART I

"Forty miles from Portland, and thirty south of Alfred. Terminus of York Harbor and Beach Railroad. Settled about 1624. Originally called Agamenticus. Endowed with a city charter and government by Sir Ferdinando Gorges, April 10, 1641, under the name of Gorgeana. The first English city upon the continent of America. Thos. Gorges was the first mayor. It was organized in 1652 into a town under the name of York, from the English town, being the second in the State. It was the shire town of Yorkshire county (by order of the Legislature of Massachusetts), which included the whole province of Maine, from 1716 to 1735; then shire town with Portland (then called Falmouth) of the whole province from 1735 to 1760; then shire town of the County of York from 1760 to 1800. In 1802 Alfred was made a shire town with York, and continued so until 1832, when all the courts were removed to Alfred. Population: 1850, 2980; 1860, 2825; 1870, 2654; 1880, 2453; 1890, 2444; 1900, 2668. Valuation: 1860—polls, 614; estates, $702,218; 1870—polls, 614; estates, $771,776; 1880—polls, 625; estates, $716,798; 1890—polls, 735; estates, $1,228,716; 1900—polls, 735; estates, $1,815,471; 1904—polls, 760; estates, $2,323,440."

THE ABOVE has been given in the Maine Register as the geographical location, and Historical Epitome of York for the last fifty years. Earlier writers tell us that at least three hundred years ago it was known on the maps as Boston. The "Hub" was where York Harbor and Village now are, before there was a wharf built in Boston at the mouth of Charles River. Capt. John Smith, who in 1614 explored the coast of Maine as far eastward as the Penobscot, had given it the Indian name of Agamenticus. He projected and drew up a map with the Indian names of the rivers and principal harbors and islands along the coast, and presented it to Prince Charles, heir apparent, afterwards King Charles I of England. He changed many of the names upon it to

English names. Agamenticus as laid down on the map was changed to Boston. This was in 1616, two years after Capt. Smith's explorations. Also on the same map appeared the name Plymouth—where the Pilgrims landed some years later. Our plantation was established under the guiding hand of Sir Ferdinando Gorges, the oldest and by far the most prominent promoter of these settlements of Colonies in New England. He had received the original New England Charter in 1606, and was the first president of the first Council organized under it for the initiative of settlements. He was also much interested in the Popham Colony, and sent his Captains, Smith and Vines, on many voyages to this coast before 1616. In 1620 he and his associates obtained a new charter from King James by which the various original grants of New England were made; and in 1622, in company with Capt. John Mason, obtained the grant of New Hampshire and Maine, extending from the Merrimac to the Kennebec river. Under this grant the first settlement was made by their united labors in 1623 at the mouth of the Piscataqua, now Portsmouth and Newcastle. And the same year a permanent settlement was made at Agamenticus, now York.

In this settlement Mason had no share, although they operated together at Piscataqua until 1634. Thus Portsmouth and York appear to be children of the same year. But as Rev. Rufus M. Sawyer in his sketch of "Agamenticus & Gorgeana, or York, Maine," published in 1866, says, "It is not quite certain when civilized men first pitched their tents at Agamenticus." Or Edward E. Hale, "What was his name? I do not know his name. Whoever he may have been he knew that his shallop had found a safe anchorage and good harbor." Standing where the Marshall House now is, he traced a navigable stream for miles. A fertile valley partly intervale from one to two miles wide and heavily wooded with pine and oak. On the eastern bank of the river, near the ocean, was an admirable site for a future city, backed by the knoll of Sentry Hill, from which, inland, could be seen a bird's eye view of the three-mile-square plantation, which in 1642 was to be enlarged to twenty-one square miles.

In 1623 the colonists sent out by Sir Ferdinando Gorges came prepared to clear away forest, procure lumber, build mills and ships, and cultivate the ground. The millwrights and carpenters had the tools of their trades; the agriculturists, their oxen, and farming implements. They began the embryo city by building cabins on the eastern bank of Agamenticus River near its mouth. This colony was in charge of his nephew, Capt. William Gorges, and Col. Francis Norton, a young officer, in whom he placed great confidence, and whom by merit alone had advanced from a common foot soldier to the rank of Lieut. Colonel.

In 1636, Capt. William Gorges was sent from England with full power as Governor of the Province, in which position he acted nearly two years. At this time Gorges really had no power to establish a government over his province. The council referred to under the Charter of 1606, and which held its right from the King alone, had dissolved, and surrendered their Charter. Doubtless the discovery of this fact caused him to recall his nephew so soon after the commencement of his administration. However, Sir Ferdinando went to work earnestly to secure a new charter from the King. He wished for one that would not only insure a perfect title to the land, but convey with it full civil sovereignty within the jurisdiction of his province. This was granted on the third day of April, 1639, and conferred upon him, as lord proprietor of the province, almost absolute power of government. He could now commission Governors and

Councillors. The first Governor chosen and commissioned was Sir Thomas Jocelyn, who declined the position. Thomas Gorges was next appointed, and sent across with a commission for himself and his associates in Council. Here follows an abstract from the "York Records Book A."

Sir Ferdinando Gorges by Commission appoints—

	Sir Thomas Jocelyn,	Knight	
	Richard Vines,	Steward General	
	Francis Champernoon		
Sept. 2d	Henry Joselin	Esquires	Councillors
1639	Richard Bonighton		
	William Hooke	Gent.	
	Edward Godfrey		

Second Commission

	Thomas Gorges		
	Richard Vines,	Steward General	
	Henry Joselin		
	Francis Champernoon		Councillors
March 10	Richard Bonighton		
1639-40	William Hooke		
	Edward Godfrey,	Esquires	

Thomas Gorges, appointed Secretary.

OATH

Here follows the oath the Councillors were required to take—swearing before God and by the Bible:

"I do swear and protest before God Almighty and by the holy contents of this Book, to be a faithful servant and Councillor unto Sir Ferdinando Gorges, Knight, my Lord of the Province of Mayne, and to his heirs and assigns to do and perform to the utmost of my power all dutiful respects to him, or them belonging, concealing their Councils, and without respect of persons, to do, perform, and give my opinion in all causes, according to my conscience and best understanding both, as I am a Councillor for hearing of causes, and otherwise freely to give him, or them my opinion as I am a Councillor for matters of States or Commonwealths, and that I will not conceal from him or them and their Council any matter of conspiracy or mutinous practice against my said Lord and his heirs, but will instantly after my knowledge thereof, discover the same and prosecute the authors thereof with all diligence and severity according to Justice, and thereupon do humbly kiss the Book."

Of the Deputy Governor and Councillors, Thomas Gorges, Edward Godfrey, and William Hooke were residents of Agamenticus; Richard Vines lived at Winter Harbor; Henry Jocelyn at Beak Point; Francis Champernoon (loving nephew) at Piscataqua, now Kittery; and Richard Bonighton at Saco. Thomas Gorges, whom Sir Ferdinando calls his "truly and well beloved cousin," arrived in the province in 1640 and was Governor about four years. He built his house at Agamenticus on the point of land known then and now as Gorges Point, which lies between the Judicature Creek and the river, about three and one-half miles from the sea. Here he resided until 1644 when he finally departed for England. The remains of the cellar of his house may still be seen.

It is said by Williamson and Dr. Belknap that Thomas Gorges on his arrival at Agamenticus found affairs, both public and private, in a lamentable state of disorder. The Lord Proprietor's buildings which had cost him large sums of money were greatly dilapidated and his personal property had been squandered. The young Governor went to work with zeal and soon had a good degree of order from out the confusion. In all his efforts he was strongly aided and heartily sustained by that eminent citizen, and friend, Edward Godfrey of the Council, "than whom no man in the province was a more earnest supporter and faithful public officer." Governor Gorges was a young man who had received a law education at the Inns Court, Westminister. As before intimated, he entered upon his government determined to discharge its duties promptly and with fidelity. He was also an active patron of trade and commerce, a considerable amount of which had grown already between Agamenticus, Piscataqua and Saco, and the colonies farther east at St. Johns and Nova Scotia. Much of the disorder

which Gov. Gorges found existent was the result of the
actions and teaching of the notorious George Burdett, who
purported to be a minister of the Gospel. He had been
brought before the First General Court for lewd and dis-
orderly conduct, but he had managed to gain a strong influence in political matters. (Burdett will be referred to later
in this work.)

However, a new era was about to dawn on the colony,
so well had Gov. Gorges and Edward Godfrey, in whom
Sir Ferdinando placed implicit trust and whose confidence
he had never betrayed, carried on their work. So well did
the settlement thrive under their management that Sir Ferdinando less than two years after receiving his grant from
King Charles, conceived the idea and carried out the design
of making the plantation of Agamenticus a *"borough"* and
then a city. This brings us to the second phase of our settlement, it being the time when corporate privileges were conferred. Williamson gives the date of "borough" charter,
as April 10, 1641, and the "city" charter, March 1, 1642.
Hon. Nathaniel G. Marshall gives the date of the city charter as March 1, 1641, which is twenty days earlier than
Williamson makes the date of the borough charter. Clayton in his History of York County says, "I am convinced
that Mr. Marshall's copy is correct in every particular."

Part II

THE FIRST Charter formed Agamenticus into a "Borough." It included a territory "three miles every way from
church, chapel, or oratory of the plantation," and gave power
to the burgesies or inhabitants to elect annually a mayor and
eight aldermen, and to hold property to any amount. The
mayor and the board of aldermen were authorized to make
by-laws, to erect fortifications and garrison houses, and to

hold municipal courts for the trial of all misdemeanors and civil causes once in three weeks. History and historical tradition tell us that the inhabitants of incorporated Agamenticus were much pleased, and highly appreciated the privileges granted their town and were disposed to guard them with jealous care against all encroachments of the general court. Therefore, when the Court convened in June at Saco, Edward Godfrey and three of the aldermen, with delegates from the burgesies, went before that tribunal, and entered their protest against any interference with their corporate rights and privileges. They said that, while they acknowledged the authority of the Provincial Charter of the Lord Proprietor, and cheerfully rendered submission to all the requirements of the government established under it, they did not wish their appearance at Court then, or at any other time, should be considered as in any way prejudical to their borough rights and privileges, and they asked that their protest might be authenticated by a notary and entered upon the records, which was done according to their request. These "borough privileges" were soon superseded by the more enlarged privileges of a city. Sir Ferdinando, who had all along made the place the special object of his interest and loving care, on March 1, 1641, conferred upon it a city charter. The first election of mayor and aldermen under this charter was held March 25, 1642. At this first election held by the voters of the city of Gorgeana, which then according to Williamson had a population of about three hundred, Thomas Gorges was elected mayor, and Edward Godfrey, Roger Garde, George Puddington, Bartholmew Bartnett, Edward Johnson, Arthur Bragdon, Henry Simpson and John Rogers were elected aldermen. Thus Agamenticus became the *first incorporated English city on this continent*, with the graceful name of GORGEANA.

As earlier stated, the corporate limits of this city embraced an area of twenty-one square miles. The whole lay in the form of a parallelogram on the northern side of Agamenticus river, extending up seven miles from its mouth and five miles upon the seashore. The officers consisted of a mayor, twelve aldermen, twenty-four common councilmen and a clerk, annually elected by the freeholders on the twenty-fifth of March. The mayor and aldermen were ex-officio Justices, and had the appointment of four sergeants, whose insignia of office was a white rod, and whose duties it was to serve all judicial processes. The courts were two—one held every Monday by the mayor, aldermen and recorder or clerk, for the trial of all offenses not extending to life, and all civil suits excepting titles to lands not exceeding ten pounds; the other was a court holden twice a year by the recorder for preserving the rights of the corporation and the punishment of the abuse of public trusts. Appeals were allowed to the Lord Proprietor or his Deputy Governor in person. Bancroft, speaking of Agamenticus, said, "Tho' in truth but a poor village she became a chartered borough and Sir Ferdinando, like another Romulus, resolved to perpetuate his name and under the name of Gorgeana the land around York became as good a city, as seals and parchment, a Mayor and Aldermen, a Chancery Court and Courtleet, Sergeants and white rods, can make of a town of three hundred inhabitants, and its petty officers."

The city of Gorgeana and the early settlements, religiously, were under the direction of Episcopalians. Gorges was instructed by the Court of England to establish the Episcopal form of worship throughout his province as appears in the following extract from the Charter: "Our will and pleasure is, that the religion now professed in the Church of England, and ecclesiastical government now used in the

same, shall be ever hereafter professed, and with as much
convenient speed as may be settled and established in and
throughout the province." Thus Gorgeana was to be the
seat of Ecclesiastical power, as well as civil; and also the
residence of the Bishop, and other Episcopal dignitaries. It
is not certain whether she was ever blessed with a settled
curate or rector of that order. Doubtless Episcopal worship was enjoyed for there was a "Church Chapel or Oratory." And we hear of several ministers of the same faith
in the province of Maine at that time. Robert Jordan of
Casco, conducted Episcopal worship in different places for
nearly thirty years. In 1675 he moved to Portsmouth and
died there in 1679 at the age of sixty-eight years. He left
a will providing for his widow (Sarah Winter) and their
children, John, Robert, Samuel, Dominicus, Jedidiah, and
Jeremiah. Richard Gibson, a scholarly man and popular
preacher, labored also at Casco, Portsmouth and the Isle
of Shoals for six or seven years, beginning in 1637. He
probably visited Gorgeana frequently in the last years of his
ministry, as it was but eight miles distant, and at the present
day Rev. Harold M. Folsom, Rector of St. John's in Portsmouth, "breaks the bread of life" at St. George's and Trinity, located in the proposed modern town of "Gorges." This
Mr. Gibson it would seem was somewhat of a politician, for
he attempted to make the Islanders at the Shoals revolt from
Massachusetts and come under Gorges government. Other
Episcopal clergymen preached at times in the early settlement of Maine. Consequently it would naturally follow that
that form of worship was frequently, if not continually, observed at Gorgeana, the seat of power. But now and then
a Puritan minister found his way to, and labored in, this
proud little city, or among the people of Agamenticus before
the city was founded, for according to Belknap the first Col-

onists were very reckless and licentious. Mention is made
of Rev. Mr. Thompson, a pious and learned minister, who
came to this country in 1637. Savage says of him: "He
was a very gracious, sincere man, a very holy man, who had
been an instrument of much good at Agamenticus." However, at this period in our history there were troublous times
in England. As Edward C. Moody truly states it in an address delivered before the York Association in 1894: "A new
power had arisen in England, Charles I had lost his throne
and about to lose his head. Oliver Cromwell, Protector of
the Faith, ruled England, and a dark shadow hangs around
Gorgeana." Sir Fernando took an active part in the cause
of the King. He was taken captive by Cromwell and imprisoned; he suffered the loss of his property and died in 1647.
Under this state of affairs, many of the people of the Province
of Maine sought a union with Massachusetts. And the great
Charter of the Bay Company was enrolled before the General
Court in Boston and so interpreted as to give Massachusetts
full claim to all the territory embraced in the Gorges Charter,
and Commissioners were soon on their way to reorganize
the government of the Province of Maine. On receipt of
the news of Sir Fernando's death, Edward Godfrey was
elected Governor of the territory, which belonged to Gorges,
and he was acting as such when the Commissioners from
Massachusetts, selected by the General Court under their
new interpretation, arrived. Mr. Marshall, in his address
says: "Mr. Godfrey and his associates resisted to the utmost of their ability this encroachment on their rights, and
appealed to the Court of England for redress, but the King,
his friend, was shorn of power to aid him, Cromwell was in
the ascendant, and he, probably remembering Gorges as his
active opposer in the struggle from which he had recently
come out victorious, was not inclined to render the friends of

Gorges any favor. The result was that all the possessions of Gorges were transferred to the Massachusetts Bay Company, and Godfrey, his associates and all our ancestors residing here became subject to that Company. This happened in the year 1652." We are told that Godfrey yielded gracefully and signed the articles of submission that were required. The Massachusetts Bay Company then entered into full possession.

Our City charter was revoked and the name of York was given by which we have since been known. A recent attempt to restore part of the name to part of the territory to be called the town of Gorges, as is known did not materialize. "We took our name from what was once the proudest city of Britain," Moody in his address said. The City of York in Britain was founded by the Emperor Agricola, eighteen hundred and fourteen years ago, and was the political and military capitol of the realm. There the most noted body of troops of Rome that then ruled the world was stationed. It was called the "Victorious Legion" and occupied the city upwards of three hundred years. There the Governor resided and administered justice. It had numerous temples and public buildings, and had attached to it the name of "Another Rome," and here, too, in this city in the fourth century occurred a most notable event which has made its mark on the history of mankind, for it was at York that Constantine the Great, the first Christian Emperor of Rome, was so proclaimed, and through his influence, Christianity became the established religion of the Empire. The walls and towers of Old York still stand, tho' ivy covered monuments to the ancient glory and power of the city whence we took our name." What is there in a name? Mr. Marshall says of the change, "As if the cruel company could hardly spare us many letters of the alphabet for a name, they gave us the short, snappish name of York; and the beautiful, liquid, euphonious name of 'GORGEANA,' after an existence of ten short years, was forever wiped out."

In the place of Sir Ferdinando's city the Massachusetts Commissioners incorporated the town of York, which embraced the same limits as remain substantially unchanged up to the present day. Frank D. Marshall, Esquire, of Portland, a grandson of Hon. N. G. Marshall, in his Historical sketch of York, written in 1903, says, "Aside from the lots parcelled out to the first settlers, there remained a great tract of wild and primeval land, mostly lying back from the river and coast. This was the "Common Lands," held by the town and from which *for good cause*, lots were granted by vote of the freeholders and laid out to new settlers, and worthy residents. The grant would be by brief vote, of which the following is a fair example:

"Granted to Mr. Sam[l] Doniel, fifteen acres of land between the land of Stephen Preble de[sed] and ye Little Fresh Brook, called the fresh water, if he can find it clear of all former grants." Subsequently the grantee would see that his grant was duly "laid out" and surveyed by the town surveyor, and entered on the town records. Occasionally the vote was coupled with the condition that the grantee should "come and settle in this town." Such were frequent immediately following the devastation in 1692. Among the earliest and choicest grants were those "for the use of the ministry," some of which are still held by the First Parish. By 1732, the remaining Common Lands lay well inland around Mt. Agamenticus. In 1732, three hundred shareholders were constituted and became the Proprietors of the Common Lands. This body held meetings and retained its organization until 1820. By that time all of the original tract, however distant from the coast, that was embraced in the grants of Gorges had become the possessions of individuals. From this partial digression we will return to 1653.

In about 1645, there arrived within the city limits a new element of strength. The revolting of the Scots had made it almost imperative for many of the Cavaliers in order to have their lives to look for a home across the sea in the western world, so along the banks of York River toward its source a hamlet grew up known to this day as "Scotland." The descendants of Griscom, McIntire, Robert Junkins, Pierce, Thomas Donnell, Joseph Grant, who were banished by Cromwell in 1645, and other Scotchmen, who immigrated in 1647, still live there, and have been for more than two hundred and fifty years prominent in town affairs. The Town Commissioners appointed by the Massachusetts authorities were: Edward Godfrey, Abraham Preble, Edward Johnson and Edward Risworth; the latter was also appointed clerk of the waits and County Recorder. Henry Norton was chosen Marshall and Nicholas Davis, Constable. John Davis was licensed to keep an inn, ordinary or tavern. Edward Risworth was chosen the first Representative to the General Court in May, 1653. The Articles of Submission to Massachusetts were signed at the dwelling-house of Nicholas Davis, November 22nd, 1652. The following are the names of the signers: Philip Adams, Sampson Angier, John Alcock, Nicholas Bond, George Beanton, Joseph Alcock, Samuel Alcock, Richard Banks, Arthur Bragdon, Richard Codagon, John Davis, Thomas Curtis, Nicholas Davis, John Davis, 2nd, William Dickson, Thomas Donnell, Henry Donnell, Robert Edge, Andrew Everett, William Ellingham, William Freather, Hugh Gale, Edward Godfrey, William Gomsey, John Gooch, John Hooker, Philip Hatch, Robert Hethers, William Hilton, Edward Johnson, Robert Knight, ——— Lewis, William Moore, Henry Norton, John Parker, George

Parker, Abraham Preble, Francis Raynes, William Rogers, Edward Risworth, Edward Start, Sylvester Storer, Mary Tapp (acts only), John Turisden, Jr., Edward Wenstome, Thomas Wheelwright, Peter Wyer (Weare), Rowland Young. As was noted, Gorges' Charter provided for the establishment and conducting of the Episcopal religion, or what was more generally known as the Church of England.

Cromwell was a non-conformist and was called a Puritan at that time, and he was a firm dissenter from the doctrine and rites of the Established Church. The Massachusetts Bay Company to whom the freeholders of Gorgeana had submitted was composed principally of Puritans; hence that Company found it less hard to rob Gorges' heirs of their rights than it would have been had they both been Puritans, or Episcopalians; had the religious views of both parties been reversed it is very doubtful whether Gorges would have been disturbed. Such a view seems to be sustained from the fact that on the downfall of Cromwell's "Commonwealth" and the accession in 1660 of King Charles, an Episcopalian of the strictest sect to the throne of England, Sir Ferdinando's grandson, who succeeded to his grandfather's estates, asked of the King the restoration to him of his rights. The King appointed Commissioners who came to York early in the year 1665, and after examining the several charters and claims, issued on the 23d of June of that year, a proclamation prohibiting both parties from exercising authority and placed the whole province under the protection of the Crown, and so it remained for fifteen long weary years, when in 1675, the King confirmed the title to the grandson of Gorges, both as to soil and civil and religious government. History says, "Thus after a long struggle the Gorges heirs had confirmed to them the rights for which they so long contended."

But not long did Sir Ferdinando's heir retain his hard-earned title, the Massachusetts Bay Company with that tenacity of purpose that characterized the Puritans, determined against defeat, cast about for means whereby they might regain what they had acquired in 1652, and lost in 1675. On hearing of the King's decision, they at once dispatched an agent to England to treat with the heir of Sir Ferdinando, for the relinquishment of his rights, and in 1677 the grandson of the former Lord Proprietor of the Province of Mayne, for a sum less than two thousand pounds conveyed all that great territory which had descended to him, to the Massachusetts Bay Company, and by this act their title became complete. In referring to this matter, Mr. Marshall in his address said: "Now, I do not wish to be understood as charging any blame upon the Puritan settlers of Massachusetts for this course of proceeding as a reflection upon their religious creed. But as a business transaction, I think they, aided by their creed, took advantage of the adversities of Gorges, and became possessed of his rights in a manner *uncreditable* to say the least." Thus it will be seen that York had been tossed to and fro on the wave of a stormy sea of contesting claims for nearly forty years, though the seat of government for the Province. But in 1684 the storm clouds passed away, the tempestuous sea calmed, President Danforth, authorized by the Massachusetts Bay Colony, "Ye now Lord Proprietors," confirmed to the inhabitants all "rights and privileges" to them formerly granted by Sir Fernando Gorges. The manner of conferring these rights and privileges was by an indenture, "Between Thomas Danforth, Esquire, President of His Maj'ties Province of Mayne in New England, on the one part, and Mayor John Davis, Mr. Edward Risworth, Capt. Job Alcock and Lieut. Abraham Preble, Trustees on the "ye behalf and for ye sole use and benefit of ye inhabitants of ye town of Yorke." The consideration embodied in the deed reads, "That they, the above said Inhabitants forever hereafter as an acknowledgement of *Sir Ferdinando Gorges,* and his Assigns, right to soyle and Government, do pay twelve pence for every family whose single country rate is not above two shillings, in a single rate, to pay three shillings per family annually in money to ye Treasurer of said Province for ye use of ye Chief Proprietor thereof."

As Frank D. Marshall says, "Thus it would seem that in this instance the Massachusetts Bay Company chose to rest on her title as Assignees of Gorges' heirs, rather than by her famous interpretation of the line north of the Merrimac." Abraham Preble and Edward Risworth were the most prominent of the Trustees and are remembered.

Abraham Preble, the senior, was one of the first settlers, coming from Scituate, in Plymouth Colony, in about 1641. His son, Lieut. Preble, was known as Abraham Preble, Junior, and was a Representative of the General Court. Preble is a name favorably known in Maine for many years. In the home of the writer hangs a portrait, life size in oil, of Lydia Preble of the third generation from Abraham, and wife of Samuel Moody, great-grandson of Father Moody. Of the descendants of Edward Risworth none bear his name. He was of English birth and married an English maiden, Susan Wheelwright. He became a resident of Gorgeana in 1647; was recorder of the court in 1651 and in 1653 was chosen Representative to the General Court in Boston, representing York. In 1665, he was appointed one of the Justices, but three years later under what would now be styled the "recall" he was removed by the Massachusetts Bay Company. However, in 1673, he made an apology and was reinstated and in 1680-81 he was promoted to the position of Chancellor, under the charter acquired of the Gorges heirs by the Massachusetts Bay Company. His death occurred in 1691. He appears to have been a resourceful man, and an adept in obtaining office under the faction at the time in power. Also he sems to have been a faithful public servant, performing his various duties efficiently. He stood for law, order and all that goes to make prosperity in a town and province. It is greatly to be regretted that the records of the town up to the year 1691 were destroyed in the great devastation of 1692. A few fragmentary pages were found and are restored in Vol. I.

In writing of Abraham Preble and Edward Risworth we are brought to the subject of interest—The First Courts.

PART III

I CANNOT do better than to quote from Hon. Nathaniel G. Marshall in his popular address following this introduction: "When Massachusetts Bay Company took possession of the town and County in 1652, York was made the County seat or Shire town. The commissioners convened a regular courtleet, and named as associate judges, four men, namely, Edward Godfrey, Abraham Preble, Edward Johnson and Edward Risworth, all inhabitants of the town." Of this court, Mr. Marshall in his interesting style says: "The first Court holden here under this order of things, was in 1653, and was presided over by Chief Justice, Right Worshipful Richard Bellingham, assisted by our four distinguished resident judges. Now let us pause for a moment and fancy to ourselves, if we can, Chief Justice Right Worshipful Richard Bellingham, and his four associates, with powdered wigs, and flowing robes always donned while in Court, and their numerous retainers, under charge of Henry Norton, Esquire, of this town, who was appointed sheriff for the occa-

sion. Fancy the street through our Village, and that leading to the Court Room as mere pathways on either side of
which stood the stately pine, the majestic oak, and other
monarchs of the forest. Fancy, if we can, the personal
appearance of the suitors who had cases to be tried before
the Right Worshipful and his four worthy associates. Fancy,
if we can, the form and texture of the apparel of these
suitors. Fancy, too, how the ladies appeared on that august
occasion. Form an opinion, with the aid of fancy, as to
how many yards of gro de Nap, gro de Swiss, or moire
antique, their dresses contained. What style of bonnets
they wore, for they probably did not wear *hats* then, as
ladies do now. The men wore *hats* in that age—the women
did not. Fancy, if we can, the size and architectural appearance of the temple of Justice in which this august body held
its session, and by all means if you can fix its location."

The first inferior Court under the King's Commissioners
was held in Wells, July, 1665; one of its orders was that
every town should cause to be built between that time and
the sitting of the next Court, a pair of stocks, a cage, and
a *ducking* stool, on which to punish common scolds. This
stool consisted of a long beam movable on a fulcrum, one
end of which could be extended over the river or a pond of
water of sufficient depth for the ducking. This beam could
be let down and drawn up as deemed necessary for the punishment of the delinquent, who was secured to a seat at the
outer end of the beam. Its use appears to have been required as punishment for the female sex largely.

The first Court and Council under the jurisdiction of
Massachusetts, as rightful administrator of the government,
was held in York, March 17th, 1680. Thomas Danforth,
President, Mayor B. Pendleton, Capt. Joshua Scottan, Capt.
John Davis, Capt. John Wincott, Edward Risworth, Francis

Hooke, Capt. Charles Frost, and S. Wheelwright, were commissioners for the first year. Warrants for the choice of
deputies to the General Assembly, to be holden in York,
were issued, and the session commenced March 30th, 1680.
Edward Risworth was chosen Secretary, and Francis Hooke,
Treasurer of the Province. Mayor Brian Pendleton was
appointed Deputy President, and authorized with the assistance of other members of the Council, to hold intermediate
terms of Court. John Davis of York was deputy president
in 1682. In 1684 the Assembly was composed of president,
deputy president, assistant to justices and twelve deputies.
For its adjudication were committed a variety of subjects,
laws were made and enforced, legal questions settled, estates
proven, and letters of administration granted, military commissions issued, provision for the public safety in time of
war was made, roads laid out, religious affairs of towns
supervised, and, in fact, all matters pertaining to public interest were superintended. At the opening of every session
an "Election Sermon," as it was called, was preached. Just
two hundred and twenty-nine years ago from the day of this
writing, Rev. Shubael Dummer performed this duty, that is
to say, in March, 1683. Mr. Danforth was an able and dis-
creet magistrate, also popular, and as before stated, the
"storms had passed away" and the people had become recon-
ciled to the government of the Massachusetts Bay Company.
In 1685, in the month of April, James II, who had come to
the throne of England, was proclaimed King in the town.
The former scheme of a general government for all the
colonies was favored by the King. The Massachusetts Charter was recalled, and a President appointed for the whole of
New England. Joseph Dudley was made president, early
in 1686, and his council, which was composed of seventeen
gentlemen residing in different portions of New England,

was organized at the same time. Thomas Danforth was relieved of his office, and a court consisting of one judge, two councillors and a justice from each town in the province. Dudley was succeeded by Sir Edmund Andros, whose well-known and arbitrary administration came to an end with the reign of the King in 1689. After this occurred, President Danforth took up the duties of the office, which he doubtless exercised until the new charter of 1691 came into effect. This instrument set forth and made provision that all the territory and colonies known by the names of the Colony of Massachusetts Bay, of New Plymouth, Province of Maine, Acadia or Nova Scotia, and the tract lying between Nova Scotia and the Province of Maine, be incorporated into one province by the name of the Province of Massachusetts Bay in New England. Maine as far as Nova Scotia was constituted a county under the name of YORK. In all these changes of administration, as Clayton says, "The town took a lively interest from the fact that the provincial Courts were mainly held here and this for the time being became the Capital of the Province."

Part IV

This date of 1691 brings us down to the time of the Indian wars. Being a border settlement, we or they suffered greatly from every incursion of the savages. In fact it seemed the purpose of the Indians in all three wars to entirely destroy the place and exterminate the settlers, but their efforts were unsuccessful. The colonists erected garrison houses in which they gathered and heroically defended themselves against their cunning foes, and though some were the victims to the hatred of the wily foe, the settlements extended and increased. The most disastrous attack made upon the town was on February 5th, 1692 (January 25, '63). I quote here

from Hon. Nathaniel G. Marshall's manuscript which can
be relied on as being as nearly authentic as any writer on the
subject extant: "This was a fatal year * * * on the
twenty-fifth of January (or Feb. 4) a descent was made by
a body of Indians at which nearly all the inhabitants on the
north side of the river were either slain or taken prisoners
and carried into captivity. * * * This town protected
in a measure by the villages growing up in the interior and
on either hand did not suffer much until this year 1692
* * * when it was nearly annihilated. All the property
and accumulations recorded in the preceding pages (referring to town records), the result of seventy years of toil,
were swept away and loved ones were either slain or carried
into captivity by the Indians, who were beyond doubt urged
on by the French; and it is a tradition not to be doubted, that
the Indians who made the attack were commanded by the
French officers, perhaps in disguise." So far as can be
learned, every house in the locality spoken of was put to
the flames, with the exception of the garrison houses and the
meeting house and Old Jail. One account gives it that the
foray was planned and equipped in Canada, with York as
the central point of attack, and that it was composed of
nearly as many French as Indians, in all nearly two hundred.
Clayton in his history sets the numbers at three hundred.
Reaching the outskirts of the settlement at night, the expedition halted and piled their snowshoes around and upon a
large rock which is yet pointed out and whose outlines have
been preserved by the camera. It seems strange at this
writing that so large a body of hostile men should have
come from Canada to the southwestern coast, and no warning given. After divesting themselves of their foot gear
snowshoes, they separated, a Frenchman and Indian placing
themselves at the door of each dwelling. The break of day,

or discharge of a musket, was to be the signal for the general
massacre and devastation. Among the first to be killed was
Rev. Shubael Dummer, who was mounting his horse at his
home near Roaring Rock. He had started thus early on the
way to visit a sick and supposed dying parishioner to offer
the consolation of the holy gospel and religion he professed.
The life of his wife was spared for the time being—she being
dragged away from her dead, and the burning home. I
quote from Frank D. Marshall, LL. D. "Arthur Bragdon,
Jr., a young man attending his traps, suddenly came upon
the pile of snowshoes. Realizing their import, knowing
himself surrounded by an unseen, unmerciful foe, he fled to
Fort Head at the Harbor and there hid among the rocks.
Presently an Indian dog appeared with its mouth strapped
tight, looked at him and trotted away. He knew an Indian
would soon come, guided by the dog. Again Bragdon started on, followed the shore up river and found an old canoe,
crossed over and gave the alarm to the settlers on the south
side, who fled for their lives. Had Bragdon been able by
fire or knife to have destroyed those snowshoes, doubtless
there would have occurred within sight of Old Agamenticus,
a struggle as bloody and as famous as any in the Deerfield
Valley; for the alarm given, the men of Kittery and Portsmouth would have started in pursuit. But it was a hopeless
chase, the French and Indians had the start by several hours
though impeded by their captives. Among the latter was a
sturdy youngster, who escaped. He is known in history as
Col. Jeremiah Moulton, a scourge to the Indians and a
valiant officer in the War with France."

As I rise from my seat at the writing table this February
morning and look out and down to the seashore, the land at
and around "Roaring Rock" is covered with snow, the sky
is clear and the same sun as of two hundred and twenty-one

years ago sends its beams on a fair village of cottages, villas, and hostelries. Midway is the spot where stood a "garrison house" which would have offered shelter and comparative safety to the victims of the massacre of that early morn. But it was not to be, they are now walking in the pavilions of God. And to those who were left, comfort and hope came, and ever will until the heavens pass from the earth. From this time until 1698 or thereabouts we know but little. The history of those six years is but fragmentary. Some unknown man has written of those days thus: "When I was about nineteen years of age, I was conscripted as a soldier and was ordered to be stationed at York, when I first came there, there was very little of so much as ye form of religion, and no settled ministry; but on ye contrary an abundance of levity and vanity, although it was so soon after ye destruction of a great part of ye town by ye Indians." In 1695 the inhabitants through a committee of three, Samuel Donnell, Abraham M. Preble and Arthur Bragdon, were relieved in a measure of "ye straits and necessities" by lack of a corn mill, by Capt. John Pickerin of Portsmouth, and an indenture was executed by the committee and sworn to before William Pepperell, Sr. From this some litigation was engendered in relation to timber and water rights and transmitted for thirty years, and bears fruit even to this day. In the year 1698, May 18th, Rev. Samuel Moody, who was born in Newbury, Mass., arrived in York and commenced his labors. He had been graduated from Harvard but one year. The General Court in Boston aided in his support by an appropriation of twelve pounds sterling, and the town voted "that there is a whous to bie built forth with for yous of ye Ministry Ye dimensions as foloeth twenty eight fout in length and twenty four wied with a Lentoo att one end to be two story high with three fire plesses." Twenty pounds were raised for the purpose. Thus Mr. Moody began a pastorate of fifty years amid troublous times. He relied on the voluntary gifts of his parishioners—sometimes the town would vote to "mend his fences," to "cut his grass" and to "replenish his supply of fire wood." It was voted to "garrison" his twenty-four by twenty-eight "whous" with timber of oak or hemlock, with two suitable Baskins or Flankers. In 1710 it was agreed upon to have a new meeting-house, fifty foot square, and to be built every way proportionally. This would appear to be the second house of worship. It may have been the third, and was if the Church Chapel or Oratory spoken of in the Charter of 1641 as being the central point from which the borough limits diverged was actually built. It was in this place that Capt. John Harmon, Joseph Sayward, Micom McIntire and others were given ye hinde seat in our meeting-house in ye gallery, provided they fill it." Thus they were provided with ample seating room for their families and servants, and the strangers within their gates, all of whom were expected to attend divine service at least once on the Lord's Day.

EARLY FAMILIES.

THE LOVER of genealogical research can find a wide field for the occupancy of his time in the perusal of the early records of York. But in this book that part which treats of the genealogy of our ancestral times can only be generally noted. Time, and the limited space forbids the recording of the birth, marriage and death of the Bragdons, Prebles, McIntires, Banes, the families of Came, Banks, McLucas, Averhills, Bridges, Freeman, Plaisted, Junkins, Blaisdell, Thompson, Sewall, Moulton, Currier, Grant, Swett, Talpey, Weare, Brewster, Grow, Norton, Lunt, Goodwin, Lord, Bradbury, Hutchins, Donnell, Webber, Bowden, Baker, Kingsbury, Nowell, Risworth, Barrell, Simpson, Trafton, Chase, Putnam, Parsons, Raynes, Bracy, Harmon, Moore, Emerson, Young, Varrell, Mathews, Moody, Payne, and others. It would read like the Book of Chronicles, and of many of them St. Paul might be quoted, "All these by faith for they looked for a city which hath foundations, whose builder and maker is God."

EARLY PROMINENT MEN
ABRAHAM PREBLE

IN 1642 Abraham Preble came to Gorgeana from Scituate, Mass., and became Mayor of the embryo city. And we find that he was from that time until his death in January, 1663, very active in public affairs. As early as 1645 he was a magistrate. In 1647 he was one of the Judges of the province exercising legislative authority, as well as judicial. He took a very active part in favor of the measure for bringing Maine under the jurisdiction of Massachusetts, believing that it was greatly for the advantage of the inhabitants of Maine to secure the protection of that powerful province. In 1657 he was appointed to the same office of Judge under the authority of Massachusetts, which he continued to hold until December, 1662. He was also for several years one of the commissioners for York County, which then included the whole territory of Maine. He was at one time County Treasurer. He was a man of high integrity of character and as such was often called to act the role of arbitrator. Among the children of Abraham above named and his wife, Judith, was another Abraham. He was Register of Deeds for York County. In 1702 he was appointed a judge of the judicial court for the province of Maine. He was also captain of the town or chief commander of all the military within its borders. In all he held thirteen offices. The youngest son of this Abraham and Hannah Preble was Samuel, the youngest son of Samuel and Sarah was Esaias, who was four years old when his father died. In 1766 Esaias married Lydia Ingraham, who was the grand-daughter of Joseph Holt, and Elder of the First Church. Although bereft of his father at an early age, his courage and ambition

carried him forward in the activities of life, for we find that
in 1775 he was at Cambridge with a company of minute men,
as captain. He was a member of the Convention of Massachusetts that ratified the constitution of the United States,
also Representative to the General Court from York, and a
Selectman for several years, and a colonel of the militia.
Col. Preble died in 1813, having had by his wife, Lydia, no
less than fifteen children.

Among those born in the mansion now owned and occupied by Malcolm McIntire was Lydia, who became the wife
of Deacon Samuel Moody, and William Pitt, who was born
Nov. 27, 1783, graduated at Harvard College in 1806. In
1809 he was tutor of mathematics at Harvard, studied law
in the office of Benjamin Hasey at Topsham, and with Mr.
Oft in Brunswick, and then passed on to actual practice in
York. From here he moved to Alfred, and there in 1811
he was appointed attorney for York County. He removed
to Saco in 1813 and there received from President Madison
in 1814 appointment as District Attorney for the United
States. From Saco he went to Portland in 1818 and made
that place his permanent home. He was a member of the
convention which formed the Constitution of the State of
Maine, and was one of the three judges composing the highest judicial tribunal of the new State of Maine. He resigned
from the bench in 1828; was appointed minister plenipo-
tentiary to the Netherlands by President Jackson. The
King of Holland having been selected as arbitrator in the
northeastern boundary dispute, Judge Preble was chosen to
represent the interests of this country in that important case.
The controversy was not settled until 1842, when the Web-
ster-Ashburton treaty established a definite boundary. Great
Britain claimed nearly all of what is now the County of
Aroostook. Judge Preble was very influential throughout

the whole difficulty. In 1842 as one of the four commissioners chosen by the Legislature he rendered the last political service of his life in adjusting the terms of settlement.
He was a zealous and able promoter of the enterprise of
building the Grand Trunk Railway from Portland to Canada,
which was opened to the St. Lawrence River in 1853.   He
was married to Nancy Gale Tucker, daughter of Joseph
Tucker of York, in September, 1810.   Two daughters and
one son were born to them; the son, William P., became a
lawyer, and served many years as Clerk of the U. S. District
Court at Portland.   Judge Preble's second wife was Sarah
A., daughter of Thomas Forsaith, by whom he left one son,
Edward.

GEORGE BURDETTE

THIS WILY and corrupt man was one of the prominent
men of early York—prominent in much evil.   Previous to
his flight from England to New England where he left a
destitute and distressed wife and family in 1635, he had had
trouble.   He landed in Salem and was admitted as a freeman, and being "an able scholar and of plausible parts and
carriage," was employed to preach to the church there of
which he had been received as a member.   The discipline of
the church being too strict for his loose conscience, he went
to Dover, thence he came to York, and for the period of
seven or eight months he did a good deal of mischief and
filled the cup of his iniquity to overflowing.   However, he
departed for England early in 1640 and joined the Royalist
Army; was taken prisoner and put in prison, and then his
personality disappears.   In the meantime his wife had received a yearly annuity from the Norwich Corporation.   Of
his career in Agamenticus Judge Bourne writes: "Even the
Rev. George Burdette, a man of cultivated intellect, who

had enjoyed the good opinion of his fellow prisoners * * * suffered himself to be carried away by the seductions of unrestrained liberty.   He had been repeatedly guilty of adultery and all of those misdemeanors invariably concomitant.   Females of respectable standing, wives of men of irreproachable life, were induced to forget their marriage vows and fellowship with him in his wickedness."   Thomas Gorges, Sr Ferdinando's nephew, determined to take the necessary steps to stay the influx of vice, which was fast undermining the foundation of good citizenship.   He caused an indictment to be brought against Burdette at the court held in Saco, as: "A man of ill name and fame, infamous for incontinence, a publisher and broacher of divers dangerous speeches, the better to seduce the weak sex of women to his incontinent practices."   He was found guilty and sentenced to pay ten pounds sterling to the King.   He was also indicted "for deflouring Ruth, the wife of John Gooch," and for this offence he was fined twenty pounds sterling. At that period of our history there was not much deference paid to the female character, at any rate the people or court did not hide their eyes to the transgressions of that sex. Women did not get much mercy or sympathy at the hands of the courts.

"Mary the wife of George Puddington was indicted by the whole bench for often frequenting the house and company of Mr. George Burdette, minister of Agamenticus, privately in his bed chamber, and elsewhere in a very suspicious manner, notwithstanding the said Mary was often forwarned thereof by her said husband, and the constable of the plantation, with divers others, to the great disturbance and scandal of the said plantation."   And she was required to make this public confession: "I, Mary Puddington, do hereby acknowledge that I have dishonored God, the place where I live, and wronged my husband by my disobedient, and light carriage, for which I am heartily sorry, and desire the forgiveness of this court and of my husband, and do promise amendment of life and manners henceforth," and having made this confession she was to ask her husband's pardon on her knees.

Another female who was a participant with Burdette was censured by the court and also ordered "to stand in a white sheet without other clothing publically in the congregation at Agamenticus two several sabbath days, and likewise one day at the general court, when she shall be thereunto called by one or all of the councillors of the Province."

It is not to be supposed that on those Sundays "Grace did much more abound." And whether or no the standard of morality was raised by this scene among the young or even those of mature years is a question. But Gorges was determined if possible to stay the tide of wrong, and he felt that morality and religion were strong supports to a secure and prosperous government.

HENRY SAYWORD

HENRY SAYWORD (Sayward) was born in England and came to this country in 1637. His trade profession was that of a mill wright. He was for a time resident of several New Hampshire towns, but being unable to find a location he thought desirable he extended his search to the east of the Piscataqua River, and in York found what he sought, and here he established himself by means of purchase or otherwise obtained a grant of land, rented a dwelling house and began the construction of mills "where someteyms the ould mill stoode which was erected by Hugh Gayl and Will Effingham." He was prosperous for a time and carried on a large and paying business. The exact date of his coming

to York cannot be given, but we find that between the years
1660 and 1664 the town granted him "fifty acres of upland,
eighty poles in breadth from his former bounds east, and
one hundred poles in length running due south." In June,
1667, Sayword contracted with the selectmen to build a
meeting house for the use of said town. The third article
of his agreement provides that Sayword shall "inclose the
said meeting house with good sound plank slabs three inches
thick, and to battern the said plank sufficiently on the outside, and to cover it with good inch boards on the top and
with inch and a quarter boards underneath." * * * The
seats to be removed from the old meeting house (the first
built) to the new at the town's charge, and Sayword agrees
to place them (in the new) at his own charge for the most
convenience. This contract was fully carried out by Sayword, who received from the town as compensation three
hundred and seventy acres of land, twenty of which was a
"grassy swamp"; another parcel containing one hundred and
seventy acres; also twenty poles of land to be added to his
home lot whereon he had then built a house, together with
privilege of cutting logs on certain parcels Commons lands
and other minor privileges. Thus had Sayword become a
large landholder. Some time in 1668 the Sayword mills
were destroyed by fire. This was a misfortune which seri-
ously embarrassed him financially. Thereupon he concluded
not to rebuild in York, if he could obtain a situation elsewhere with greater water power and larger facilities whereby he could enlarge his business to a greater volume than if
he rebuilt on his old site. Learning of the superior power
of the Mousam River, then known as Cape Porpus River,
he visited that locality. An examination of the water power
privilege led him at once to take measures for its possession.
On making known to the selectmen of Wells his desire to

erect mills there if suitable encouragement were given him,
he was met with a hearty welcome, and with a proposition
so liberal that he did not hesitate for a moment to accept it.
And on January 4, 1669, the town of Wells granted to
Henry Sayword, and James Johnson of York, and Thomas
Paty of Wells, "liberty to build a saw mill at Cape Porpus
River Falls, together with the privilege of the said river for
the transportation of boards and logs. Also liberty to cut
pitch pine timber on the commons adjoining the river for
the use of said saw mill." On the same day the town granted to Henry Sayword three hundred acres of upland lying
on the northeast side, and one acre adjoining the falls, on
the west side of Cape Porpus River. Thus as Judge Bourne
in his History of Wells and Kennebunk says: "York's loss
of Sayword became Wells' gain." References to Sayword
in various papers show clearly that he sustained the character
of a big-hearted and enterprising citizen, and that he was
always ready to buy, sell, lease real estate, to make contracts
or engage in any business pursuit that gave promise of gain,
but it is also evident that impulsiveness was a prominent
trait of his character, and to this may be traced his later
embarrassment, which led to bankruptcy, and perhaps might
be safely added, to his death, which occurred in the year
1678. His wife died Dec. 26, 1689; she had borne him five
children. Charles E. Sayward of Portland is a lineal descendant, as is Horace Mitchell of Kittery on his maternal
side.

Judge Bourne in his History of Wells and Kennebunk,
writing of Sayward's last years of life, says:

"Sayward was one of the best of men, but enterprise was
too prominent an element of his character. He needed
cautiousness and discretion to check his zeal. He anticipated no failure. Ardent in his pursuits, he never doubted

their successful termination. He gave himself to work as confident of a favorable issue, as if already reached; and thence from a want of considerate previous examination, disappointment came from all his exertions. He was in no degree extravagant in his domestic economy. There was no opportunity for a thoughtless and lavish expenditure. He lived on the plainest fare, and all the furniture which his wife had to carry on her household administration, was three beds, a few old pewter dishes, three keelers, two iron pots, two brass kettles, two old tubs, a tramel and pot hooks, a spit and irons, two water pails, a pair of cards, two table boards, a spinning wheel, meat trough and chest. This we should now regard as rather poor provision for comfortable life. Chairs were not then in vogue extensively. But all his struggles, notwithstanding his economy, left him in complete insolvency at the close of life; so that nothing remained for his wife and children but her dower in his real estate, and the memory of his virtues and manly character. Fifty years' hard labor closing in poverty seems to have been a severe destiny. Left almost penniless, his wife, Mary, after what she had passed through, was obliged to remove to some more public place and resort to the low business of rum selling without license, to keep herself from becoming a burden to the people.

SAMUEL MOODY

REV. SAMUEL MOODY was born in Newbury, Mass., January 4, 1675. He was the son of Caleb, who was the son of William, who came to this country from Wales, British Isles, in

He graduated at Harvard; commenced his labors as a minister in York, being ordained Dec. 20, 1700, as the successor of the lamented Shubael Dummer, and to quote from a work of Rev. Rufus M. Sawyer of Middleboro, Mass., published in 1866:

And he was just the man to beautify sinful men with the features of moral loveliness, and perfection, and raise up the pillars of a prostrate church in troublous times. He had felt the power of divine things in earlier life. He had evidently walked thoughtfully as in hearing of the ocean of eternity, and his soul

> "Could in a moment travel thither
> And see the children sport upon the shore,
> And hear the mighty waters rolling evermore."

As he looked up into the heavens,

> "The clouds were touched,
> And in their silent faces did he read
> Unutterable love."

He heard the voice of God in the wind and saw His hand in every gift. In prayer, in deep reflection, during the watches of the night, in his study as he read the Book of Books, and in meditation under the open sky, he felt the presence of a divine almighty spirit in his own soul—in his own blessed experience. The hearts of men, the change in communities, the destiny of nations, he saw were at God's disposal.

He had strong *faith*. This appears in many instances of prayer, and in the way he provided for himself and family. Added to his zeal and earnestness in his Master's service was strong sympathy for men in want or suffering, and readiness to give of his substance for their relief. Meeting a beggar, and taking out his purse, and finding it difficult to untie it—his wife having purposely made it so, to prevent

his giving before a little reflection—he concluded the Lord
intended he should give the whole, so he handed over to the
beggar both his money and his purse. But he had other
virtues than those of benevolence, zeal and faith. There
were stern features to his character. He was bold and fearless. Col. Ingraham's wife was a very fashionable lady,
and appeared at church occasionally in a very showy dress.
According to the fashion of that day, one Sabbath morning
she came *"sweeping into church,"* in a new dress very much
inflated with hoop skirts. "Here she comes," said Father
Moody from the pulpit, "here she comes, top and top, gallant
rigged most beautifully, and sailing most majestically; but
she has a leak that will sink her to hell," * * * There
are many anecdotes illustrating his various traits of character, but space will not permit their reproduction. What
he accomplished during his ministry in York cannot be fully
described. * * * The work of a faithful, devoted servant of God may be learned from the records of eternity,
but not from those of time. Yet there was a great change
visible to mortal eye and understanding in the community.
Now family worship was observed in nearly every dwelling.
When Mr. Moody came to York it was given up to levity
and wickedness; now it was filled with love, joy and peace.
Then the church numbered twenty, now it contained three
hundred and seventeen members. * * * What a change
to be produced under God principally by the labors of one
man. He closed his labors at seventy-two "in great distress
of body." During his last hours, Joseph, his son, sat behind
him on the bed holding him in his arms. When he ceased
to breathe and the people began to remark that he was gone,
his son exclaimed with a loud voice, "And Joseph shall put
his hand upon thine eyes." He then closed his father's eyes
and laid the lifeless body back on the bed. His grave is but

a few rods from the old meeting house which was built the
year he died, and beside the graves of those he loved. On
the stone at its head is this inscription:

Here lies the body
of the Revd.
Samuel Moody, A. M.
The zealous, faithful, and successful pastor of
the First Church of Christ in York;
Was born in Newbury, January 4, 1675,
graduated 1697, came hither May 16, 1698,
Ordained in December 1700, and
died here Nov. 13, 1747, for his
further character read the 2nd
Corinthians 3rd chapter,
and first six verses.

Mr. Moody was first married to Hannah Sewall, the only
daughter of John Sewall of Newbury. She died Jan. 29,
1728, at the age of fifty-one years. They had three children,
namely, Joseph, minister of the Second Congl. Parish in
York, Mary, who became the wife of Rev. Joseph Emerson
of Malden, and Lucy, who died in infancy. Father Moody
wrote several treatises and books, which were published;
among them, "Vain Youth Summoned to Appear at (?)
Bar," 1701; "The Doleful State of the Damned," 1710;
"Judas the Traitor Hung up in Chains to Give Warning to
Professors," 1714; "The Way to Get Out of Debt, and the
Way to Keep Out of Debt," 1721.

SAMUEL AND NATHANIEL DONNELL, son and grandson,
respectively, of Henry Donnell, the common New England
ancestor of that family, who sailed from London in 1635 at
the age of twenty-three years. Henry Donnell was the first
of that name to settle in York. He married Frances, daughter of Thomas Reading, of Saco. Their son Samuel was

born in 1646. He became a judge of the Court of Common Pleas Oct. 10, 1699, taking the place of Job Alcock. He was also a Councillor in 1692 and 1700 under the charter of Massachusetts granted by William and Mary. He died March 9, 1718.

Nathaniel, a son of Samuel and his wife Alice (Chadbourne) was born Nov. 19, 1689. He married Hannah, daughter of John Preble, as appears in the section devoted to York at Louisburg. Nathaniel was a colonel in the expedition of Gen. Pepperell. He was a large landed proprietor and a large portion of the ocean frontage from York River to Cape Neddick stream was under his control. He died Feb. 9, 1780. On his gravestone in the old burying ground is this inscription :

"In memory of Nathaniel Donnell, Esq. (son of the Hon. Samuel Donnell, one of the Council named in the charter of William and Mary), who was born Nov. 19, 1689, and died Feb. 9, 1780, Æ 91.

"He was strictly just, universally charitable, and eminently pious, patient and cheerful in adversity, and without pride or vanity in prosperity, in high estimation of all his acquaintances in every stage of life. May his descendants imitate his virtues and perpetuate his name with honor to posterity."

THE FITZGERALDS. (KING DAVID)

THE PROMINENT Fitzgeralds in this country today are of comparatively modern origin in comparison with the family of that name in York, which was founded in about 1700. Patrick Fitzgerald immigrated from Ireland. His son, David, was born previous to 1740, as near as can be learned, in 1738. He was styled "King David" and in 1765 held almost kingly sway in the section round about Agamenticus.

The clan increased rapidly in numbers as the years passed on, and in lapse of a century from King David's birth had reached the number of three score. The voting members were considered a valuable asset to the party or cause with which they affiliated, "for as one went, so went all." In the early days their style of speech was peculiar, in fact as a people they were considered peculiar, and yet possessed of sterling traits of character, not the least of which was the love of home. And even in later years the descendants of Patrick are imbued with the feeling of love for home, and it is crossing to them to be called upon to carry out in full a contract that requires absence for a lengthy continuous period.

David, grandson of King David, was born in 1817. He served in the war for the preservation of the Union from 1861 to 1865, as appears in another part of this book.

It may not be out of place to say that it was a unique scene when King David marshaled the clan and in the lead of fifteen or more teams loaded with chestnut oak wood passed through Cape Neddick Village to the Landing, where it was to be shipped to market; returning in the same order of march, rejoicing in the so-called good cheer of those days.

MAJOR SAMUEL SEWALL

SAMUEL SEWALL, the noted engineer and master mechanic, was born in York, September 14, 1724. He deceased July 23, 1815. In 1761 he designed and built the first pier or pile bridge in the United States, known then and now as "Sewall's Bridge."

As early as 1742 the parish had voted that they were willing that there should be a bridge built across York River, at or near where Capt. Samuel Sewall keeps a ferry, and

after nearly twenty years the bridge was built.   Among
other prominent men who were active in the matter so far
as the First Parish was concerned, were Capt. Nathaniel
Donnell, Joseph Holt, Samuel Bragdon, Jr., Samuel Millbury, and Thomas Donnell.   The method of construction
was the erection of a whole section, or bent, at one time.
This contained four piles of the proper length, the river
bottom having been probed and marked for each required
length, this being capped by the cap sill securely.   This being
done on the river bank, at the still of the tide, it was floated
to its place and set upright.   A large and lengthy oak log
being fastened by the top inland, the butt was raised by
tackle to a height of fifteen or more feet and by the striking
of the latch lock the tackle was released and the log fell with
much force on the cap over each pile, and in time the section
was driven to the proper position.   Later Major Sewall
was employed to build a similar bridge between Boston and
Charlestown.   The building of the York Bridge caused a
sensation in the world of mechanics at that time.

Hon. Alexander McIntire was the son of Micum Mc-
Intire 3rd.   Micum McIntire, the ancestor of the York
McIntires, came from Scotland and settled in Berwick, a
precinct of the town of Kittery, and had fifty acres of land
granted him, Feb. 9, 1663.   In June, 1670, John Pierce
deeded land to the above named Micum in York.   Micum
also married the daughter of Mr. Pierce.   It was along in
these years that the McIntire Garrison House was built.
Micum McIntire 2nd settled on the southwest side of York
River opposite Micum 1st.   Micum the 3rd married an
Allen, and among their children was Alexander, the subject
of this sketch, who married and had children, the first being
Edgar A., who succeeded his father as Town Clerk.   Micum

the 1st and his son built the Garrison House. Hon. Alexander McIntire served his town, county, state and country in a faithful manner. He was Representative and Senator, Collector of Customs, a Selectman, Town Clerk, and Justice of the Peace. His son, Edgar, married a daughter of Capt. John S. Thompson. Among the many descendants of Micum were Major General Jeremiah McIntire and John McIntire, whose grandson is now Treasurer of the Town of York. In evidence of the regard that Alexander McIntire was held the following from the records of the town is appended. At a town meeting held July 3, 1852, the following resolutions were presented and unanimously adopted:

"Whereas, it has pleased the great disposer of all events to remove from among us by death, our late, able and efficient Clerk, the Hon. Alex. McIntire.

"Therefore—Be it resolved by the inhabitants of this town, in Town Meeting assembled for the choice of his successor—in view of his able and efficient services as a Town officer for more than forty years; that we feel the loss we have sustained by his death, and that his virtues as a citizen and Townsman are not forgotten by us.

"Resolved that we sympathize with his family in the loss they have sustained as a husband and father. And

"Resolved that the foregoing preamble and resolution be entered at large upon the Records of the Town."

Isaac Lyman

Rev. Isaac Lyman settled in York, 1749. He was born in South Hampton, Mass., Feb. 25, 1725. He was pastor of the First Church of Christ in York forty-five years.

Dr. Job Lyman, a brother of Rev. Isaac, both sons of Moses Lyman of South Hampton, married Abigail, daugh-

ter of Jeremiah Moulton of York. Their second daughter
married Edward Emerson, Esq., of York. Their ninth
daughter married Samuel Lunt. The family name of Lyman is now extinct in York, but there are many descendants
of Rev. Isaac and Doctor Lyman in Maine and Massachusetts.

HON DAVID SEWALL

WAS BORN in York Oct. 7, 1735, deceased Oct. 22, 1825.
He married first Mary Parker. His second wife was Elizabeth Langdon. He built and occupied the mansion at the
Village now owned by Rev. Frank Sewall, D. D., and called
Coventry Hall, after the ancestral home of the Sewalls in
England. He was a man of eminent character. In fact,
he was the foremost man in York for two generations. He
was an able lawyer, a just judge, a devout Christian, and
withal a philanthropist in the full acceptation of the term.
He was in the class at Harvard which graduated in 1755;
admitted to the bar in 1760. He was actively interested in
all matters for the advancement of the town, and for sixty
years his name is recorded on almost every page of the
record which includes the doings of the voters at town meetings. His body was interred in the "old burying ground"
and upon the stone that marks the place is the following:

"Consecrated to the memory of the Hon. David Sewall,
LL. D.

An elevated benevolence was happily directed by an en-
lightened intellect. Conscientious in duty, he was ever
faithful in its discharge. Piety with patriarchal simplicity
of manners conspired to secure him universal esteem. His
home was the abode of hospitality and friendship. In him
the defenceless found a Protector, the poor a Benefactor,
the community a Peacemaker, Science, Social Order, and

Religion an efficient Patron.   Distinguished for his patriotism, talents and integrity, he was early called to important public offices which he sustained with fidelity and honor. Having occupied the Bench of the Supreme Court of the State and District Court of the U. States with dignified uprightness for forty years without one failure of attendance, he retired from public in 1818, and died Oct. 22, 1825, aged XC years.

> Death but entombs the body,
> Life the soul."

YORK IN COLONIAL WAR — LOUISBURG

IN 1743 England and France were at peace, but mutterings of approaching hostilities were heard. Louis XV was King of France and George II ruled Great Britain. With each successive war the English colonies were engaged in strife with their French neighbors, each in earnest for the success of fatherland.

At this time a large portion of that territory now known as the "Dominion of Canada" and the Provinces, or the British possessions in North America, was under the protection of the French. In October, 1743, Governor Shirley of Massachusetts in a letter to Col. William Pepperell of Kittery, who commanded the York County Regiment, said that he had received word from England that peaceful relations were likely soon to be dissolved. Col. Pepperell sent a copy of the Governor's letter to all the Captains in his command, and added his own words as follows: "I hope that He who gave us breath will give us courage and prudence to behave ourselves like true born Englishmen."

Louisburg in 1736 had become a fortified seaport, six million dollars had been expended from 1715 to the above date to make it so, and it was a most important strategical position in the defense of French colonies along the Gulf and St. Lawrence River. Situated on the island of Cape Breton, which seems to guard the approach to the gulf and river, the French had re-named what was known in 1713 as "English Harbor" and called it "Louisburg," after the then reigning King Louis XIV. It is interesting to read the details of the elaborate work of the French engineers in making this place what France had designed it to be—the strongest fortress in America, but space will not allow, or time to recount it in this article which primarily intended to deal with "York at Louisburg."

When war was declared by France in March, 1744, and by Great Britain in April, and preparations by the government of the Province of Massachusetts looking to the sending of an expedition against what was a "thorn in the flesh of New England—Louisburg," the governments of New York, the Jerseys, Pennsylvania, Connecticut, Rhode Island and New Hampshire were asked "to accompany and follow" the force of the Province with men and vessels. The command of the expedition was given to Col. William Pepperell, who at the time of his appointment was forty-nine years old. His rank was that of Lieutenant General, which commissions he had received from three Provinces, Massachusetts, New Hampshire, and Connecticut. Col. Jeremiah Moulton of York was in command of the 3d Regiment, Capt. John Harmon was at the head of Campany 6 of the 1st Regiment, which was Col. Pepperell's. Dr. Burrage says he has not been able to find a list of Harmon's men—but it is known that Benjamin Harmon was his Lieutenant, and Joseph Adams his Ensign. Both Moulton and Harmon had seen hard service in the wars with the Indians, which the French had instigated.

All the troops rendezvoused in Boston for transportation. Jonathan Sayward of York was captain of one of the transports. In expressing his desire to take part in the expedition Capt. Harmon wrote to Col. Pepperell as follows:

York, February 16, 1744.

To the Hon. William Pepperell, Esquire, Brigadier General at Kittery, per Capt. Beal.

Hon'd Sir:

This waits on you with my duty, wishing you all the success and comfort that prosperity can afford you, in the great trust reposed

in you.   May the conduct of Heaven always attend you in every
scene of life.   The Providence of God blessing me with so good a
measure of health, and my inclinations being strong to wait on you
to Louisburg, I am persuaded there is something yet for me to do
there before I leave the world.   And as your smile is all I crave
in order to my going with you, I shall look for my reward either
in the coming world, if I am called off in the cause of my King and
country, or as you see I deserve if ever I return to New England.
If you will favour me with a line in answer, I shall look upon it as
a token of your regard.   I beg leave, Honored Sir, to subscribe
myself,

> Your dutiful humble servant,
>
> Johnson Harmon.

Capt. Nathaniel Donnell of York also commanded a company in the 1st Regt. and of its roster the following names
have been preserved: Josiah George, Sergeant Dotson, Shubael Boston, Joseph Boston, Jonathan Sayward, John Clement, David Monson, —— Leavitt.

Francis Raynes was one of the prominent York men who
took part in the siege, also Zebulon Preble, whose descendants live at Brixham.   Seventeen of Capt. Harmon's "snow-
shoe" men enlisted in February, and ten under Ensign James
Donnell.   York had an enrolled militia at that time of 350
men.   Of these, twelve under Capt. Sewall signed a paper
setting forth that they were intending to enlist, but wanted
to know who would be their captain.   Joseph Webber was
a sergeant, Daniel Young a corporal, Joshua Ramsdell and
James Hays also served, and John Kingsbury, of whom
Frank D. Marshall, Esquire, of Portland, writes: "I had a
great-great-great-grandfather, John Kingsbury of York, who
as a boy of eighteen was at Louisburg, and there lost a leg.
Years ago I came across a receipt given him by L. D. Leopold, surgeon, who performed the operation of amputation.
*   *   *   Kingsbury stumped around on his wooden leg for
more than sixty years afterward; was a Selectman, Justice
of the Peace, and one of the committee on the Crisis of

1774." It is to be regretted that the names of all the men from York who participated in the expedition are not extant, for it can not be doubted that the influence of men like Jeremiah Moulton, who was a member of the Provincial Council, Judge of the Court of Common Pleas and Treasurer of York, of Capt. Harmon, Doctor Bulman and others, would go far in matter of the response of York in making good in personnel and numbers.

In concluding this story I will take up the services of the Chaplain and Surgeon of the expedition, who were both York men. I should have spoken earlier of John Sweet, who was Surgeon's mate at the request of Doctor Alexander Bulman, who was an eminent physician and surgeon of his day.

After the capture of the fortress and city much sickness prevailed, and from November to January, 1746, there were 561 burials in Louisburg, and Gen. Pepperell's command had been reduced to less than one thousand men who were fit for service. This large degree of sickness wore on Dr. Bulman and he was stricken with a critical illness. Gen. Pepperell, writing to Mrs. Pepperel, said: "And now, my dear, I must tell you something of the distress and anguish of my soul. My prudent and valiant Dr. Bulman, although he has held his health finely until about six days past, was taken with a nervous fever and given over. I expected the day past he would not have lived, but blessed be God there is some hope this morning. The Lord in great mercy continues him to us, if it is His holy will." Not long after the sorrowful news was brought to York of the death of Dr. Bulman, and thus passed across a "prudent and valiant man," who was sincerely mourned in York and adjoining towns, in Boston and wherever he was known.

Rev. Samuel Moody, who was pastor of the First Church of Christ in York, was seventy years old at the time of the organization of the expedition, and at the request of Gen. Pepperel became the Chaplain.   He must have had a strong constitution to enable him to go on this tiresome voyage of six or seven hundred miles under the circumstances and surroundings incident to such undertakings.   Some of his friends tried to dissuade him from his purpose; but he said, "No, there never was a bullet made to hit me."   He entered upon the expedition with great zeal, and predicted that Louisburg would be taken, and that he should cut down the cross and images of Papal worship.   On stepping on board the transport at Boston he seized an axe, exclaiming "The sword of the Lord and of Gideon," and after the place was taken he shouldered his axe and went up to the images and actually cut them down as predicted.*   In the mass house there. he preached the first Protestant sermon ever heard on the island, from these words: "Enter into his gates with thanksgiving, and into his courts with praise; be thankful unto him and bless his name.   For the Lord is good; his mercy is everlasting; and his truth endureth to all generations."—Psalms, 100, 4-5.

It would appear that almost an uncommon series of providential interpositions gave the strongest fortress in America into the hands of the Provincial and British forces.   It is said that "Father Moody's" son Joseph, who was supplying the pulpit of his father during his absence, was at Louisburg in spirit if not in person, and on the day of the surrender made one of those wrestlng, overcoming, conquering prayers, a type of those of the patriarchs and prophets of old.

It was at a dinner given by Gen. Pepperel, after the surrender of Louisburg, and in commemoration, that Mr. Moody

* Appendix in memoir of Rev. Joseph Emerson.

craved that remarkable blessing at the table, which was at once concise and to the admiration as well as happy disappointment of all present. Sir William, well knowing with others of Mr. Moody's prolixity on such occasions, was fearful that the dinner might get cold, or the British officers offended, or both; yet knowing his arbitrary and independent disposition, no one would take the liberty to suggest to him that he be brief in addressing the Throne of Grace. When all was ready, the chief in command spoke to Mr. Moody that dinner was ready. He, all unconscious of their feeling, approached the table, and lifting up his hands, they were agreeably surprised when he expressed himself in this apt and laconic manner, which his friends took down in writing: "O Lord, we have so many things to thank Thee for that time will be infinitely too short to do it. We must therefore leave it for the work of ETERNITY. Bless our food and fellowship on this joyful occasion, for Christ's sake. Amen."

YORK IN THE REVOLUTION

THE WAR of the Revolution or Independence began July 4, 1776. Previous to that the Americans had been fighting in defence of their rights as British subjects. Washington had said: "When I first took command of the Continental Army, I abhorred the idea of Independence." Who shall say that here in York, in a legal town meeting more than three years before the writing of Thomas Jefferson's immortal document, was not put forth the first Declaration? The record says (Vol. II, Page 166) that Dec. 28, 1772,

"At a legal town meeting holden in York, Joseph Simpson, Esq., was chosen Moderator.

"1st. Resolved. That as the Inhabitants of this town are faithful and loyal subjects of his most Gracious Majesty, King George, the third, they are well entitled to his most gracious favor, and to be protected and secured not only in their natural and constitutional rights as Englishmen, Christians and subjects, but in all the rights and privileges contained in the Royal Charter of this Province.

"2nd. Resolved. As the opinion of this Town, that divers of those Rights, Liberties, and Privileges have been broken in upon and much infringed to the great grievance of this town, and justly alarming to the Province.

"3d. Resolved. That in the opinion of this Town, it is highly necessary some just and reasonable measures be adopted for the speedy redress of such grievances, so burthersome and distressing to us, which if made known to our most gracious Sovereign, we cannot but flatter ourselves (as our cause is just) that he will be pleased to remove them.

"4th. VOTED, that our Representative at the General Court use his utmost endeavors and influence for the speedy redress of our Grievances, in such wise, moderate and prudent way and manner as shall appear to him most likely to take effect and as his wisdom and judgment shall dictate.

"VOTED. That the Clerk give out a Copy of the Proceedings of the Town at this meeting to the Selectmen, who are desired to transmit the same to the Selectmen of Boston. With the thanks of this Town to that Town for the early care they have taken of our invaluable rights and the Zeal they have for preserving the same.

"DANIEL MOULTON, *Town Clerk.*"

The main part of our declaration made one year and twenty odd days subsequent to the First, is found in Vol. 2, pages 169 and 172 of the Records, and is as follows:

"At a meeting of the freeholders and inhabitants of the town of York regularly assembled at the Town House on Monday, the 20th day of January, 1774. The Hon. John Bradbury, Esquire, was chosen moderator. The town immediately proceeded to choose a committee, namely, the Hon. John Bradbury, Esq., Thomas Bragdon, Esq., Capt. Joseph Holt, Capt. Daniel Bragdon, Capt. Edward Grow, Capt. John Stone, and Mr. John Kingsbury, to consider in what manner the town sentiments may be best expresesd on the present important crisis and make report to this meeting on adjournment. Voted this meeting be adjourned to tomorrow, two of the clock afternoon. Upon adjournment, viz., Tuesday, Jan. 21st, two o'clock of the afternoon. The said Committee appointed by the Town to consider in what manner sentiments may best be expressed on the present crisis; beg leave to report. The Committee reported, which with the amendments are as follows:—

"1st. That the people in the British American Colonies, by their Constitution of Government have right to freedom and an exemption from every degree of oppression and slavery.

"2nd. That it is an essential right of Freeman to have the disposal of their own property and not to be taxed by any power over which they can have no control.

"3rd. That the Parliamentary duty laid upon teas landed in America for the express purpose of raising a revenue is in effect, a tax upon the Americans without their consent.

"4th. That the several Colonies and Provinces in America have ever recognized the Protestant Kings of Great Britain as their Lawful Sovereigns and it doth not appear that any Parliament have been parties to any contract made with American settlers in this howling wilderness.

"5th. That this Town approves the Constitutional Exertions and struggles made by the opulent colonies throughout the continent for preventing so fatal a catastrophe as is implied in taxation without representation and that we are, and always will be, ready in every constitutional way to give all assistance in our Power to prevent so dire a calamity.

"6th. That the dread of being enslaved ourselves and of transmitting the chains to our posterity, is the principal inducement to these measures.

"7th. VOTED: That the sincere thanks of this town are justly due, and hereby are given to all such persons in this and the several Provinces and Colonies on the American Continent; especially to our brethren of the Town of Boston, so far as they have constitutionally exerted themselves in support of their just privileges and liberties.

"Which was read paragraph by paragraph and accepted, and thereupon

"VOTED that the Town Clerk transmit a fair copy to the Town Clerk of Boston; and then the meeting was dissolved.

"DANIEL MOULTON, *Town Clerk.*"

The concluding part of the grand old record which gives us a view of the character of our ancestors of those times is on page 177, Vol. II, and was written a month before that paper which contains illustrious names headed by John Hancock.

"At a meeting of the Freeholders and other inhabitants of the Town of York, qualified to vote in Town meetings, regularly assembled on Wednesday, June 5th, 1776, The Hon. John Bradbury, Esq., chosen moderator.

"Unanimously voted, that the Representative of this Town now at the General Court, be advised: That if the Honorable Congress should, for the safety of the Colonies, declare them Independent of the Kingdom of Great Britain, they, the said inhabitants, will solemnly engage with their Lives and Fortunes to support them in the measures."

Speaking of these several meetings and votes, Hon. N. G. Marshall in his address says: "You will observe copies of these resolves and votes were directed to be sent to Boston. Now if Mr. Jefferson had written his declaration in Boston (and who can say he did not) some would be so ungenerous as almost suspect that he might possibly have had a peep at our declaration before he wrote *his.* Suppose Mr. Jefferson's declaration had preceded ours a length of time as long as ours preceded his, what would be said at this day? Would it not be said ours was copied substantially from his? Who gave our ancestors the idea of 'taxation without representation?' Was it Mr. Jefferson? How many in this 'howling wilderness' knew much about

Mr. Jefferson? Who gave him the same expressed ideas? Did he obtain it from our ancestors, Who knows, In justice to the noble patriot, Thomas Jefferson, and our noble ancestors, I will presume that the spirit of liberty dictated to him and them the same ideas, which found utterance in exact similarity of expression. *Our ancestors were a set of noble men.* The careful study of their transactions as spread out upon our early records, show they were men of no mean calibre. They acted and put themselves upon the record fearlessly. With them there was no circumlocution, no fawning to secure position or favor can be charged to them. When they learned what was their right, they went straight to the mark, and did their known duty, fearlessly disregarding consequences."

It appears that these patriotic resolutions that had been adopted by the voters of York were well maintained during the struggle following. Word was received from Lexington in the late evening of that battle day. Early next morning the inhabitants met, a company of more than sixty men was enlisted, and furnished with arms and munitions as well as knapsacks filled with provisions. The command was given to Johnson Moulton, and they marched fifteen miles that day toward Boston and also crossed the same ferry at Portsmouth, which two of them when returning from the war crossed and paid with *one fare.* They were scant of money, having between them the amount asked for one passage. The larger man asked the ferryman if his burden could cross free and on receiving an affirmative response at once placed his companion on his shoulder and embarked, keeping him there until a landing was made on the eastern shore.

The town of York had the honor of putting into the service of the field the first soldiers from Maine. Capt. Moulton continued in the service and was made Lieut. Colonel of Scammon's Regiment. He became Sheriff of the County. Many of his descendants live in York and are enterprising and respected residents. The several actions the town took while the war was in progress may be found in the town records. In 1775, a military watch was ordered kept at night at the mouth of the river. In 1777 a bounty of six pounds was offered to every member of the militia who would enlist in the army. In 1778, it was voted to purchase shoes, stockings, and shirts; this was the year of Valley Forge, of which more later.

The Selectmen at the beginning of the war were Dr. Edward Swett, Edward Grow, Joseph Grant, Samuel Hains, and Jeremiah Weare. History in the form of the Maine records in the Massachusetts archives has preserved the names of the patriot soldiers of York. Her sons fought on nearly every battlefield of the war and the voters of York were zealous patriots and appropriated money and liberally furnished supplies. In the Massachusetts Archives, Vol. 10, page 81, may be found the roster of Capt. Samuel Darby of Old York Company belonging to the 2nd Massachusetts Regiment, John Bailey, Colonel, of the ninety-nine at Valley Forge. I will give the names of those from York:

"A Return of Capt. Samuel Darby's Company: In Col. John Bailey's Regiment, Belonging to the Massachusetts Bay in the Army of the United States.

"Valley Forge, Jan. 25th, 1778.

"Samuel Darby, Old York; Eliakin Hilton, Ensign; Daniel Webber, Sergeant; John Young, Corporal; Stephen Young, Corporal; Privates: James McDonald, Edward Moore, Joseph Parsons, Spencer Perkings, Daniel Preble,

John Perkings, William Preble (Killed in Battle), Abraham Preble, Henry Sayward; (Deserted) Paul Webber, Nathaniel Young.

"A true Rool,

"SAMUEL DARBY, Capt."

The eminent antiquarian, Nathan Goold, Esquire, says:—
"Capt. Samuel Darby, belonged in York, Me. He was a Captain in Col. James Scammon's Regt. that marched to Cambridge soon after the battle of Lexington and served in Gen. Heath's Brigade, in Gen. Putnam's Division, until Dec. 31. He commanded a company in Col. Prescott's 7th Continental Regt. in 1776 and joined Col. Bailey's 2nd Massachusetts Regiment January 1st, 1777. He was commissioned Major in Lieut. Col. Brooks' 7th Massachusetts Regiment Nov. 1st, 1778, and afterwards served in Col. Michael Jackson's 8th Massachusetts Regt. His wife's name was Mary, and he died in 1807."

Capt. Darby must have served several years in the army and the foregoing service named shows that he was a gallant officer, and one of those brave men that we have a right and are proud to call our own. In the company of Capt. James Donnell of York, who was furloughed in the winter of 1777-78, was Henry Sewall, first lieutenant; Jonathan Donnell and Zachariah Gatchell, sergeants; John Gibson, sergeant major; Benjamin Trafton, corporal; Matthias Beal, drummer, and Daniel Bragdon, Will Couch, Joshua McLucas, Daniel Sargent, James Williamson, and Daniel Preble. In Capt. Silas Burbank's company, Charles Sargent. In the company of Capt. Billy Porter, was John Freeman and John Freeman, Jr. In the company of Capt. Daniel Wheelwright of Wells, Josiah Bragdon, Josiah Parsons, Richard Adams and Jotham Baker, were lieutenants, a sergeant and corporal, and Stephen Bridges, John Beal, Abraham Facundus, Peter Grant (who died January 25th, 1777), Shubael Nason, John Sutton, Oliver Plumbery, Abraham Pribble, Archibald Rutlege, Abraham Sawyer, and Ebenezer Young. In Capt. Nicholas Blaisdell's company were John Bedel, sergeant; John Cellars (John Cartisle, Ceaser Prince, John Philips), William Conway and John Davidson. In other companies were Solomon Bloome, Timothy Donnell. The foregoing hailed from York, with the exception of Capts. Burbank and Wheelwright and Blaisdell, and were in regiments other than Col. John Bailey's, viz., Cols. Brewer, Tupper, Wigglesworth and Voses.

Thus may be seen that forty men from York endured with fortitude the sufferings of that dreadful winter of 1777-78, It is not given to any language to describe adequately the scenes of those dreary days at winter camp. Those brave men, with a loyalty unsurpassed, a courage undaunted, fought many battles. The enemies they encountered were not armed with "cannon, sword or musket." The foes they met were "hunger, cold, disease and death." The record shows that the men of York through all the years of the war for our Independence, were trustworthy, loyal and brave, and this was evidenced at the siege of Boston, at Ticonderoga, Saratoga, Valley Forge, Monmouth, and elsewhere. In that struggle short enlistments and consequent and oft-made changes in the personnel of our forces brought about a condition which at times seemed to endanger our success, but "thrice armed is he who has his cause aright," and Washington and his associates knew it and never paused or faltered, "but laid the best they had upon the altar."

YORK IN THE WAR OF 1812

THIS WAR was not popular in the New England coast towns. York was not an exception in this respect. But a volunteer company known as the "Sea Defencibles" was organized, and the harbor was guarded by a battery at Fort Head near the Marshall House. The services of this company were recognized by the United States Government and a bounty in the shape of a land grant certificate was awarded each member. The writer recalls seeing the certificates of three members of the company; they were Ivory Simpson, of Scotland, Ebenezer Chapman, Raynes Neck, and Charles Moody, of York Village. Moses Brewster, grandfather of James S. Brewster, was a privateersman, as was Capt. Jonathan Talpey, who was taken prisoner and confined in Dartmoor Prison. He was the father of Mr. Appleton H. Talpey. Rufus Baker, Jonathan S. Barrell, Joseph Berry, Henry Donnell, Francis Goodwin, Benjamin Lucas, Skipper Lunt, George Moore and Joseph Thompson, were each in the land service, and William Stacy in the navy.

An incident of the war locally; written by Frank D. Marshall is herein reproduced:

"It happened that in the summer of 1814, the British fleet with H. M. S. Bulwark, seventy-four guns, flagship, was blockading Portsmouth and adjacent ports. The primary object was to destroy shipping at the Kittery Navy Yard. The British had captured a small pink-sterned schooner named the 'Juno,' put swivel guns aboard and with an armed crew were capturing and burning unsuspecting coastwise craft. One Sunday while the 'Juno' was pursuing a fisherman up the coast several of the townspeople saw the chase and with muskets hurried out to the 'Knubble.' Concealing themselves, they signalled the pursued to stand in close. In she came by the point, and the 'Juno' followed. As the latter passed the half dozen men behind the rocks opened fire. Where a Donnell fired a red-shirted sailor fell. The British ineffectually returned the shots, although a bullet spatted upon the flat rock which Donnell had placed before himself. The 'Juno' was forced to bear off and the fisherman escaped. The shooting and death of the British sailor was confirmed by captives on the 'Juno,' but who were soon after released. All this fusilade led to further alarm. A man rushed to the doorway of the First Parish Meetinghouse but stood silent until Rev. Mr. Messenger finished his prayer. He then announced, 'I think the British are landing on the "Nubble."' The congregation was dismissed, the York Artillery, an independent company, mustered and with its single field piece started to meet the enemy. When the company had reached Long Beach the cause of the alarm became known and the march ended. The spirit which hastened those untrained militiamen to meet British seamen was the same which impelled their fathers toward Lexington on that April morning, 1775. They thought, with good reason, that the enemy was at hand. Yet they did not know in what numbers; nor did they care. Forthwith they went out to meet them, prepared to do their best."

YORK IN THE CIVIL WAR

"Thy sons in war their lives did give."

IN THE WAR for the preservation of the Union York did noble work in men and money. As from time to time the need was presented the town officials would call the voters together in town meeting, and the "sinews of war" would be appropriated without stint. A full record of every meeting could be given, but room is not available within the covers of this abridged history.

Following are the names of York residents in 1861, who responded to the several later calls for volunteers, supplemented by some incidents remembered by the writer. This roll has been secured with care, aided by Mr. J. S. Brewster, and data from the Adjutant General's Reports. It is hoped that every patriot's name who served is included. It would be interesting to read and know the experiences of each, but in few cases this can be noted.

Ezekiel Austin
George W. Berry
Charles H. Banks
Bradford W. Blaisdell
George Blaisdell
Joseph Blaisdell
William Blaisdell
Charles Bragdon
Frank Came
Wilbur Center
Charles H. Chapman, Navy
Josiah Chase
Joseph Cochie
Thomas Cochie
John Dudley

John Dennett, Navy
Rufus Donnell, Navy
Andrew L. Emerson, Navy
David Fitzgerald
John W. Freeman
Charles L. Grant
John P. Grant
Charles A. Goodwin
Ivory L. Goodwin
Joseph Hill
Charles H. Hooper
William Hooper
Hampden C. Keen
Joseph E. Littlefield
John M. Lowe

Horace Lunt
Joseph W. Manson
William H. Manson, Navy
Daniel H. McIntire
Jeremiah L. McIntire
Thornton McIntire
Albert Moulton
Daniel Patch
Solomon Poole
Charles D. Preble
Charles H. Ramsdell
Paul R. Ramsdell
William H Redding
Moses Rowe
Joseph A. Sewall
Daniel W. Simpson
George O. Simpson, Navy
Albert R. Walker
Charles W. Walker
John H. Walker
Wilson M. Walker

Charles Welch
John F. Welch
Luther D. Welch
Joseph Winn
William H. Woodward
Hiram D. Stover, Navy
George W. Lord, Navy
John F. Weare
William Powell, Navy
C. A. Bowden, Navy
Henry Bowden, Navy
John F. Dixon
Isaiah Boston
Charles Stewart
George H. Hutchins
Henry Dow
John T. Hill
Harmon Varrell, Navy
James S. Brewster
William H. Brewster

Of the foregoing Josiah Chase was the sole commissioned officer in the land forces from York. He was corporal (non com.) in Company E, 27th Maine Regt. Infantry, and later commissioned as lieutenant Co. B, First Maine Battalion. Charles W. Walker was sergeant, John Wesley Freeman, corporal, Company K, First Maine; Andrew L. Emerson and Rufus Donnell were ensigns in the Navy; John Dennett, master's mate; James S. Brewster was in both branches of the service, in the U. S. S. Agawan, with George Dewey, lieut. commander, now Admiral of the Navy, later in the Army, a member of the 20th Maine Vol., and was wounded at the battle of Five Forks; Paul R. Ramsdell, Albert B. Walker, who was a sergeant, and D. Webster Simpson under the immediate command of Lieut. Dahlgren in Kilpatrick's raid on Richmond were taken prisoners, and died in Libby prison. Henry Dow was captured later and met his death in a prison pen. A careful research shows that Charles Donnell Preble and John Moore Lowe were the first from York to enlist. They enlisted at Kittery in the service of the State of Maine in a company raised by Dr. Mark F. Wentworth. They were not mustered into the U. S. Army, but as a state independent company were stationed at Fort McClary, Kittery, for three months. Under an early call Horace Lunt went to the front. The three other sons of Richard and Clarissa Walker—Charles W., John H., and Wilson M.—each enlisted, the latter serving with Gen. Banks at Port Hudson. Bradford W. Blaisdell was severely wounded at Cold Harbor.

John F. Weare, a native of York, was captain of Company C, 40th Regiment Mass. Volunteers, and was shot through the body at the battle of the "Wilderness." He afterward lived in Chicago, and died there a few years ago. His body is interred in the cemetery at Cape Neddick.

George E. Blaisdell, son of Joseph and Elvira Blaisdell, was in Co. E, 23d Mass. Regt. He died in Boston, January 5, 1865. He was on his way home from the front, a victim of southern fever. He was buried in York, Jan. 9, 1865, with military honors. A platoon of infantry from Fort McClary was in attendance and gave a volley as the casket was lowered in the ground. His brother, Bradford W., was wounded at the battle of Cold Harbor, as has been stated.

Mr. S. Judson Adams of Cape Neddick while not in the service was taken prisoner by Southerners.

Master's Mate John Dennett, who after the close of the war entered the service of the U. S. Revenue Marine, became a Captain in that branch of government service. He was on the "Seminole," commanded by Commander Ronaldo, U. S. N., at the celebrated capture of the British blockade runner, a steamer, the Sir William Peel. Capt. Ronaldo's seizure was protested by the British minister at Washington. There is a long story in connection with this capture, it being a rich prize, she having on board one thousand bales of compressed cotton, which had been exchanged by the Confederates for munitions of war. Ensign Stephenson, Master's Mate John Dennett, and Sergeant McKie of the Marine Guard were placed in charge.

Ensign Andrew L. Emerson served under Farragut at the battle of Mobile Bay, and other engagements.

Ensign Rufus Donnell during his term of service was stationed off the harbor of Charleston, S. C., as the executive officer of the armed brig "Perry" in the blockading squadron.

York Association of Veterans and Sons

In order to cherish the memory of those who served in the Civil War, and to foster the spirit of loyalty to the country and the flag, a few of the survivors of the war conceived the idea of forming an organization for the purpose stated, realizing that their numerical strength was not sufficient for the establishment of a regular Grand Army Post. After considerable discussion the plan of an Association was evolved, and October 30, 1897, *"The York Association of Veterans and Sons of Veterans"* came into being, with Charles W. Walker as President, Daniel A. Stevens, Secretary, and J. Alba Sewall, Treasurer. The following is the roster of the members at that time, including the officers named:

John M. Drury, Charles L. Grant, John P. Grant, Edward J. Sylvester, David Fitzgerald, John L. Hatch, James S.

Brewster, John H. Varrell, Harmon Varrell, Charles H. Ramsdell, Charles Hildreth, Charles Stewart, Edward Shea, Hampden C. Keene, Jasper J. Hazen, Josiah Chase, Daniel H. McIntire, Albert Moulton, John W. Freeman, M. J. Adams, Charles Banks, A. L. Emerson, John M. Lowe, John Dennett, Horace Lunt, Wilson M. Walker, John Junkins, George Caswell, Jere L. McIntire, O. B. Schofield, Charles H. Wilson.

Sons

E. D. Twombly, H. D. Philbrick, George F. Preble, Charles E. Noble, Eugene Lee, George Banks, Ross Banks, W. G. Banks, Will T. Keene, John D. Keene, Albert G. McCullum, John Q. Adams, John E. Woodward, Frank Keene, E. A. Sewall.

Since its formation the Association has received yearly by vote of the town the maximum sum allowed by statute to aid in defraying the expenses of the exercises of Memorial Day.

THE OLDE GAOL

PREVIOUS to the placing of the whole Province of Maine under the laws of Massachusetts Bay, a law had been passed in 1646 providing that "each county shall have a house of correction, and that the prisons may be used for houses of correction"; and also enacted that all persons committed "shall first be whipped not exceeding ten stripes." In accordance with this act in the year 1653 the Province raised money to build the gaol, or prison, and it was built at once. Henry Norton was the first sheriff of the Province under the laws of Massachusetts, and assumed, it is supposed, the control of the new prison. In 1695, the county of York having been depleted in men and money by the Indian devastation of three years previous, issued a motion to the General Court setting forth their inability to raise money for their defraying county charges by reason of their poverty, and praying that ye fines in the hand of their sheriff may be granted them for repairing their gaol. The result of the motion was this order: "This Court do order that Mr. Treasurer do pay to the Treasurer of York ten pounds out of fines in the sheriff's hands towards repairing of the County Prison." Later the care and maintenance of the gaol was with the "Court of General Sessions," and the sheriff and the jailor were subordinate and answerable to that body. The sheriff was allowed not exceeding ten pounds per year, and the turnkey or gaoler was allowed two shillings and six-pence for turning the key, and for "diet" three shillings, and nine-pence for each prisoner per week. Until 1760 the gaol served as the prison for the whole province of Maine. From that date to 1802 it was the County Gaol of the County of York, and

up to August 16, 1860, it was in use. So for more than
two hundred years the old prison served as a place of con-
finement for evil doers under sentence. The southwesterly
room could be used as a court room for an inferior court
with Bench and Bar at the westerly end. The higher courts
were generally held in the meeting house, the present First
Parish Meeting House and its predecessor. No doubt there
have been respectable men whose only offence was lack of
funds to pay a small debt, occupying the cells, as well as
murderers, and hardened criminals of various sorts and conditions.

On the small knoll in front of the north end near where
the six-inch Parrot gun is now in position were the stocks
and whipping post. The place where the post stood was
plainly visible a few years since, Prisoners who could give
bonds were given the "liberty of the yard," the yard not
being an enclosure, but a tract of certain defined limits extending each way from the building, and for the spiritual
well-being of the prisoners one of the limits was to the door
of the First Parish Meeting House, "to the end persons
having the liberty of the yard may attend public worship."
That there wer numerous attempts and successful "breaks"
of jail is the story of record and tradition. That of Stephen
Peirce in Marc , 1750, was notable, carrying with it litigation that rea hed the General Court of Massachusetts,
brought by the appeal of the sheriff, Joseph Plaisted's administrator, who by the lower court had been ordered to
pay Samuel Walton of Somersworth, fifteen pounds, four
shillings and two-pence. It appears that in the year 1750
one Stephen Peirce of York, a cordwainer, was attacked
and imprisoned in York at the suit of Samuel Walton of
Summersworth, N. H., in the sum of one hundred pounds,

equal to 13-6-8. Peirce broke prison and escaped. Following is given the record of facts in the matter, taken from Baxter's "Documentary History of Maine":

"The Petition of Joseph Plaisted of York Administrator of the estate of Joseph Plaisted Esq. late of York in said county of York Dec. Humbly sheweth that the said Joseph Plaisted was sheriff of said county of York several years and while he was such, viz., in the year 1750, one Stephen Peirce of York aforesaid cordwainer was attacked and imprisoned in York aforesaid at the suit of Samuel Walton of Summersworth in New Hampshire went to recover one hundred pounds old tenor equal to 13-6-8 lawful money, and broke prison and escaped, since which the said Samuel Walton brought his action against the said sheriff and recovered his damages and costs, which ought to be paid by the County on account of the insufficiency of the Gaol. Therefore, your Petitioner prays ye advisement of this court concerning the premises and that ye costs and damages aforesaid may be paid out of the County Treasury and your Petitioner shall pray, etc. JOSEPH PLAISTED.

Copy Examined.

P JNO. FFROST, Cler."

York S. S.

At a Court of General Sessions of the Peace held at York within and for the County of York the first Tuesday of April, 1753, read and the question being put, whether the prayer of the petition be granted, it passed in the negative, and ordered that this petition be dismissed.

Attest—

JNO. FFROST, Cler.

Copy Examd p Jno. ffrost, Cler.

Petition of Joseph Plaisted to Governor Council & House

of Reps. To His Excellency, William Shirley, Esq. "Captain General and Governor in chief in and over his majesties province of the Massachusetts Bay and to the Honble his maj^{ts} council and House of Representatives for said province in Gen^{ll} Court assembled October 16, 1754.

The Petition of Joseph Plaisted of York in the County of York, yeoman Administrator of the estate of Joseph Plaisted, late of York, Esqr Dec.

Humbly Sheweth,

That in Jan'y, 1750, the said said Joseph Plaisted Esqr being sheriff of said County of York, one Stephen Peirce of York aforesaid cordwainer was arrested and committed to ye Gaol of said County in York by virtue of a writ of attachment at the suit of Saml Walton of Summersworth in New Hampshire Genl for one hundred pounds old tenor due by a note of hand, which writ was returnable at the Infe^r Court of common pleas held at York afores^d, on the first Tuesday of April 1751, at which court in April 1751 the said Sam^{ll} Walton upon said writ recovered judgment against ye said Stephen Peirce by ye sum of 13-6-8 Lawful money, damages and one pound 1612 for cost and had execut^a upon said judgm^t which was returned in no part satisfied. But before the sitting of ye court into which the said writ of attachment was returnable the said Stephen Peirce with the assistance of some evil minded persons broke through the stone wall of the prison, took out the iron grate of the window in the night time about the 20th of March, 1750, and he the said Stephen (together with another prisoner committed there for felony) escaped from the said Gaol against the will of the said Joseph Plaisted, the sheriff, and could not be recovered, notwithstanding the said sheriff used his utmost endeavors to retake him. After the return of the exe-

cution * * * said Walton appealed to ye Super^r Court
of Juicature held at York for said County in June, 1752,
and upon that appeal the said Sam^ll Walton recovered Judgment against ye said Joseph Plaisted, Esqr for ye sum of
15-4-2 damages and costs 5, 8, 3, at which Judgment the
said Joseph Plaisted Esqr thinking himself greatly wronged
and injured for that the escape of the said Stephen was not
a voluntary escape as to ye sheriff nor a negligent escape but
by and with the assistance of others to ye sheriff unknown
who with force and strong hand in riotous manner in the
night broke through the prison wall by means whereof ye
said Stephen escaped and not by or with ye will or negli-
gence of ye sheriff and for which the said sheriff humbly
conceived he was not answerable or liable by law to make
good the damages any more than he was obliged to build a
Gaol at his own cost and thereupon with ye care of the
Honble Sup^r Court pursuant to law gave bond to review the
said action at the then next Supe^r Court of Judicature to be
held in York for said County. (The associates on the bond
were Henry Simpson, and Johnathan Bean, each in the sum
of forty pounds. Editor.) Soon after which he was taken
sick and languished until about ye 25th August, 1752, when
the said Joseph Plaisted, Esqr dyed not having served a
writ of review of that case for want of opportunity, and
afterwards, namely, about ye beginning of January 1754
the said Saml Walton dyed, the said judgment not being
satisfied nor the action reviewed. Since which ye Admin^rs
of the said Sam^ll Walton have claimed of your Petitioner
Adm^k of Jos. Plaisted Esqr dee^d ye sums recovered by said
Judgm^t which your Petitioner thinks he ought not to be
obliged to pay— Your Petitioner prays leave further to
observe that since the death of the said Joseph Plaisted,

Esqr your Petitioner for presenting of any farther cost or trouble about ye case apply^d to ye court of General Sessions of the Peace for said County held at York on ye first Tuesday of April, 1753, shewing forth the premises that the said escape was through the insufficency of the Gaol praying that the said court would order satisfaction to be made out of the County Treasury— but they refused to do it— so your Petitioner is without remedy unless aided by this Honble Court about and concerning the premises. Wherefore your Petitioner humbly prays that he may be enabled by the authority of the Honble Court to have his remedy either against the County Treasury for all his damages and costs. Or that he may be enabled to review the aforesaid action *   *   * Or that he may have such other relief in the premises as to this Honble Court in their great wisdom and justice shall seem meet, and your Petit^r as in duty bound shall ever pray.

JOSEPH PLAISTED,
Administrator.

In the House of Representatives Nov. 14, 1754.

Read and ordered that the pet^r serve the adverse party, viz., the administrator of Samuel Walton Dec. with a copy of the Petition that he shew cause (if he have any) on the first friday of the next sitting of the Court why the prayer thereof should not be granted.

Sent up for Concurrence— T. HUBBARD, Spk.

In Council Nov. 15, 1754. Read and Concerned.

THOS. CLARKE, Dp^ty Secry.

Answer to the Petition of Joseph Plaisted, Adm^or

To His Excellency, William Shirley, Esqr, Captain, General and Governor in chief in and over his majesty's province of the Massachusetts Bay. The Honble His majesty's council and House of Representatives for said Province in Gen-

eral Court assembled Feb. 4, 1755. The answer of George
Walton, Esqr, Moses Carr and Elizabeth Walton, executors
of the testament of Samuel Walton, late of Somersworth in
the Province of New Hampshire, Deceas^ed To the Petition
of Joseph Plaisted of York in the County of York, yeoman,
* * * in the matter of an escape of one Stephen Peirce,
etc. The Respondts humbly conceive it is not resonable to
grant this petition so far as concerns them— 1st. Because
there was a fair Tryal upon Appeal when full evidence was
committed to the jury * * * which in case of a New
Tryal can't possibly be done, for the Respond^ts are wholly
strangers to the circumstances of the escape, as well as to
the name of the witnesses by which proper proof was made,
the Testimonies being given Viva Voce in Court and no foot-
steps remaining how or where to come at them. The principal of which were persons then living at the prison, are
long since removed by death or other ways * * * For
it can't be conceived had the case really been as the Petitioner represents it, that, that court considering the provision
made by the Province Law in such cases would have rejected
his motion. But the Case in truth (as the Respond^ts have
it from others) was thus, the Prisoner was a Shoe-maker,
the Sheriff permitted him to work at his Trade in the Prison,
had his Tools and Billets of Wood for his fire, by which he
cut away the wood and wrenched out the Grates in the
window of the Room in which he was confined at which
Window he made his Escape— Suggestion therefore of
Riotous Assistants with force of strong hand breaking
through the Prison Wall, and that he got out of the Prison
by that means is without foundation, which many of the
said Justices knew, by what they heard in the time the fact
was done, and afterwards on the Trial, which was doubtless

the Reason of the Sessions denying relief * * * The
Delay of this Motion so long, is some objection against it,
the said Sam¹ Walton had had no apprehentions of it in his
time, considered the said Judgment as part of his Personal
Estate and doubtless had some Regard to it in the Disposition of his Estate, * * * as to that part of the Petition Desiring a Remedy against the County Treasurer the
Respondᵗˢ have nothing to say. But upon the whole as to
the Review prayed for, submit it, that the Petition is un-
reasonable.

Geo. Walton
Moses Carr
Elizabeth Walton
Executors.

Deposition of Abiel Goodwin

The Deposition of Abiel Goodwin of York in the County
of York testifieth and saith that the next day after it was
reported that Samuel Ball and Stephen Pearce had broake
out of York Gaol which the Deponᵗ thinks was some time
in March 1750 he was sent for by the then Keeper Mr.
Sheriff Plaisted since decᵉᵈ to mend the Breach upon which
he the Deponᵗ immediately came and did it,— And upon
examining the Breach found it was at one of the Windows
where the Wall as he judges was about two feet and an half
thro'. The Window was Double Grated with Iron Grates
placed into Iron Bars one set of Grates and Bars being
placed in the inner edge of the Window and secured in the
Oak Plank with which the Walls are cealed. The other set
of Grates and Bars was about midway of the Wall and
secured in the same. The manner of the Breach as the
Deponᵗ judges was thus, the prisoners first got out the inner

set of Grates and Bars whether by the help of a stick of Wood which he saw there in the Gaol or other ways he can't tell but to the best of his remembrance one of the Grates was broake with the help of which as the Depon^t judges they Pick^d out the Stones and Lime between the Oak Cealing aforesaid and the next pair of Grates, (the Stones being in the middle of the Wall something small), and made such way as to slip the Bars into which the Grates were plac'd on end and so made way to creap out.

ABIEL GOODWIN.

York, Feb. 3, 1755.

York S. S. Feb. 3, 1755.

Then Mr. Abiel Goodwin personally appearing solemnly made oath to the truth of the within written Deposition by him subscribed.

Before DAN^L MOULTON

Jus. Peace.

In continuance of action by the General Court on Plaisted's Petition the Council took the matter in hand:

In Council Feb'y 12, 1755. Read again together with the Answer of the Executors of Saml Walton Dec^d. and ordered that John Greenleaf and Benj. Lincoln Esq^{rs} with such as the Honble House shall join be a Com^{tee} to consider this Pet^n hear the Parties and report what they judge proper for this court to do thereon. Sent down for concurrence.

by Ord^r of the Board

J. OSBORNE.

In House of Represent— Feb'y 12, 1755.

Read and Concurred and Col. Hale, Mr Bradbury & Mr Niles are joined in the Affair.

T. HUBBARD, Spk^r

Report of the Committee

The Committee— to whom was Refer'd the petition within mentioned having fully considered the same with the papers accompanying it are of Opinion that the prayer of the petition be so far granted that the petitioner in his capacity afores[d] be impowered to bring forward a writt of Review at the next Superior Court to be holden for the County of York in an action wherein the S[d] Joseph Plaisted dec[d] was the Original Defen[dt] against the Exec[rs] of the Testament of Sam[l] Walton dec[d] and all further proceedings on the former judgment in the meantime be stayed.

P Order John Greenleaf.

In Council Feb'ry 21, 1755.   Read and Ordered that the above Report be accepted and that the Pet[r] in his capacity aforesaid be and hereby is impowered to bring forward a writ of Review at the next Superior Court of Judicature to be holden at York.   *   *   *   And all other proceedings on the former judgment are staid in the meantime   *   *   *

Sent down for Concurrence—

Thomas Clarke, Dep[ty] Secry.

In the House of Rep. Feb. 21, 1755.   Read & Concurred.

Consented to W. Shirley.

What the final outcome of the matter was I have not been able to ascertain.   In the historical foreword of the catalogue of the Olde Gaol Museum written by Frank D. Marshall several escapes are mentioned, one of which I will bring into this account:

"Spiked to the underside of the flooring, which may be seen between the dungeon and the north wall, is a heavy hardwood plank.   This recalls the story of the escape of two criminals on a December night in 1823, for beneath the plank can undoubtedly be found the hole cut with a shoe-knife through hard beech flooring, and through which the escape was made. The gaoler and his assistant on that night heard the shout of a man in the cell and rushing in found one of the prisoners wedged in the hole to his armpits. In his eagerness to escape, another prisoner had jumped upon the shoulders of his companion and so hurt him that he cried out. The gaoler rushed to the outside of the building to prevent the escape of two prisoners who had already gone through the hole. He saw them running over the hill toward the burying ground and pursued. One disappeared and the other shortly outran the gaoler and escaped. Some weeks later the gaoler received a letter from one of these men, telling him that the moment he jumped over the wall of the burying ground he crouched under it and that the gaoler unknowingly jumped over him in pursuit of the other man. He thanked the gaoler for kindness shown and expressed gladness that he was not discovered, for he said he would never have been recaptured alive and was prepared to disable the gaoler. He also donated a small sum of money which was due him towards purchasing a new bell for the First Parish Church, to replace the cracked one which he described as 'that cussed sounding thing.' Years later the name of this man might be seen upon the door-plate of a substantial Boston residence."

It was from this gaol that Seymour went forth to his hanging at Stage Neck, the story of which is told in this book.

It is without doubt the oldest public building of the days of the Colonies in this country, and under the watchful care of the York Improvement Society stands up against the ravages of time for many years.

THE FIRST PARISH MEETING HOUSE

THE FIRST Meeting House of the Parish was erected sometime prior to 1699 nearly on the site of the house of Mr. G. Frank Austin. It was standing at that date. As all records of the Parish were destroyed in 1692 the time of its building cannot be given.

In May, 1710, the town voted to build a new meeting house, on the northeasterly side of the country road by the burying place, on land given for the use of the ministry, and have it finished by the last day of November, 1712. That the house was built is shown by the town record, which reads: "York, July 15, 1713, Laid out to Nicholas Sewall, half an acre of land for a tan yard, granted to him the 23d day of March last by said town of York, with the privilege of the spring of water, between the *new* and the *old meeting house,* where the said Sewall's tan yards now are, and is bounded as followeth, viz: Beginning at a stake standing at the north ward corner of Mr. Moody's little field, on that side of the way, and runs from thence six poles to a white oak stake marked on four sides, (by Moody's land); thence northeast thirteen poles to a stake standing by *the way that leads to the old meeting house from the country road,* and is bounded by said road to the stake first above mentioned." In the two meeting houses all town business was transacted, and the courts held at least up to 1732. The first direct action taken to build the present structure was in 1744 as appears from the Parish records: "At a Parish meeting regularly assembled the 19th day of April, 1744, Voted that there be a Meeting House built in this parish by subscriptions, of seventy feet long, and fifty feet wide, and twenty-five feet studd, and be set in the same place where the old Meeting House now stands." But through the delinquency of the subscribers the house was not founded until 1747 and during that summer completed. In 1838-39 the house was remodeled and great changes were made in the exterior and interior of the building, the most striking within, where the gallerys, the elders' seats, the high pulpit and sounding board were removed. The entrance, which had been on the side, was changed to the end next the Court House. The work was in charge of a committee consisting of Charles Moody, Joseph P. Junkins, Eben Chapman, Paul Langdon, Charles O. Emerson. The house was reopened and dedicated July 3, 1839. Rev. John Haven preached the sermon from the text found in Genesis 28-17. In opening he said: "We assemble this day for the first time in this temple, remodeled for the worship of Almighty God. The object which has convened this audience, is one which accords with every pious sentiment of the soul * * * Accordingly, we meet at this time, to consecrate the interior of the building to the worship and service of the majesty of heaven. We shall have no august and imposing ceremony to awaken the imagination of the thoughtless, and dazzle the eye, but the solemnities will be characterized with the simplicity which marks the ordinances of the gospel dispensation * * * The reopening of a house of worship is an event which crowds the mind with recollections of the past, and points onward to that scene, when the grand results of all God's plans for this world, Christ's sufferings, and the Spirit's agency, shall be announced. When we remember the throngs which assembled in this venerable structure in its primitive glory; the success which attended the gospel especially in its early history; the generations which have come and gone since

the corner-stone was laid; the worthy men who have contended for the faith once delivered to the saints; and when
we take into consideration the circumstances which have
called us together, and the future purpose to which this house
is to be devoted, we may exclaim with the ancient servant
of God, 'How dreadful is this place. This is none other
than the house of God, and this is the gate of heaven.'"
*   *   *   "Who is left among you that saw this house her
first glory?" They are gone, minister and people, in less
than one hundred years they have been gathered to the
graves of their fathers.

> "Our fathers where are they,
> With all they call their own?
> There where the fathers lie
> Must all the children come."

But our spirits will live when this world shall be known
only in the past.

The most elaborate and extensive remodeling was made
in 1881-2. At a Parish Meeting held April 11th, 1881, it
was voted to repair and remodel the meeting house, and on
motion of Dr. Wilson L. Hawkes a committee consisting of
Washington Junkins, John B. Fernald, Samuel P. Young,
John E. Staples and Edward C. Moody were chosen to carry
out the vote of the Parish. The committee organized with
the choice of John B. Fernald, Washington Junkins, Chairman and Treasurer, and Edward C. Moody, Secretary. At
a subsequent meeting of the Parish the membership of the
committee was increased to seven by the addition of Edward
S. Marshall and Wilson M. Walker. The exterior and interior of the building were entirely changed. Previous to
1881 the building stood lengthwise parellel with the road,

the tower and steeple being on the western end, the entrance
at the eastern end. The building was changed from its
original site to the extent of bringing the tower facing the
highway, and the entrance end toward the cemetery. This
work was performed by contract. Edward S. Marshall,
Edward B. Blaisdell, and Edward C. Moody were awarded
the contract, and gave bonds in the sum of one thousand
dollars to perform the work in safety to the building, particularly as regarded the steeple. This work being duly
accomplished, and the steeple apparently not swerved any
perceptible distance therefrom, the committee decided to take
the steeple down, which was done and in accordance with
the plans drawn by Architect Silloway of Boston the present
tower and spire were built, the distance from the base to the
apex being twenty feet higher than originally. The main
entrance was made in the base of the tower, and one on the
northern end for the pastor's use. The interior was entirely changed. The gallery formerly used by the choir was
removed, the pulpit was transferred to the northern end of
the auditorium, with the organ and choir seats at the left
of the platform. The re-dedication took place in 1882.
Ex-President of Bowdoin Joshua L. Chamberlain delivered
the address. The committee on remodeling presented the
following to the First Church of Christ in York, through
the Deacons, Charles Colburn Barrell and Frank Phillips
Emerson:

York, Maine, Sept. 27, 1882.

Gentlemen:

We who have attached our names to this communication
were chosen by the First Congregational Parish in York, a
building and repairing committee, to have in charge, direct
the measures adopted, the means afforded, for repairing the

meeting house of our parish. In the absence of any action
by the parish as a body corporate and party in interest for-
mally presenting the remodeled meeting house to the church
of which you are worthy members, as we trust, and that you
represent in the subject matter, on which we address you;—
we take great pleasure in placing in your care and keeping
for solemn dedication this house of the Lord. "The tribe
of Levi shall have charge thereof, but hither let all the tribes
come up and worship." It is not needed, and yet perhaps
it will be well to say that in the outlay which has been made
we have exceeded the fartherest bounds anticipated by the
most progressive member of our ancient parish, but we can
truly say that the added beauty of our church edifice is com-
mensurate with the burden it brought, and will so be regarded as the days go by. True it is that loving and kindly
hands have aided us in making the "Old York Meeting
House" a pleasant home on Sabbath days for ourselves, our
children, and we hope, our children's children, and the
strangers within our gates. The ladies of the First Church
and Parish have one and all done right well; a distinction,
should we make it, would be invidious. The misses emu-
lated the example of their elders, and soon, how soon, they
will be the ladies of the First Parish. We can but think,
as we have this brief word with you, of one of our number,
who passed from among us to those beyond. Col. Washington Junkins, the chairman of the building and repairing
committee, died before the work he was so much interested
in, to which his persuasion and enterprise gave impetus, was
finished, and as we think of him our thoughts are kind. It
would be idle to say, more idle to believe, that all this good

work has gone on to completion without difference of honest opinion, now let us all truly say "Peace be within thy walls."

(Signed)   JOHN B. FERNALD,
            JOHN E. STAPLES,
            EDWARD S. MARSHALL,
            WILSON M. WALKER,
            EDWARD C. MOODY,

Committee.

To Charles C. Barrell,
    Frank P. Emerson,
        Deacons First Cong'l Church,
            York, Maine.

THE COURT HOUSE, NOW TOWN HALL

FROM THE earliest record obtainable we learn that up to 1713 the town had no fixed place to transact its business. If in 1653 the old meeting house was standing, and when the first court was holden, it was probably held there.

In March, 1715, at a meeting it was "Voted that our general town meeting shall be holden upon the second Tuesday in March, hereafter, at *our meeting house,* beginning at 9 o'clock in the forenoon."

Also on the 19th of June, 1732, a town meeting was holden in the meeting house in the First Parish, and up to 1732, there all town business appears to have been done. A town meeting was held in May, 1726, where action was taken toward the erection of a building to accommodate the courts of justice and for the use of the town.

It was "Voted, that if the justice of the quarter sessions (now County Commissioners) order the building of a *Court House* in the town, this town shall bear one-half the charge of building said house, provided said town may have the use of said house for holding town meetings, and keeping the grammar school."

On the 5th of December, 1733, $100 was raised towards building a Court House, and on the 20th day of the same month a committee was chosen to join the "Courts committee," to "appoint a place to set said house upon." In January, 1734, it was "Voted, that this town will join with the County in building a Court House, in this town, which house shall be for the use of the County to hold courts in and for the use of this town to meet in, on all public times." This action had become necessary from the fact that in 1731 the First Parish was organized, and the town had no control over, or right to use parish property, but at times the two parties reciprocated, as the record says—A *parish* meeting was holden in the *town house* on Dec. 26th, 1735, and on May 23, 1745, the town meeting was adjourned to the meeting house.

This Court House was located on a plat of land between the four old elm trees recently standing in front of the present Town Hall and the house of Jeremiah McIntire, for as Judge David Sewall wrote on the inside of the cover of a volume of our Probate Records—"Four elm trees set out between Town House and Meeting House April 15, 1773." This building was used for seventy-seven years as a town house.

York had been the shire town of the Province of Maine from 1716 to 1735; then Portland was made a shire town with it for the whole province up to 1760; then shire town for the County of York from 1760 to 1802, when Alfred was made a shire town with York. It was at about this time many complaints were made of the unsuitable condition of the old town house for holding courts, and the want of accommodations for the various parties who usually attend court, and the result was that the terms of the Supreme Court in 1800 and 1801 were held in Wells, in that part now Kennebunk. Strong efforts were made in the General Court to have the towns of Alfred and Kennebunk constituted shire towns for the County. Our people and those of Kittery and Berwick were much wrought up over the matter, and measures were brought about whereby the County gave $500, York $600, and individuals in York and Kittery gave liberally to the fund for building the Court House, which was done in 1810 and 1811, and courts were held here until 1832, when they were on account of our geographical position all removed to Alfred, except at times Probate Court would be held in York in July and August, up to 1863. Mr. Marshall in his address delivered Feb. 22, 1874, at the dedication of the practically new town hall, says: "From 1832 to 1873, upwards of forty years, this building had been used for almost every conceivable purpose—town house, hearse house, school house, etc., without a friend to care for it, a target for *play balls* and harder missiles of unruly boys and 'children of a larger growth,' 'with none so poor as to do it reverence,' until it had become a byword and a standing disgrace to the town." The interest of the County in it had been purchased by the town, and at its annual meeting and a subsequent meeting in 1873, money was raised to rebuild and remodel it. Hon Nathaniel G. Marshall was chosen an agent to take charge of the work. At the beginning and during the process of reconstruction several town meetings were called. In the warrant of one was an article to see if the town would vote to move the building to a lot at Cider Hill. During the meeting a motion was made and seconded to carry that matter into effect. A motion to "lay that motion on the table" was made, but the maker of the first motion objected, saying, "Mr. Moderator, that can't be done, there ain't no table here, and beside all that the motion ain't writ out." However, the meeting disposed of the question by passing a vote to "indefinitely postpone."

In 1893 the building was enlarged by an addition of sixteen feet on the northern side, in the upper hall great improvement was made under the auspices of the "York Association," aided by the town, and Feb. 22, 1894, the Association gave a supper, and appropriate exercises were held in the enlarged and beautified upper hall. Edward C. Moody

by invitation delivered an address and in speaking of the
room as it was in court days said: "Some of you in your
thought can see this room as it was in 1873, the entrance
being by a wide flight of stairs from the lower hall at my
left. Just in front of the landing, ascending a few steps,
was the jury room, a corridor from the landing to the hall
of justice, and on either side were raised seats for spectators.
In the center were seats for the members of the bar, flanked
on each side by the sheriff boxes, and jury benches. In the
southern end was the place of dignity and awe, the desk of
the judges, just in front of which was that of the clerk, and
at his other hand the prisoners' dock and the witness stand.
Running from a point just back of the sheriff's box to the
judge bench was a row of seats on each side. * * *
This hall has been the theatre of many exciting scenes.
Audiences have here listened spellbound to orators of renown.   Here were formulated military plans for 'training
days.' Here Major General McIntire, the pride of the
Maine Militia, of superb military bearing, issued his orders,
and just outside Capt. Thompson of Artillery fame in a fit
of righteous indignation broke his sword on the limbers of
a gun carriage. * * * Now, to you young men and
women, who will meet here, as we trust, twenty years from
tonight, and you boys and girls who will then be the young
men and women, I beseech you guard well this hall which
from time to time will be improved and beautified. Let no
disloyal sentiments here be publicly uttered, no disloyal act
perpetrated, and if in the future as in the past, duty calls,
gather as loyal sons and daughters for the protection of your
country and your flag; and never let it be said that a son of
York dishonored the Stars and Stripes, and as Hannibal
swore on the knees of his father eternal hostility to the

Romans, so here swear you by the memories of those who have gone before to ever be faithful to your good old town, and all its interests, and then doing your duty, 'every winter of discontent shall be made glorious summer' by the sons and daughters of York."

YORK IN THE CONSTITUTIONAL CONVENTION

A CONVENTION of Delegates were assembled at Portland on the 11th day of October, 1819, and continued in session until the 29th day of same month for the purpose of forming a constitution for the new State of Maine. Three delegates were in attendance from York: Elihu Bragdon, Jeremiah Bradbury and David Wilcox.

Elihu Bragdon was the son of Daniel and Mary (Came) Bragdon of York; born May 3d, 1767. He was Representative to the General Court from 1808 to 1819, State Representative in 1820-1-5-6, Justice of the Peace 1821 to 1832, Coroner for York County, 1825, Selectman for nearly thirty years. He married Abigail, daughter of Cotton Bradbury; had a son, James, born Oct. 9, 1789, a Selectman, Sheriff, Jailor, and a Representative in the Legislature at the time of his death Nov. 6th, 1831.

Jeremiah Bradbury was born in Saco, Oct. 22, 1779, the son of Thomas and Dorothy (Clark) Bradbury. He studied law and was admitted to the York County Bar in 1805, and opened an office in Saco; removed to Biddeford in 1810, to South Berwick in 1812, and to York in 1815. He was Collector of Customs at York from 1813 to 1820; appointed by Gov. King Clerk of the Judicial Courts in 1820, removed to Alfred in 1821; was Clerk of the Courts in York County from 1820 to 1841 with the exception of one year; removed to Calais in 1841, where he continued in the practice of law until his death in 1848 in November. He married Oct. 28th, 1810, Mary Langdon, daughter of Seth and Olive (Jordan) Storer of Wells. Eight children were born to them, the oldest being Bion Bradbury, born at Biddeford Dec. 6th, 1811, who afterward was Collector of the Port at Eastport, Democratic candidate for Governor of Maine in 1863, and afterward Surveyor of the Port at Portland. David Wilcox was Deputy Sheriff for York County from 1821 to 1825, Weigher in the Custom House, York District, from 1823 to 1827, Inspector of Customs from 1829 to 1830, Justice of the Peace from 1823 to 1832, Postmaster from 1823 to 1828, and Coroner from 1830 to 1832.

The Constitution was signed Oct. 29, 1819. Mr. Bradbury of York declined to sign. And it was provided that: "This Constitution shall be enrolled on parchment, deposited in the Secretary's Office, and be the supreme law of the state, and printed copies thereof shall be prefixed to the books containing the laws of this state."

It may not be out of place in this connection to relate that previous to the convention of 1819, several meetings of citizen delegates had assembled to take into consideration the question of separation from Massachusetts. These were in 1788-1793 and '94 in Portland, but they proved abortive. In 1816 a Convention was called at Brunswick. York was represented in this Convention by Messrs. Bragdon, Bradbury and McIntire. It appears to have been a lively gathering of Democrats and Federalists, the Democrats generally in favor of separation, the Federalists opposed. The committee on credentials, an important one (then as now), did not agree. "Judge Widey suggested that some certificates might not be signed by the town clerk, what then?" Capt. Tolman replied, "Those would be like the old woman's tub without any bottom, who said 'It was no tub at all.'" On October 9th without large accomplishment the Convention adjourned to the 20th of December. Of this meeting, if held, I find no record.

But the leaven had begun to work. In January, 1820, Hon. David Cony addressed a letter to ex-President John Adams, in part as follows:

"Sir: The circular enclosed regards a subject which has several times, within forty years past, been brought before the public * * * *Shall Maine separate from Massachusetts?* I should feel particularly grateful to know your opinion." * * *

Ex-President Adams in reply, Feb. 1, 1819, wrote in part: "Dear Sir:

* * * "The question you state to me is of so much importance and the decision of it leads to consequences so extensive that a volume might be written in favor of the affirmative, and another in favor of the negative. My forces are not competent to the composition of either, my judgment poor as it is, and my inclinations strong as they are, are all on the side of union. * * * But I can tell you how it will be when there arises in Maine a bold, daring, ardent genius, with talents capable of inspiring the people with his own enthusiasm, and ambition. He will tear off Maine from Massachusetts and leave her a state below mediocrity in the union. My advice therefore is to remain as you are long as you can." Mr. Adams' advice was not followed. The "ardent genius" arose in the person of William King of Bath, who was President of the Constitutional Convention, and the first Governor of Maine.

CIVIL LIST — COLONY

REPRESENTATIVES UNDER CHARTER

Edward Risworth,   1653-1666   Peter Weare,   1665-1666

CIVIL LIST

REPRESENTATIVES IN GENERAL COURT OF MASSACHUSETTS
AND LEGISLATURE OF MAINE FROM 1690 TO 1913

Samuel Donnell,	1690-91	Josiah Bragdon,	1812-13-15
Jeremiah Moulton, }		Peter Weare,	1812
Moses Turprey, }	1692	Isaac Lyman,	1816
William Screvine,	1694	Capt. Thomas Savage,	1817
Abraham Preble, }		Cotton Chase,	1819
Ezekiel Rodgers, }	1698	Charles O. Emerson,	1825 to 1828
From 1768 to 1724 no record.		Josiah Chase,	1829-35-43-54
Peter Nowell,	1724	Nathaniel Webber,	1831-32-44
Samuel Came,	1725-43	Solomon Brooks,	1834-36-37-40
Jeremiah Moulton,	1726-28	William McIntire,	1838-39
Johnson Harmon,	1727	Theodore Wilson,	1841-42
Richard Millbury,	1729 to 39-45	Samuel Webber,	1845-46
Samuel Clark,	1741	George M. Freeman,	1847-48
Capt. Thomas Bragdon,		Alexander Dennett,	1849-50
1747 to 1750-63-69-70-71-72-73		George Bowden,	1852-53
Joseph Plaisted,	1752	Charles Came,	1855-56
John Bradbury,	1753-1762	William H. Swett,	1857-58
Jonathan Sayward,	1765 to 1768	Samuel E. Payne,	1859-60
Daniel Bragdon,	1774-75	Asa McIntire,	1862
Joseph Simpson,	1776-77	Josiah D. Bragdon,	1864
Col. Edward Grow,	1778 to '84	Charles C. Barrell,	1866
John Swett,	1785-86	Charles Junkins,	1868
Capt. Esais Preble,	1787-89-96-98	Joseph Bragdon, Jr.,	1870
Hon. David Sewall,	1790	George W. S. Putnam,	1872
Joseph Tucker,	1791 to 1793	George M. Payne,	1874
Nathaniel Barrell,	1794	Josiah D. Bragdon,	1876
Joseph Bragdon,	1795-99-1800-5	James A. Bragdon,	1878
Major Samuel Derby,	1801 to 1804	Daniel B. Harris,	1880
Alexander McIntire,		Samuel W. Junkins,	1884
1806-7-8-15-16-20-23-30-33		Edward S. Marshall,	1889
Elihu Bragdon,		Fremont Varrell,	1892
1807-9-10-11-12-13-15-18-19-		Joseph W. Simpson,	1896
20-23-24		John E. Staples,	1901
Jere Clark,	1809	Richard F. Talpey,	1905
Joseph Bradbury,	1810-11-12-13-15	Josiah Chase,	1909-11
Joseph Weare, Jr.,	1810-11	Arthur E. Bragdon,	1913

CIVIL LIST — UNITED STATES

Presidential Elector—David Sewall, 1788.

Collector of Internal Revenue—Nathaniel G. Marshall, 1862 to 1870.

Chief Accountant of Portsmouth Navy Yard—Edward C. Moody, 1873-74.

Provincial Congress—Daniel Bragdon, 1774-75.

COLLECTORS OF CUSTOMS

Richard Trevett,	1791	Luther Junkins,	1853
Joseph Tucker,	1795	Washington Junkins,	1860
Samuel Derby,	1804	George Bowden,	1860
Jeremiah Clarke,	1809	Jeremiah S. Putnam,	1861
Alexander McIntire,	1811	Edward A. Bragdon,	1870
Jeremiah Bradbury,	1815	Joel Wilson,	1886
Thomas Savage,	1821	George W. Currier,	1891
Mark Dennett,	1829	Edward W. Baker,	1898
Joseph P. Junkins,	1840	Edward H. Banks,	1902
Jeremiah Brooks,	1841	George E. Marshall,	1905
Nathaniel G. Marshall,	1849	Herbert D. Philbrick,	1908

CIVIL LIST — PROVINCE AND STATE

1698 to 1913

TOWN CLERKS

James Plaisted,	1698	Edgar A. McIntire,	1852 to 1856
Followed by Abraham Preble.		Washington Junkins,	1856 to 1863
Joseph Moody,	1723 to 1732	Charles I. Hutchins,	1864 to 1865
Jeremiah Moulton,	1733 to 1743	Samuel P. Young,	1865 to 1873
Abraham Nowell,	1744-45	C. O. Clark,	1873 to 1874
Daniel Moulton,	1745 to 1782-84	Nathaniel G. Marshall,	
Joseph Simpson,			1875 to 1879
	1782 to 1783-1784 to 1794	Joseph Bragdon,	1880 to 1892
Joseph Tucker,	1795 to 1801	Bradford S. Woodward,	
Moses Lyman,	1802 to 1808		1893 to 1895
Alexander McIntire, 1809 to 1815-		Allen C. Moulton,	1895 to 1899
1818 to 1821-1827 to 1837-1839		A. B. Bragdon,	1900 to 1901
to June, 1852, when he de-		George F. Plaisted,	
ceased.			1901 to the present time

JUDGES OF COURT COMMON PLEAS

Job Alcock,	1692	Samuel Came,	1731
Samuel Donnell,	1699	Joseph Moody,	
Abraham Preble,	1699		1731, resigned 1732
Samuel Moody, 1724, appointed		Jeremiah Moulton, Dec. 15, 1732,	
to succeed Abraham Preble,		to fill vacancy.	
who died March 24, 1724,			
aged forty-nine years.			

STATE SENATORS

Alexander McIntire,	1835-36	Nathaniel G. Marshall,	1861-62
Solomon Brooks,	1843-44	John C. Stewart,	1891
William McIntire,	1853-54	Joseph W. Simpson,	1905-7

COUNCILLORS UNDER MASSACHUSETTS

Job Alcock,	1692	John Bradbury,	1763-72
Samuel Donnell,	1700	David Sewall,	1776-78-80
Samuel Came,	1733-41	Joseph Simpson,	1780-81
Jeremiah Moulton,	1735-51		

COUNTY COMMISSIONERS

Joseph Bragdon,   Samuel Junkins,
        1874-75-76-77-78-79   1901-2-3-4-5-6-7-8-9-10-11-12

MEMBERS EXECUTIVE COUNCIL

Edward C. Moody,   1879 Edward S. Marshall,   1897-99

STATE TREASURER

Joseph W. Simpson,   1913

SHERIFFS OF COUNTY

Henry Norton,	1653	Jotham Moulton,	1771
Abraham Preble, Jr.,	1713	Johnson Moulton,	1784
Jeremiah Moulton,	1724	Nathaniel G. Marshall,	1854-1857
Jeremiah Moulton, Jr.,	1752		

CLERK OF COURTS

Daniel Sewall,   1794-1812 Jeremiah Bradbury,   1812-1838

THE PASSING OF THE CUSTOMS DISTRICT OF YORK

In his message to the third session of the 61st Congress, Dec. 6, 1910, President Taft said: "There are entirely too many customs districts and too many customs collectors. These districts should be consolidated, and the collectors in charge of them, who draw good salaries, many of them out of proportion to the collections made, should be abolished or treated as mere branch offices, in accordance with the plan of the Treasury Department which will be presented for the consideration of Congress. As an illustration, the cost of collecting $1 of revenue at typical small ports like the port of York, Me., was $50.04 or $510 per year. Subsequently the Congress authorized the carrying out of the plan suggested. And under the order of the President the last day of his one term of office, March 3, 1913, the Customs District of York was abolished, and thenceforth all business arising at York will have to be transacted at Portsmouth, N. H., the nearest port of entry. Miss Adaline Talpey Marshall, who has been Deputy Collector of the Port since October, 1905, delivered the effects of the office to Deputy Collector Looney of Portsmouth, N. H. Mr. H. D. Philbrick had been Acting Collector since Jan. 15, 1911.

The York Customs District was one of the oldest in the country. At the first session of the Congress of the United States in June, 1789, a law was passed with a preamble declaring it to be "necessary for the support of Government, for the discharge of the debts of the United States, and the encouragement of manufactures, that duties be laid on goods, wares, and merchandise imported." This law imposed specific duties on a long list of enumerated articles and an ad valorem duty upon others. The duties on goods imported in American vessels were ten per cent less than if brought in foreign vessels. Thereupon in 1790 Customs Districts with ports of entry and delivery were established on the seaboard and northern and eastern border, and early in 1791 Secretary of the Treasury Alexander Hamilton recommended Richard Trevett as a suitable person to organize and establish a working institution the Custom House at York. He was nominated by President Washington for Collector, confirmed by the Senate, and his commission dates March 21, 1791. He was followed by the persons named down to Jan. 15, 1907:

Name	Date of Temporary Commission	Date of Permanent Commission
Trevett, Richard		March 21, 1791
Tucker, Joseph	July 26, 1793	January 28, 1794
Derby, Samuel		December 21, 1803
Clarke, Jeremiah		March 2, 1807
McIntire, Alexander		February 8, 1809
Bradbury, Jeremiah		February 23, 1813
Dennett, Mark		February 9, 1833
		March 8, 1837
Junkins, Joseph P.		July 3, 1840
Brooks, Jeremiah	March 19, 1841	July 2, 1841
Junkins, Joseph P.	April 1, 1845	February 26, 1846
Marshall, Nathaniel G.	July 16, 1849	September 27, 1850
Junkins, Luther		December 22, 1857
Bowden, George G.	July 10, 1860	February 21, 1861
Putnam, Jeremiah S.	May 15, 1861	July 20, 1861
	July 20, 1865	February 15, 1866
Bragdon, Edward A.		April 21, 1870
		May 2, 1874
		May 2, 1878
		May 19, 1882
Wilson, Joel		July 12, 1886
Currier, George W.		July 31, 1890
Baker, Edward W.		August 28, 1894
Banks, Edward H.	March 10, 1899	January 19, 1900
Marshall, George E.		March 12, 1903
Philbrick, Herbert D.		January 15, 1907

Later Joseph Lowe was Deputy at York and Samuel Webber at Cape Neddick.

David Wilcox was Weigher and Inspector for five years.

In 1865 during the second term of Dr. Putnam, on the recommendation of William A. Cromwell of South Berwick, an Inspector of the Treasury Department, the positions of Deputy Collectors were abolished. Following the resignation of Mr. Banks Andrew W. Junkins was Deputy Collector. At the death of George E. Marshall, Adaline T. Marshall became Acting Collector, and on Mr. H. D. Philbrick's appointment she became Special Deputy.

YORK HARBOR & BEACH RAILROAD

UP TO 1860 the only inland mode of public travel with the outside communities was by a stage line between Kennebunk and Portsmouth managed by Isaiah Farwell. This line had succeeded in part the through line by stage from Portland to Boston. Three times a week Mr. Farwell passed through each way. In 1872 and '73 the old line was discontinued. John P. Grant followed Mr. Farwell and he by William Grant, he by Grant and Stewart. In the fall of 1882 a public meeting was called but not largely attended for the purpose of discussing the question of obtaining better facilities for the transportation of people and freight which the fast increasing business of the town seemed to demand. A paper setting forth in detail the business of the town was compiled and John E. Staples, Edward S. Marshall, Henry E. Evans and John C. Stewart were chosen a committee to wait upon Mr. E. B. Phillips, the President of the Eastern Railroad Co., and present the facts and also to urge the advisability of that company extending a line from Portsmouth to York. Mr. Phillips received the committee kindly and listened to what they had to say, verbally and orally, and then informed them that the Eastern Railroad Company was in no condition to finance the scheme. He said: "When the time comes that the Eastern R. R. needs two tracks from Portsmouth to Portland, then we may consider the advisability of building a line through York; but at present we need four tracks between Boston and Portsmouth more than we need two beyond Portsmouth. On the way home the committee discussed the situation thoroughly and decided to build a railroad on their own account, and as one writer has it, these four railroad kings, Marshall, Stewart, Evans and Staples, began work at once. They employed Civil Engineers Foss and Merrill of Concord, N. H., to make a survey, they paid the surveyors, cut the bushes, carried the chain for the survey of four different lines between Kittery Depot and York Beach. At the session of the Legislature of 1883 a charter was obtained and the above named with Jeremiah P. Simpson and Dr. F. E. Potter of Portsmouth, N. H., were the incorporators. Dr. Potter declined to act, and Samuel W. Junkins of York, and Dr. Evan B. Hammond of Nashua, N. H., were elected. The organization was completed by the election of Edward S. Marshall, President, John C. Stewart, Clerk, and they with Staples, Evans, Simpson, Junkins and Hammond were chosen Directors. A stock book was opened and subscriptions invited. Mr. Marshall subscribed for sixty shares, the others twenty each, the shares being placed at a face value of fifty dollars. At the next annual meeting Samuel W. Junkins was made Treasurer. The Boston & Maine Railroad Company having secured control of the Eastern Company, efforts were made in that direction for aid in building the road. Hon. Frank Jones of Portsmouth was a director of the Boston & Maine, and he became personally interested in the matter, having subscribed to the stock, and through his influence Mr. Bissell, the chief engineer of the Boston & Maine, came to view the several routes that had been surveyed. After a careful examination of each he reported to Mr. Jones and the company upon the feasibility of all. The charter would expire on Feb. 1st, 1885, if no location was made. Up to this time the officials of the road had remained the same with the exception that Mr. J. P. Simpson had been made Treasurer in place of Mr. Junkins. Jan. 15, 1885, a location was adopted and filed, thus the charter received a continuance for two more years. In December, 1885, the old officers were re-elected and no more was done until Sept. 21, 1886. At that time Mr. Marshall resigned as President and Dr. Hammond was elected, thereupon he added nine thousand dollars to his subscription, and Mr. Marshall raised his to five thousand; thus far the subscription amounted to twenty-six thousand dollars. It has been said that "to these two men more than to any others is due the successful completion of the undertaking." The town declined to aid in any respect, even refusing to endorse company's bonds for twenty-five thousand dollars, although offered a first mortgage of the road as security. Much of the right-of-way was given by the landholders. Edward C. Moody gave one hundred dollars for the purchase of the site for a station at Long Beach. October 22, 1886, the specifications were completed and bids for the construction asked for. These bids were to be opened Nov. 1st. They were for a narrow guage railroad from York Beach to a point near Butler's Crossing about a half mile east of Kittery Depot. Mr. Jones seeing that the building of a narrow guage road was nearing a certainty, at once sent word to the directors to suspend all contracts or further action until a conference could be held between them and the directors of the B. & M.; this was done. A committee from the directorate of York H. & B. met a similar committee of the B. & M. and an agreement was made subject to final assent of the board of directors of each road, to wit: The Y. H. & B. Company would give a right of way from Kittery Junction to the terminal of the road in York, and take fifty thousand dollars worth of the stock. The Boston & Maine would furnish the balance of the necessary funds to complete the road and take stock certificate, as bonds were to be issued, also provide all rolling stock and equip them at actual cost, give the Y. H. & B. road the free use of the road from Kittery Junction across the river to Portsmouth Station, also all terminal facilities in Portsmouth, until the Y. H. & B. stock should pay a dividend of two and a half dollars per share or five per cent., and they would construct a road of standard guage. The first contract was let December 6, 1886, and work began at once. August 8, 1887, the first train was run to Long Beach. The next week the terminal called "Union Bluff" was reached. This is now known as York Beach. The cost of the road approximated three hundred and ten thousand dollars.

ALMSHOUSE AND NEW HOME

PREVIOUS TO 1838 the indigent portion of the population known as paupers and requiring the support of the town as such, were cared for in a somewhat doubtful manner, under the "bidding-off" system, that is to say, the unfortunates were auctioned to the different parties who for reasons of a little gain that might be coaxed or driven from the pauper so bid off by relatives with charitable intentions, and others for various reasons. But as a whole the plan was a hardship for the poor unfortunate. At the date above stated the idea was realized of building or purchasing an almshouse and securing land for a farm as being considered a more humane way for the care of this class of people. After a number of exciting meetings were held, it was finally voted to purchase a farm with buildings, or procure land and erect buildings thereon if a farm with suitable buildings was not available. The Chapman farm at Raynes' Neck was bargained for, but the owner on reflection declined to deed the property. Then land was purchased of Mrs. Abigail Emerson and a set of buildings built and the poor requiring a home at the expense of the town were gathered from their several "bid-offs" and placed therein under the care of a Superintendent and his wife, Mr. and Mrs. John Banks. After being occupied more than fifty years, it was found that extensive repairs or a new house on a better location was a necessity, and at a town meeting held Dec. 13, 1890, the following vote was passed:

VOTED: That Joseph Bragdon, Wilson M. Walker, J. P. Simpson, Lemuel Mitchell, James A. Bragdon, Charles Junkins, Almon H. Merrow, John F. Plaisted, Charles A. Grant, Josiah D. Bragdon, be a committee in relation to the improvement of the Town Farm buildings, whether it be best to repair or build new, and if to do either, to investigate the cost and location of the same, and to report their proceedings to the next annual town meeting. The committee reported as follows, and at the annual meeting, March 9th, 1891, their report was accepted and further action taken as follows:—

* * * And your committee would submit the following recommendations for your consideration at this present meeting, March, 1891.

First. That a committee of three or five shall be chosen, one of whom shall be a practical builder, as a building committee, and that this committee under instructions from the town shall have power to arrange for the location of the building or buildings, as the case may be, and to contract with responsible parties for the erection of the same, to be completed prior to the annual Town Meeting in March, 1892.

Second. That the town vote a sum of money not exceeding five thousand dollars ($5000) to carry into effect the foregoing recommendations.

York, March 9, 1891.

Signed by Committee ....

VOTED to raise four thousand dollars to be expended for building an almshouse upon the recommendation of the foregoing committee.

VOTED that a committee of five be chosen by nominations from the floor for a building committee, and Edward B. Blaisdell, Henry Grover, Henry E. Evans, Lemuel Mitchell and Bradford S. Woodward were nominated and chosen said committee.

The New Home was opened for the reception of inmates,

Oct. 28, 1891, and the old house was at once vacated. Bradford S. Woodward was the first superintendent at the New Home.

George W. Currier, Esq., auditor, in his report dated Feb. 21, 1892, says: "The town is to be congratulated upon having a home for the unfortunately poor, which will compare favorably with any similar institutions in the State, and it is a credit to the liberality of the town. Generous donations were received from various organizations and private individuals, towards furnishing the house." A barn connected with the "New House" was built in 1894 at an expense of $1500. The old buildings were disposed of at public auction by those chosen to build the barn, which consisted of William H. Chase, Bradford S. Woodward, Edward E. Young, Edward B. Blaisdell and Edward C. Moody.

SUPERINTENDENTS OF TOWN FARM FROM ITS ESTABLISHMENT

John Banks	Alvah Trafton
George Norton	Josiah Norton
George Woodward	Addison G. Norton
Joseph Plaisted	William H. Grant
Henry Grover	John F. Todd
Theodore Beal	Timothy Furbish
Thomas A Whittle	William P. Titcomb
James Warren	Bradford S. Woodward
Joseph Woodward	William H. Chase
Johnson B. Moulton	George M. Robinson
Gardner Swett	Stephen Adams
Charles H. Sayward	

THE YORK HOSPITAL

THIS INSTITUTION was founded and incorporated November 5th, 1904, under the laws of Maine.

Clerk of the Corporation, Albert M. Bragdon.

Wilson L. Hawkes, Jasper J. Hazen, Frank W. Smith, Edward C. Cook, Seabury W. Allen, E. H. Siter, and Louis F. Bishop, all allopath physicians and surgeons, were the first trustees.

The Davidson estate was purchased at a cost of $15,000.

Changes by remodeling interior, and repairs, $3,000.

Construction of Nurses' Home, $2,000.

There are no bequests.

Under the lead of Mrs. Newton Perkins in 1905 a Japanese fete was planned, and materialized, and among other noted guests were the two prominent envoys of Japan who attended the Peace Conference at Portsmouth, Baron Komura and Count Takahira. A few days after the hospital trustees received from each of these men a check for $500. Later Count Witte, the Russian envoy, sent $200. These gifts and the proceeds of the fete, and several contributions brought the sum available for hospital purposes to $6,000.

"The Marianna Bryan Lathrop Memorial District Nurse" was established by Mrs. Thomas Nelson Page in memory of her mother, and is connected with, but not a part of the hospital. It has an annual interest value of $800 specifically designated to the payment for services of a district nurse. The trustees of this fund are Thomas Nelson Page, Bryan Lathrop, Arthur T. Aldis. The District Nurse makes visits among the poor, and emergency cases, making about one hundred and fifty calls each month.

The hospital furnishes yearly about 1200 days' service to approximately 100 patients, sixty per cent. of which is free. The York Hospital opened its doors to the public on July 22, 1906. There is no doubt as to the usefulness of its mission, and of the benefits it bestows charitably and by fee to those who seek relief, and it is now the recipient of a yearly stipend from the state of $1200, and the town of $1500.

Yearly by subscription Mrs. Samuel Seabury Allen has secured a tidy sum for the use of the institution.

ELECTRIC PLANT

AFTER GIVING the matter careful consideration, in 1894 Hon. Edward S. Marshall decided to erect a plant for the production of electricity for light, heat and power purposes. He chose as the site a situation near the station of the York Harbor & Beach R. R. The plant was completed and in operation about August 1, 1895.

It was incorporated under Legislative Act as the Agamenticus Light and Power Company in 1899. June 1, 1910, it was incorporated as the Agamenticus Electric Light Co.

In 1911, July 1st, the last named corporation was taken over by the York Light and Heat Co., George F. West, President, and called the "York Division," of which Fred W. Marshall was made Superintendent. The town entered into an agreement with the company for street lighting.

February 19, 1910, was the beginning of all-the-year service, the current for some three or four months being taken from the Twin State Corporation in Dover.

YORK COUNTY NATIONAL BANK

THE GROWTH of York's summer population had so increased that among others who did not fail to take the initiative were Edward S. Marshall, Wilson M. Walker and James T. Davidson, who believed the time was ripe and opportunity present for the establishment of a National Bank in York. Thereupon a charter was obtained and the Bank established Feb. 6, 1893, with the following directors, James T. Davidson, Wilson M. Walker, Charles A. Grant, Jeremiah P. Simpson, George M. Simpson. The capital stock was $60,000.

James T. Davidson was chosen President; Wilson M. Walker, Vice President; Albert M. Bragdon, Clerk and Cashier.

In 1894 the bank building was erected. The growth of the business has been almost phenomenal. In 1893 the deposits were $59,000. In 1912 the deposits were more than $550,000.

The present directors are Mrs. Elizabeth B. Davidson, Albert M. Bragdon, Capt. John Dennett, Frank D. Marshall, and Joseph W. Simpson; with Elizabeth B. Davidson, President, John Dennett, Vice President, Albert M. Bragdon, Cashier.

From its establishment the affairs of the bank have been ably managed in a modern and yet conservative manner. The only ripple to ruffle the smoothness of the flow of business was in April, 1909, when the first (and last to date) run on the bank was made, April 5, 1909. On April 3rd the selectmen directed the Treasurer of the town to withdraw $9,000, a part of the so-called Clark fund. A number of individual depositors also withdrew their funds. On the

5th, Monday morning, about forty men congregated before the Bank building intending to withdraw their deposits. A few did so. However, the result of the day was that a greater amount of money had been deposited than was withdrawn. On the 6th, Tuesday morning, parties from out of town appeared to demand their money; but on seeing $30,000 in gold and bank notes upon the counting tables decided that it was "well to let a good thing alone."

Thus ended the run on the bank.

To the reporter of the Boston Herald, Mr. Bragdon, the Cashier, said: "It was a dastardly attempt to ruin a bank to satisfy personal spite." Mr. Bragdon also said that he had received telephone messages that morning from the Shawmut National Bank in Boston and two banks of Portsmouth offering all the money they needed, but they had not been obliged to accept the kind offers.

The York Transcript said:

"If those individuals who had in mind the wrecking of the York County National Bank had used their common sense as much as they used their tongues, they never would have undertaken to carry out such a foolhardy scheme.

"It seems beyond comprehension that men of common sense and good understanding could have attempted to make a run upon a bank which has made the greater part of its loans among the very people who attempted to make a run. Any man with a fair understanding would know that the result would simply be that the bank would call in its loans.

"This would mean that in order to withdraw perhaps $125,000 the bank could call from the very same people, loans amounting to over a quarter of a million. Such an action on the part of the bank would simply stagger the financial condition of the town, and would embarrass financially the very men who desired to ruin the bank."

YORK REALTY COMPANY

In accordance with Sections 16, 17, 18 and 19 of Chap. 48, R. S., the York Realty Company was organized for the purpose of holding, leasing, managing, and improving real estate. Also to own and convey buildings of any kind, and interests therein, also for the purpose of selling stocks and bonds, and securities of any other corporation.

The articles of association were signed Aug. 15, 1903, by Joseph P. Bragdon, John C. Stewart, Josiah Chase, Walter M. Smith, J. Perley Putnam, Edward S. Marshall, Frank D. Marshall, and George E. Marshall. Subsequently John C. Stewart, Walter M. Smith of Stamford, Conn., Josiah Chase, Edward O. Emerson of Titusville, Pa., J. Perley Putnam, Francis Lynde Stetson of New York, and Edward S. Marshall were elected directors. Later Samuel W. Junkins was chosen a director. The directors organized with the choice of John C. Stewart, President, and J. Perley Putnam, Treasurer; Frank D. Marshall had previously been elected Clerk. The corporation proceeded to erect the Realty Building; the President, Treasurer, and Edward S. Marshall being the Building Committee. The building and site cost approximately $27,000 and was and is the first structure built of brick in York for office and commercial purposes. In April, 1913, the property was purchased by Ernest F. Hobson.

NEWSPAPER

York's first newspaper under the name of "The York Courant" was started and established Sept. 4th, 1891, in Chas. H. Junkins' store, by George F. Plaisted, with the following announcement:

To Our Readers:

This is the first issue of a newspaper ever printed in the Town of York.

We believe it is an important stride in the welfare of our good old Town.

In assuming full management of the paper, we do so with mingled feelings of pride and embarrassment, and, while we will not use extravagant language as to what we will do, we can safely promise that we shall use our best endeavors to make a paper worthy of your support and patronage.

Our columns will be open to criticism and comment.

Letters of a vindictive nature will not be published.

We will be ever ready to defend the innocent and expose wrongs without fear or favor as to person or rank.

Politics will be a thing unknown in these columns.

No blackguardism, no personal imputations without proof.

We will work to improve our paper and to increase its usefulness.

We shall be alive and alert to the best interests of the public.

With these few remarks we launch out into the newspaper world asking the support of the public.

George F. Plaisted.

Mr. Plaisted in the salutatory at the beginning of the second year said:

"On entering Vol. II, we said, 'How well the Courant has prospered both in size and appearance we leave our readers to decide. For ourself we are highly pleased with its growth and general outlook.'

"As a journalist we cannot entertain a hope of matching the illustrious Horace Greeley, only in one point. He did the best he could. That is what we propose to do, and will endeavor to fill the space as well as he did in proportion to the field and our ability."

Subsequently the plant was purchased by the York Publishing Company, Edward S. Marshall, Trustee, and the publication carried the name of "The Old York Transcript & York Courant." Previous to this time a paper established by Edwin D. Twombly called the Transcript had a fair circulation, but the consolidation of the papers was deemed advisable.

At this writing Edward C. Hawkes is President, Myron F. Cox, Treasurer and General Manager of the Company.

WATER COMPANY

A MOST important factor in all that makes for the health, wealth, and prosperity of York is its unrivalled supply of pure water for domestic and public use. The York Shore Water Company was organized under a charter granted by the Legislature of 1895, approved by the Governor March 5th. The incorporators named were Josiah Chase, Lindley M. Webb, William R. Howard, Wilson L. Hawkes, Hartley W. Mason, John E. Norwood, Jeremiah P. Simpson, John L. Chase, and John H. Varrell. Josiah Chase was made President, and Wilson L. Hawkes, Treasurer. At an early day the company was placed on a sound financial footing and preparations made to take water from "Chase Pond," now known as "Chase Lake." Every needed effort has been directed to the maintaining of the sanitary condition of the lake, reservoir and surroundings, and the analysis of the contents at stated times evidences the purity of the water supplied by the company. What the summer business of York would become if deprived of this inestimable boon is difficult to even conjecture. The management is liberally disposed, and many a lawn would be seared and brown but for this liberality.

This appears to be one of the instances where a corporation gives all the advantages claimed under municipal ownership, without public responsibility attached.

SCHOOLS

THE EARLIEST record we have in relation to official action in the matter of schools is that of 1701, when the selectmen employed Nathaniel Freeman as a schoolmaster for £8 per year and 3d per week for teaching reading and 4d a week for writing and ciphering. He commenced his duties May 5th. The next year his salary was raised to £10, with same prices for other branches as in 1701. In 1709 the selectmen were instructed by the town to hire a schoolmaster for seven years "to teach all in the town to read, write and cipher."

"Att a Legall Town Meeting holden in York March Ye 21, 1709-10 Abra M Preble Jun Chosen Town Clerk for the year Insewing. Arthur Bragdon Sen Small Came Richard Millbury and Joseph Young and Joseph Moulton chosen Select men votd our Select men for the Time Being are hereby Impowered and desiered to hier a Scool Master for the full terme of seven years to Keep Scool in our said town of York to Teach all persons belonging to sd Town to Read write an sifer: and sd Scool Master to be paid yearely for his service as our sd Select men shall a Gree

ABRA M PREPLE Town Cl."

Above is copied verbatim from Book 1, page 452, of York Records.

In 1711 Mr. Freeman was engaged for the seven years expiring 1719. He agreed to teach from eight o'clock in the morning to twelve M. and from one to five P. M. for £30 per year, payment quarterly, one-third of which was to be in provisions, the balance in money. Also to provide him quarter the town was to build him a house 22 feet by 18 with a brick chimney. The school was to be free to all above five years of age. In 1717 a vote was passed to employ a *grand school master* for one year to instruct the children in *learned things,* and from time to time action was taken in the interests of education. In 1723 Rev. Samuel Moody had a class in Latin. Previous to 1760 a building had been erected near the parsonage for a schoolhouse where Master Moody taught; this was the nucleus from which District No. 1 was evolved. The schoolhouse that was destroyed by fire in 1838 was succeeded by the one that is now a part of the stable of D. N. Armstrong. Previous to the abolishment of the district system by the Legislature there were fifteen school districts in York, as follows: No. 1, Center; 2, Raynes Neck; 3, South Side; 4, Scotland; 5, Brixham; 6, Beach Ridge; 7, Bell Marsh; 8, North Village; 9, Ground Root Hill (West); 10, Ground Root Hill (East); 11, Cape Neddick, East; 12, Scituate; 13, Cider Hill; 14, Pine Hill; 15, Cape Neddick. In the year 1850 when the Bell Marsh district was abolished there were 1150 scholars enrolled in the town. In 1849 a private boarding school was established by Isaiah P. Moody, which was well patronized, with an average yearly attendance of resident and non-resident pupils to the number of fifty.

FREE HIGH SCHOOL BUILDING

In the warrant for the annual town meeting in 1893, Article 12 read as follows: "To see what sum of money the town will raise for a Free High School for the ensuing year, by request of G. E. M. Smiley and twenty-four others." And on that article two hundred and fifty dollars was appropriated, and with the amount of stipend allowed by the state "a high school on wheels" was started and continued up to 1902 with a varied degree of success. In the report of

Edward C. Cook, Superintendent of Schools, for the year 1899, he said: "The high school has had another most prosperous year, and has worked out for itself its destiny. It has become an indispensable part of our school system. * * * A new building is necessary. * * * A nucleus is already in prospect toward a high school fund. * * * A proper home should be erected for this infant institution which is fast becoming a source of pride to the town, which by making better citizens of her children will bring back to York her ancient glory as the foremost town in this section. It is earnestly hoped that favorable action in this matter will be taken at this March meeting.

HIGH SCHOOL BUILDING

In the warrant for the annual meeting, March, 1900, Article 20 was "To see if the town will appropriate a sum of money to build a building for the High School, or take any action thereon. By request of Edward C. Cook and six others. Following is an abstract from the Town Record:

Annual Meeting, March 12, 1900.

Article 20. It was moved that the sum of three thousand dollars be raised to erect a high school building; this motion was amended to read ten thousand dollars, which amendment was carried 125 to 88.

Voted that a committee to consist of the superintending school committee, the superintendent of schools when elected, Edward S. Marshall, John C. Stewart and James T. Davidson, be elected to take into consideration the matter of a proper high school building, procure options on suitable localities, ascertain the probable cost of lot and buildings, at the expense of the town, and report in writing to the town at a special meeting to be held not later than May first.

Voted that the ten thousand dollars be raised by issuing town bonds, same to run ten years at three per cent interest. 158 to 0.

The special meeting above mentioned was holden on April 30, 1900, after the choice of lot had been made by ballot.

On motion by Hon. E. C. Moody it was voted "That the superintending school committee, the superintendent of schools, and James T. Davidson, Edward S. Marshall, John C. Stewart, be and are hereby constituted a building committee to have in charge the erection of a high school building, at an expense not exceeding ten thousand dollars, and they are instructed to issue proposals for building of same in accordance with plan and specifications that are adopted and to award the contract in such manner as they deem for the interest of the town."

Annual Meeting March 11, 1901.

Article 22. To see what action the town will take in relation to building the Free High School Building, on petition of Charles W. Junkins and eleven others.

On Article 22, voted that the building committee be authorized to purchase an additional acre and three thousand dollars was appropriated to purchase the three acres, the same to be laid out to the satisfaction of the committee.

Voted that the committee be instructed to have the building completed for the fall term of school.

A resolution was passed favoring a brick building.

Voted that the town issue five thousand dollars worth of

bonds on and under the same conditions as the ten thousand dollars issued last year.

Voted to reconsider and that the same lay upon the table.

Annual Meeting March 10, 1902.

Article 20. To see what action the town will take to raise money to finish the High School Building or take any action relating to the same.

On Article 20, voted that the Selectmen and Treasurer be and are hereby authorized, instructed and empowered to issue bonds of the town of York bearing three per cent. interest payable semi-annually; that said bonds be payable one thousand dollars each year, and that the amount of said bonds be sufficient to meet the $10,000 this day appropriated for the high school building, the $20,000 due next year, and, if satisfactory to the present holders, the $15,000 due in 1911.

The committee under some difficulties, and in face of the fact that the vote had been "reconsidered and laid upon the table," a somewhat unusual parliamentary situation, went ahead. Nathaniel B. Shattuck, Charles W. Junkins, Herbert D. Philbrick, School Committee, Edward C. Cook, Superintendent of Schools, Edward S. Marshall, James T. Davidson and John C. Stewart being in charge.

At the special meeting of April 30, 1900, a choice of site for the building was chosen from four locations named, Grant's field, York Beach, Parish, and Marshall. On the third ballot Grant's field was selected. The approximate cost of lot, building, and furnishings was $24,000.

It was dedicated in the early fall of 1902.

The Clark Fund amounts to $20,000.

THE NEW BRIDGE

On petition of the Selectmen of the Town of York to the Legislature of Maine as follows:

To the Honorable Senate and House of Representatives in Legislature assembled:

The undersigned Selectmen of the Town of York, hereby respectfully represent that public convenience and necessity require the laying out and constructing and maintenance of a highway across York River at York Harbor in said Town of York with a suitable bridge as a part thereof. WHEREFORE acting for and in behalf of said Town they pray that your honorable body may grant the passage of an Act authorizing the construction of said highway and bridge across tide waters aforesaid—

And as in duty bound will ever pray.

> J. PERLEY PUTNAM,
> HARRY H. NORTON,
> JOSEPH P. BRAGDON,
> *Selectmen of York.*

That body authorized the County Commissioners of York County to lay out a way and bridge across York River to be built by the Town of York, as by Chapter 50 of the Private and Special Laws of the State 1905.

A petition to the County Commissioners was entered in April, 1905. The County Commissioners of York County were authorized to lay out a highway and bridge. Thereupon the following petition was entered as stated:

To the County Commissioners of the County of York:

The undersigned residents and taxpayers of the Town of York in said County of York hereby respectfully represent that public convenience and necessity require the laying out of a County way between some point in York Harbor on the County way leading from York Village through York Harbor to Norwood Farm to another point southwesterly over tide water to the County Way leading from Sewall's Bridge to Seabury R. R. Station to Kittery Point, and respectfully petition that you would fix the time for a hearing and that you would lay out a way between such points in said two County ways as shall be most convenient, said way to pass over Harris and Bragdon Islands, in York River.

Seabury Wells Allen	Charles H. Young
John I. Banks	Charles H. Junkins
Charles F. Blaisdell	Lowell S. Grant
W. H. Hogarth	George F. Plaisted
Charles W. Plaisted	Willis G. Moulton
Charles Bragdon	Arthur E. Bragdon
George H. Simpson	E. C. Cook

and one hundred and fifty-four others.

In answer to the petition the County Commissioners gave a hearing on the 18th day of May, 1905, and after a full hearing of all the facts, testimony and arguments by them presented * * * "do hereby adjudge and determine that common convenience and necessity do require the laying out of said way as prayed for." * * *

Given under our hands, this second day of January, A. D. 1906.   SAMUEL W. JUNKINS,

EDWIN A. HOBSON,

LEWIS W. PENDEXTER,

County Commissioners of York.

And now it is considered and ordered by the Court of County Commissioners that all action on the original petition be, and the same is hereby closed and ordered recorded.

Attest.

WILLIS T. EMMONS, *Clerk.*

A report was made by the Commissioners in January, 1906, whereby the way and bridge was ordered and the Town given two years to begin and complete the construction of the same. This action was the basis of the call for a Town Meeting held October 13th, 1906, the warrant containing an article "To see if the Town will vote to build a highway and bridge across York River in said Town." VOTED to build the way and bridge as set forth, "Yes" 174, "No" 123. Also as appears by the record of George F. Plaisted, Town Clerk, as unamended, a motion was made and carried "That the Town accept the bid of E. B. Blaisdell of York to construct said highway and bridge for the sum of thirty thousand dollars." By an order issued by George E. Bird, Esquire, a Justice of the Supreme Court of Maine, Feb. 15th, 1910, the Town Clerk was commanded to amend the record of said town meeting so that it will read, "Voted, *Not* to accept the bid of E. B. Blaisdell for thirty thousand dollars." It would seem that a change in the record was deemed necessary from the fact that Mr. Blaisdell had completed the highway and bridge and had been obliged to bring suit for the sum of thirty-nine thousand five hundred dollars ($39,500), the contract sum he had agreed upon with the Town through a committee originally as appointed October 13th, 1906, consisting of the Selectmen, Joseph P. Bragdon, Henry S. Bragdon, Harry H. Norton, and Charles H. Young, Joseph W. Simpson, Charles Weare, J. Perley Putnam, which committee organized Oct. 13th, 1906, by the choice of Charles H. Young, Chairman, J. Perley Putnam, Secretary. Subsequently the three Selectmen withdrew from the committee and declined to take any further action toward the construction of the bridge.

The contention of the Selectmen appeared to be that the committee of four were to act with the Selectmen; that there was not a committee of seven. At a meeting of the Bridge Committee, so called, held Oct. 17th, Joseph P. Bragdon, H. H. Norton, Henry S. Bragdon, Charles H. Young, Charles E. Weare, Joseph W. Simpson and J. Perley Putnam were present. After discussing the above matter it was voted to employ counsel. At a meeting held Oct. 22d by adjournment the 17th, in the absence of J. Perley Putnam, J. W. Simpson was chosen Secretary pro tem. At this meeting the Selectmen withdrew from the committee, informing them that they would act no further with the balance of the committee. At a meeting of the committee Nov. 16th, an injunction was read which had been served on Mr. Young, restraining the committee from awarding the contract for the bridge:—

VOTED: "To employ Hon. John C. Stewart of York, and Hon. Enoch Foster of Portland as counsel." And from that day to this, injunctions, mandamus, Government hearings, suits at law, and special town meetings, accompanied the work as it progressed, and on its completion the committee notified the Selectmen of York to that effect as follows:—

YORK, ME., May 16th, 1908.

To the Selectmen of York:

You are hereby notified that the new county way and bridge across York River, which was laid out and ordered built by the County Commissioners, and was voted by the Town of York, Oct. 13th, 1906, is completed in all respects and is open for public travel.

The contractor has complied with all the specifications and requirements of his contract with the Inhabitants of

York as appears by the certificate of the engineer in charge. The committee appointed by the Town, Oct. 13th, 1906, to build said way and bridge, has performed its duty, said bridge and way being open for public travel, its care and maintenance are for the Town and its proper officers. The total cost of said work is $49,765.63 as fully appears by certificates filed with the Town Treasurer.

We respectfully call attention to the fact that provision must be made forthwith by the Town, relative to a drawtender for said bridge. All appliances for hoisting the draw are in place, the same in good working order, and we are informed that there will be occasion to hoist for the purposes of navigation at an early day.

Very respectfully yours,

CHARLES H. YOUNG,

CHARLES E. WEARE,

JOSEPH W. SIMPSON,

J. PERLEY PUTNAM,

Committee.

The increase in cost over contract price was brought about by changes ordered by the War Department and various expenses as follows:

Edward B. Blaisdell, Contract.............	$39,500 00
E. B. Blaisdell, changes by War Dept.....	6,990 43
Plans by E. B. Blaisdell.................	1,394 71
A. W. Gowen, services as Engineer........	545 35
Edward C. Moody, supervising driving of piles	60 00
John C. Stewart, legal services and expenses	575 14
Frank D. Marshall, legal services and expenses	455 93
Symonds, Snow, Cook & Hutchinson, legal services and expenses	25 00
J. Perley Putnam, expenses..............	73 52

Charles H. Young, expenses..............	24 50
Charles E. Weare, expenses..............	24 50
Joseph W. Simpson, expenses............	15 00
Ellen M. Welch, typewriting.............	55 45
Old York Transcript, advertising.........	16 80
Chas. H. Young, Court expenses of G. F. Plaisted	9 30

$49,765 63

In reply to the notification by the committee of the completion of the bridge, the Selectmen wrote as follows:—

YORK, ME., May 20th, 1908.

Messrs. Charles H. Young, Charles E. Weare, Joseph W. Simpson, J. Perley Putnam, York, Maine.

Gentlemen :—

A communication bearing your signatures under date of May 16th, 1906, relative to an alleged way and bridge in this Town is before us, we beg to call your attention to a letter from us to you bearing date, March 18th, 1908, which explains our position and views touching the subject matter of your last letter. We do not understand that the Inhabitants of the Town of York are liable for, or in any way interested in the alleged way and bridge referred to.

JOSEPH P. BRAGDON,

HARRY H. NORTON,

HENRY S. BRAGDON,

Selectmen of the Town of York.

The following is a copy of the letter of March 18th referred to in the letter of May 20th:

YORK VILLAGE, March 18th, 1908.

Messrs. Charles H. Young, Joseph W. Simpson, J. Perley Putnam, Chas. E. Weare.

Your communication bearing date March 11th, 1908, is before us, we do not recognize your right or authority to act in any way, relating to the way and bridge matter to which you refer in your communication or that you are authorized to accept any way or bridge in this Town, for and in behalf of the Inhabitants of the Town of York. We must decline in behalf of the Town of York to recognize any pretended acceptance of the same. We do not understand that the Inhabitants of the Town of York have ever entered into any valid contract for the construction of said pretended way and bridge, or that you had any authority to do any act or thing whereby the Town might become liable in this matter. We understand that no such way or bridge has been legally laid out or located or that the Town is liable in the matter in any way. If, as individuals you have undertaken to construct a private way and bridge the responsibility therefor, as we understand it, rests upon you individually

Yours very truly,

J. P. BRAGDON,
HARRY H. NORTON,
HENRY S. BRAGDON,
Selectmen of York.

The committee were without funds. Here it may be said that under the vote of the Town authorizing the Treasurer to hire money to meet pressing liabilities, John C. Stewart borrowed of the Bath Savings Bank $25,000 to build the bridge, on the 9th day of March, 1907. He turned the money over to the building committee consisting of seven. It was receipted for by four. The following demand was made on the committee:

YORK, MAINE, April 9, 1907.
To Charles H. Young, J. Perley Putnam, Joseph W. Simpson and Charles E. Weare:

We the Selectmen of York find that the late Treasurer of
the Town of York, John C. Stewart, without authority has
placed in your possession a large sum of money belonging
to the Town of York, amounting to the sum of twenty-five
thousand and eighty-five dollars and sixty cents. We demand of you and each of you that you immediately pay said
money, or cause the same to be paid to Edward E. E.
Mitchell, Treasurer of the Town of York.

JOSEPH P. BRAGDON,

HARRY H. NORTON,

HENRY S. BRAGDON,

Selectmen of York.

As appears by the following, a majority of the committee
paid over to E. E. E. Mitchell the amount demanded by the
Selectmen :—

YORK VILLAGE, ME., April 20th, 1907.

Received of Charles H. Young, Joseph W. Simpson, J.
Perley Putnam and Charles E. Weare, as a majority of the
committee elected by the Town of York, Oct. 13th, 1906,
to build a bridge across York River, the sum of twenty-five
thousand eighty-five dollars and 60/100, said money being
the same received by said committee under date of March
9th, 1907, from John C. Stewart, Treasurer of York, to be
used in the construction of the bridge and approaches voted
by said town Oct. 13th, 1906, as aforesaid.

EDWARD E. E. MITCHELL, *Treasurer.*

From June 14th, 1907, to April 25th, 1908, the committee
drew various orders on E. E. E. Mitchell, Treasurer of York,
in favor of E. B. Blaisdell, the contractor, and Angevine E.
Gowen, the engineer in charge; the last being drawn April
25th, 1908, in favor of Edward B. Blaisdell for the sum
of nine thousand two hundred ninety-eight dollars and nine

cents ($9,298.09) in full for contract price of bridge and way as ordered by the County Commissioners across York River. None of which were paid by the Treasurer, he requiring the signatures of at least two of the Board of Selectmen. Following is the rescript of the Supreme Court:

EDWARD B. BLAISDELL VS. INHABITANTS OF YORK.

York County.

Rescript, Cornish, J.

This is an action of assumpsit brought by the plaintiff to recover the sum of $51,066.71, the amount alleged to be due him under two contracts, one dated December 5, 1906, and the other October 17, 1907, made with the defendant town for the construction of a way and bridge across York River between the towns of Kittery and York, as laid out by the County Commissioners.

The petition to the County Commissioners described the proposed way as follows: "A county way between some point in York Harbor on the county way leading from York Village through York Harbor to Norwood Farm, to another point southwesterly over tide water to the county way leading from Sewall's Bridge to Seabury R. R. Station to Kittery Point . . . Said way to pass over Harris Island and Bragdon's Island in York Harbor."

Held:

1. That the petition describing a way must, under R. S. Chap 25, Sec. 1, describe it with reasonable definiteness in order to give the County Commissioners jurisdiction. The chief reason for this requirement is to give all parties over whose land the proposed way is to be laid, and all others whose interests may be affected thereby, such information through the public notice on the petition as will enable them to be present and be heard.

2. That while under the language of this petition alone
the termini might seem too vague and indefinite, as was
determined in Bliss vs. Junkins, 165 Maine 128; yet, when
applied to the geographical situation and to the location on
the face of the earth as brought out in the evidence, the
termini are proven to bet set out with such reasonable certainty as to meet the fair intent and requirement of the
statute.

3. That while the distance between York Village and
Norwood Farm, which marks the easterly base line, is more
than one mile, and between Seabury Station and Kittery
Point, which marks the westerly base line, is four or five
miles; yet only a short portion of either side could be utilized,
as the way was to cross the two islands in a southwesterly
direction. The islands served as on which the bridge and
the way were to rest and from which the way was to pass,
and any other persons whose interests could be affected by
the location, must have been fully appraised of the proposed
route, the test which must not be lost sight of in applying
the legal rule.

4. That the fact that Samuel W. Junkins, one of the
County Commissioners, was at the time of the laying out
of the way the owner of one-fourth undivided interest in
Bragdon's Island, disqualified him from acting on the petition. But as the board had jurisdiction of the subject matter, subsequent proceedings cannot be attached collaterally.
The action of the board was voidable but not void. Where
jurisdiction is lacking, a collateral attack is permitted. Otherwise, the proceedings are binding unless quashed certiorari
or set aside on appeal. Here the record shows jurisdiction
in the board to commence proceedings, those proceedings
stand unrestricted, and in this collateral action they must be
regarded as binding and conclusive.

5. That the special town meeting of October 13, 1906, was legally called and its doings valid. The original return of the constable recites that he posted attested copies of the warrant, "one at the Congregational Church in Brixham, one at the Town Hall and one at the Cape Neddick Post Office in said York"; but he did not add that these were public and conspicuous places."

There was no necessity of adding those words in this case. The places of posting being named, the Court can take judicial notice of the fact that those places are public and conspicuous.

6. That at that special meeting of October 13, 1906, after voting to build the bridge, the vote appointing "a committee of four to act in conjunction with the selectmen" should be construed to mean one committee of seven, composed of the three selectmen and the four others named; that two committees were not created, one composed of the three selectmen and the other of the four men named, these two committees to act concurrently or not at all; but a single committee of seven.

"In conjunction with" meant "in association with," "combined with," "united with."

7. That it was the duty of the committee of seven to take the necessary steps to carry out the vote of the town in building the bridge. As the selectmen refused to act with the others, it was the duty of the remaining four, the majority, to proceed without the assistance of the minority, and their action was legal and binding upon the town.

8. That the first contract of December 5, 1906, made by the plaintiff with the majority of this committee of seven in behalf of the town was valid; and the plaintiff was authorized to proceed thereunder. The communications from the

selectmen to the other four members of the committee and
to the contractor, protesting against the legality of the contract and its performance, were unauthorized and futile, as
the selectmen, as such, had no power in the matter. They
possessed only such authority as was conferred upon them
by the town when they were appointed members of the bridge
committee, and that authority was to aid in the construction
of the bridge.

9.   That the fact that the town made no appropriation for
building the bridge at the meeting of October 13, 1906, does
not affect the legality of the contract. If the contractor saw
fit to proceed with the work, and rely upon future appropriations or upon collecting his debt by others means, he had
a legal right to do so.

10.   That the town never took any legal action rescind-
ing the contract. At the annual meeting of March 11, 1907,
all articles looking toward the making of another contract
and appropriating money therefor were indefinitely post-
poned. But these had to do with the future and not with
the past. No vote was taken concerning the existing contract, and the plaintiff's rights thereunder remained unchanged.

11.   That the effect of the vote of the town at the annual
meeting of March 11, 1907, dismissing from further service
the committee of four previously appointed to act in conjunction with the selectmen was to reduce the bridge committee from seven to three. The town had the right to
revoke the authority previously conferred as it was a mere
naked authority. But the three selectmen previously appointed were not removed, and their powers continued if
they saw fit to exercise them. The contract itself, however,
was not affected by this vote, nor the plaintiff's rights there-

under. The fact that the selectmen continued their policy of non-participation was of no consequence. The work continued without their supervision, under the eye of the engineer who was legally employed, was never discharged, and who finally accepted the work.

12. That the duplicated contract of October 17, 1907, entered into because of certain changes and additions required by the War Department, was void; because the four members who signed the contract in behalf of the town had previously been dismissed from action, and therefore had no authority to bind the town.

The plaintiff was bound to ascertain and take notice of the power of the selectmen, and if the persons seeming to act had no authority, he cannot recover. Even the use of the bridge by the town would not bind it to pay for unauthorized work, although the same was beneficial.

13. That while the original contract on which the defendants are liable was for $39,500, the plaintiff was relieved from performing certain work under it when the supplemental contract was made, the cost of which was agreed to be $2,128.22, leaving a balance of $37,371.78. From this should be deducted $3,947.71, the amount received by the plaintiff from John C. Stewart as town treasurer. This leaves a balance of principal $33,427.07. The payments were due at certain specified times, and as demand was made therefor at the due dates, the plaintiff is entitled to interest for the default.

Computing the interest on the various sums due under the first contract from their due dates to May 15, 1913, and disregarding entirely the amount of the second contract, gives $11,109.92 as interest.

The entry should therefore be

Judgment for plaintiff for $45,936.99 with interest from May 15, 1913. July 1, 1913.

PROPOSED DIVISION OF THE TOWN

FROM TIME to time subsequent to 1884 the question of the division of the town of York was mooted, and in 1907 an active movement was made looking to the establishment of a new town within that portion of York lying between the Atlantic Ocean on the southeast, the Post Road on the northwest, to the juncture of the road leading to G. W. Currier's, thence direct to Wells line, on the southwest by Preble's or Little River, on the northeast by town of Wells.

A public meeting was held in Algonquin Hall Jan. 17th. It having been ascertained that "notice of any petition affecting the rights or interest of any town or county may be given to such town by serving it with a true copy of the petition at least fourteen days before the session," and being advised by the Assistant Attorney General to await the sitting of the next Legislature, no further action was taken.

In 1908 due notice was served on the town that a bill would be introduced in the coming Legislature asking for the setting off of a part of the territory of York into a new town. And on the 16th of February, 1909, Hon. Benjamin F. Hamilton in the Senate introduced a Bill, An Act to divide the Town of York and establish the Town of Yorktown. The Bill entire is as follows:

STATE OF MAINE.

In the year of our Lord one thousand nine hundred and nine. An Act to divide the Town of York and establish the Town of Yorktown.

Be it enacted by the People of Maine as follows:

Section 1. All that part of the town of York lying southerly of the following described line, namely, beginning on the line dividing the towns of York and Wells at a point where Josias River crosses said line, thence running in a southwesterly direction in a straight line to the town line dividing the town of York from the town of Kittery at a point on the northwesterly side of the road leading from York Corner to Portsmouth, N. H., and commonly called and known as "the Post Road," together with the inhabitants thereof, is hereby set off from the town of York, incorporated into a separate town by the name of Yorktown, and said town of Yorktown is hereby invested with all the powers and privileges, and subject to all the duties and obligations incident to other towns of the State.

Section 2. The several inhabitants of the town of Yorktown shall be holden to pay all taxes which have been legally assessed upon them by the town of York, and the collectors of taxes for said town of York are hereby authorized and required to collect and pay all taxes to them all ready committed according to their respective warrants. All money now in the treasury of said town of York, and all sums which shall hereafter be received from taxes heretofore assessed shall be applied to the several purposes for which they were raised, and in case of any excess said excess shall be apportioned to the towns of York and Yorktown in proportion to the valuation of the property and polls as made April, 1908, and the Treasurer of the town of York shall pay over to the Treasurer of the town of Yorktown such sums as are found to be due said town of Yorktown. The Commissioners of the County of York shall make the apportionment.

Section 3. The existing liabilities and obligations of said town of York shall be drected as follows:—The town debt shall be borne by said towns in proportion to the valuation

of their respective territories as of April, 1908. The obligations of the town of York shall be borne by each town in
the foregoing proportion, except its contract with the York
Shore Water Company, which shall be borne by each town
in proportion to the number of hydrants used by each. All
paupers now supported by the aid of the town of York shall,
after division, be maintained and supported by the town in
whose territory they resided when they became paupers including the paupers now supported on the town farm, and
insane hospital. Each town shall henceforth bear all expenses for the care and maintenance of all roads and bridges
within its respective limits.

Section 4. The high school building and lot with all the
equipment connected therewith shall be the property of the
two towns jointly, said high school shall be maintained by
the two towns in proportion to the valuation of the respective towns, and all appropriations therefor shall be based
upon the valuation taken by the assessors of the respective
towns in April next preceding the town meetings at which
an appropriation is made therefor. The management and
control of said high school shall be with the Superintending
School Committee of the two towns acting jointly. All
trust funds now or hereafter held or given for the maintenance of the high school in the town of York shall be under
the direction and control of said Superintending School
Committee of the two towns acting jointly.

Section 5. All the other property of the town of York,
real and personal, shall be the property of the town in which
it is now located. It shall be appraised by the County Commissioners of York County and each town shall be charged
with the appraisal thereof. The difference between the appraisal of the property taken by each town shall be paid by

the town taking the larger amount and it shall be divided between the two towns in proportion to the valuation of their respective territories, taken by the Assessors in April, 1908. The books and papers and records of the town of York shall be retained by the town of Yorktown and each town shall have access to the same.

Section 6. Any justice of the peace or notary public of the County of York may issue his warrant to any legal voter of the town of Yorktown directing him to notify the inhabitants thereof to meet at a time and place specified in said warrant, giving at least seven days' notice therefor, for the choice of town officers, and to transact such business as towns are authorized to do.

This bill was referred to the Committee on Towns.

Petitions for the division of the Town of York, by Henry C. Hussey and others, and W. H. Hogarth and 28 others, John F. Todd and 35 others, all of York, were presented in the Senate by Senator Hamilton.

Remonstrances against division were presented in the House, signed by Joseph P. Bragdon and 65 others, Samuel F. Paul and 85 others, George M. Simpson and 58 others, William B. Card and 40 others, Jeremiah McIntire and 78 others, Bradford S. Woodward and 45 others, E. A. Welch and 9 others, all of York, and Francis A. Peters of Boston.

In the House of Representatives Feb. 17 among other papers from the Senate was An Act to divide the town of York and establish the town of Yorktown, which had been referred to the Committee on Towns by that body. On motion of Mr. Chase of York it was tabled for printing pending concurrence in matter of reference. In the House Feb. 23d, on motion of Mr. Chase of York, An Act to divide the town of York and establish the town of Yorktown was taken from the table, and on further motion by Mr. Chase it was referred to the Committee on Towns in concurrence with the action of the Senate Feb. 16th. Notice of a public hearing on the question was ordered by the Committee on Towns, Hon. Patrick Therriault, Chairman, and the same was held in the Senate Chamber, Thursday, March 11th, 1909. The session of the committee lasted until ten o'clock P. M. There were two score people in attendance for and against it from York. The petitioners were represented by Hon. J. C. Stewart, Hon. B. F. Cleaves, and Hon. Oscar E. Fellows, while Hon. James O. Bradbury and George F. Haley, Esq., (now supreme judge), appeared for the remonstrants. Some twenty witnesses testified. Dr. Stewart opened for the proponents, practically telling the story of the petitioners, closing by saying that from the causes named property is decreasing in value. He also stated that while the new bridge had further accentuated the trouble, it did not produce the division sentiment. Hon. Joseph W. Simpson said that the division was a matter of life or death to the town. Property had depreciated, and he declared that he could almost guarantee a million-dollar increase in the new town in twenty years. He also said that the inception of the movement for division was by an anti-bridge man; Mr. William H. Hogarth. H. T. Nichols of New York, testified to the need of good roads and electric street lights, not obtainable under present town arrangement.

Dr. S. W. Allen of Boston corroborated what had been said regarding the lack of public spirit, and Frank H. Ellis' testimony was on the same lines. Edward S. Marshall also testified.

Samuel W. Junkins, Esq., was the first witness against division. He stated that a large majority of the inhabitants of the town of York and the proposed town were opposed to division, and he acknowledged that value had fallen off.

Joseph P. Bragdon as the star witness followed. In reply to questions by Mr. Bradbury he said he was chairman of the Board of Selectmen. He said the map offered by the proponents was a copy of one more than forty years old. He refreshed his memory from notes and said if the town was divided in accordance with the provisions of the bill, "Yorktown" would have a valuation of $2,071,702, and forty miles of road to maintain, and "York" a valuation of $321,-686, and one hundred miles of road. He said that three-quarters of the people in the proposed new town were opposed to division, and that there never existed any feeling of antagonism against the lower section on the part of the upper section or vice versa. He also read a resolution adopted at a town meeting protesting against the division.

Henry S. Bragdon, also a member of the Board of Selectmen, gave similar evidence as the Chairman's. Selectman Harry H. Norton agreed with the testimony of his colleagues, however, adding that most of the quarreling came from residents of the lower part of the town. J. Arthur Parsons agreed that the general sentiment of the town above and below the "dead line" is against division. He also said there was no ill feeling between the upper and lower portions, and that the quarreling is all done in the lower part of the town. Charles L. Grant, Bradford S. Woodward, Arthur E. Bragdon, J. Howard Junkins, A. C. Farwell, Samuel F. Paul, John E. Barrell, C. A. Goodale, also testified in opposition. Among other York people present were E. B. Blaisdell, C. H. Young, S. A. Preble, W. S. Putnam, H. D. Philbrick, R. F. Talpey, W. H. Hogarth, Will C. Hildreth, Malcolm McIntire, E. H. Banks. The summing up of the case for the remonstrants was by Hon. James O. Bradbury, and Hon. Oscar E. Fellows closed for the proponents, and the chairman declared the hearing closed, and adjournment was made.

In the Senate under "Reports of Committees" March 18th, a majority report for the Committee on Towns, on Bill "An Act to divide the town of York and establish the town of Yorktown," that same ought not to pass. (Signed) Colcord, Kellogg, Merrill, Hamlin, Bearce, Varney, Donnell.

A minority report from the same committee submitting same in new draft under same title. (Signed) Therriault. The foregoing reports were read, and on motion by Mr. Therriault of Aroostook, pending acceptance of either were tabled and ordered to be printed.

In the Senate March 23d—On motion by Mr. Therriault of Aroostook, Senate Document No. 445, "An Act to divide the town of York and establish the town of Yorktown," was taken from the table, and the Senator further moved that the minority report be accepted. Thereupon Senator Kellogg of Penobscot obtained the floor and spoke in opposition to the acceptance of the minority report. In part he said: "Now at the hearing the petitioners had for witnesses, J. C. Stewart, E. S. Marshall, J. W. Simpson, and one or two others, resident property owners. They also had two non-resident property owners. The claim of the resident property owners why they should have a division was that the seashore section could not get sufficient appropriations for improvements. One of the non-residents favored the division because he could not have trees set out alongside the road and sidewalks built to the golf links; the other could not tell why he wanted the town divided. I presume he had not been told what to say by the petitioners. How-

ever, he thought that the town should be divided. Now,
the opponents to the division had for witnesses the Chairman of the County Commissioners, three Selectmen, two of
whom live with the County Commissioner below the dividing
line. They also had eight or ten other witnesses, all of
whom are business men and who are interested in the welfare of the town. All but two of these live south of the
line by which it is proposed to divide the town of York.
There was a remonstrance against the proposed division
signed by 382 persons, two-thirds of which live south of
the line. * * * I hope, gentlemen, that you will sustain
the report of the majority of the committee."

Senator Hamilton for the minority report said in part:
"I was opposed to the first bill which the committee heard.
I was opposed to the division line which was first introduced
here in the Senate and referred to their committee. Since
then an amendment, as you will see by looking at your
record, has been made which wonderfully changes it; and
I will call each of the Senators' attention to the new draft
which wonderfully changes it. * * *

"MINORITY REPORT.

"An Act to divide the town of York and establish the town
of Yorktown.

"Be it enacted by the People of the State of Maine as follows:

"All that part of the town of York lying southerly of the
following described line, namely: Beginning at northerly
line of the Portland Road, so called, at the Kittery line,
thence by said northerly line of said Portland Road to the
thread of Cape Neddick River; thence southeasterly by said
thread of Cape Neddick River to the Atlantic Ocean; thence

by said shore line of the town of York to the boundary line between the town of said York and Kittery; thence north-westerly by said Kittery line, together with the inhabitants thereof is hereby set off from the town of York, incorporated into a separate town of 'Gorges,' and said town of Gorges is hereby invested with all the powers and privileges and subject to all the duties and obligations incident to other towns of the state, said town of Gorges is to assume and pay for the new bridge, so called, across York River at York Harbor, so that said town of York shall have no further concern or expense concerning said bridge. (Sections 2-3-4-5-6 remain as originally reported with exception of the substitution of the name 'Gorges' wherever that of York-town appears.) Now if you divide this town as it is indicated in the new draft, those people who live next the sea-shore in those summer residences will certainly boom that town, and you will find it one of the most elegant places to live in in the state. We welcome them there to invest their money * * * and that is why every Senator from York County is interested that they should have it where they can go ahead and not be handicapped. The men that come there and bring their money to build these homes care not how much tax they pay if they can have their homes beauti-fied and made pleasant. * * *

"In reference to the bridge matter, I want to say, there are many law suits upon that bridge, and it is costing some-body a good deal of money and the town will have to pay it in the end in my judgment."

The question being put on the motion by Mr. Therriault of Aroostook that the minority report be substituted for the majority report, the yeas and nays were called for and ordered, and the vote being had, resulted as follows: Those voting *yca* were Morey, Baxter, Boynton, Eaton, Emery, Gowell, Hamilton, Hastings, Irving, Knowlton, Looney, Lowe, Macomber, Milliken, Minott, Mullen, Osgood, Reynolds, Shaw, Smith, Staples, Therriault, Warren, Wheeler, Wyman (24). Those voting *nay*, Donigan, Hill, Howes, Kellogg, Walker (5). So the motion prevailed, the bill took its several readings and pending its second reading was amended by adoption of Senate Amendment "A." Therefore, the bill took its second reading and was passed to be engrossed.

March 24th, in the House, under first reading of Senate bills majority and minority reports of the Committee on Towns to which was referred An Act to divide the town of York and establish the town of Yorktown, the majority reporting "ought not to pass" and the minority reporting "ought to pass," came from the Senate. On motion of Mr. Chase of York, pending action on either report they were tabled together with the bill, and specially assigned for to-day (March 24). Under this assignment Mr. Chase of York moved that the House non-concur with the Senate in adopting the minority report. Mr. Marshall of Portland said: "Mr. Speaker, just a word. I hope the House will concur with the Senate in the adoption of the minority report, and that the motion of the gentleman from York will not prevail. I know the local conditions there, and I thoroughly and honestly believe that the welfare of both communities and the welfare of the County of York will be promoted as the Senate has determined."

Mr. Chase of York obtained the floor and in extended and able remarks favored the non-concurrence of the House. He presented an array of statistics favorable to his contention, and said: "Now I will say a word in relation to the subject of dispute between the different parts of the town. I was born in the town of York and have lived there a large part of the time, and these disputes they tell about are something new to me—that I never heard of myself— *   *   * A large majority of these remonstrants live within this last arranged district.   A majority of the 382 I say live in that section.   They don't want this thing.   The people are almost up in arms about it.   I ought to know something about that town.   I cannot imagine why the gentleman from Portland (Mr. Marshall) should be so persistent in looking out for York when he lives in Portland.   I don't know—yes, I do know who is pushing him.   That makes no difference.   I am the sole representative of the town of York in this Legislature.   *   *   *   I think so far as the citizens are concerned nine-tenths of the voters representing nine-tenths of the property are absolutely and utterly opposed to this whole thing."

The question being on the motion to non-concur with the Senate, Mr. Chase of York called for the yeas and nays, which was agreed to.   The result of the vote was yeas 35, nays 93, not voting 22.   So the motion to non-concur was lost.   Thereupon Mr. Smith of Berwick moved that the House concur with the Senate in accepting the minority report.   He also moved that the rules be suspended, and that the bill take its several readings at the present time, and pass to be engrossed.   The bill then received its first and second readings.

On motion of Mr. Smith, Senate Amendment A was adopted in concurrence.

Mr. Chase of York offered House Amendment A by adding the following: "Provided, however, that this act shall not take effect until it has first been accepted by a majority

of the legal voters of said town of York at a town meeting
of said town of York legally warned and holden for that
purpose at the town house in said town   *   *   *   then this
act shall be void."

Mr. Marshall of Portland said: "I had supposed that the
division of the town was for the purpose of allowing a certain portion thereof around the seashore to go ahead and
prosper and develop itself along its own lines.   *   *   *   It
seems to me this defeats the whole proposition."

Mr. Chase—"I call the attention of this House to the fact
that one of the witnesses, Mr. Edward S. Marshall, the man
who has put up this whole job, the father of the gentleman
from Portland, admitted before the committee in my hearing and in the hearing of the committee that a majority of
the voters in the whole town were in the lower part which
they want set off.   *   *   *   Now, I want to know in all
fairness, in the name of decency, what those people of York
have done that this thing shall be placed upon them, and
why a majority of the voters should not have the privilege
of deciding whether their town shall be torn in pieces or not.
I want to know if there is one particle of decency and fairness or honor among the men of the House.   I call for the
years and nays."   The motion was agreed to and the roll
called resulted in yeas 56, nays 75, so the motion was lost.

Mr. Allen of Jonesboro moved that the subject matter be
referred to the next Legislature, and also moved that the
vote be taken by calling for the yeas and nays, which was
done; resulting in 59 yeas and 77 nays, so the motion of
Mr. Allen was lost.   Thereupon Mr. Chase of York offered
Amendment "B," providing that the act should not take
effect until it had been accepted by a majority of the voters
within the limits of the proposed town of Gorges.

Mr. Marshall moved that the amendment lie upon the table and the motion was lost.

Mr. Pattangall of Waterville—"Mr. Speaker, I arise for the purpose of moving the previous question. In my opinion the amendment offered by the gentleman from York is so harmless and so eminently fair that even the lobby ought not to be consulted in regard to it."

The question being on the adoption of House Amendment "B," the yeas and nays were, yeas 99, nays 33, so the amendment was adopted, and the bill was assigned to March 25th for its third reading.

In the House March 25th, Mr. Peters of Ellsworth moved to reconsider the vote of the 24th whereby Amendment "B" was adopted.

Mr. Burleigh of Augusta offered a substitute amendment, "Provided, however, that this act shall not take effect unless a majority of the tax-payers who were assessed a tax for the year 1909 upon a poll or property within the limits of the proposed town of Gorges vote to accept this act at a legal meeting of said tax-payers."

Mr. Pattangall of Waterville: "I would like to inquire of the gentleman from Augusta if under that amendment the women of Gorges would vote on this question."

Mr. Burleigh: "I understand they could; and I see no reason why they should not."

Mr. Pattangall: "Any woman living in New York and owning property in the proposed town is allowed to vote."

Mr. Burleigh: "Yes."

Mr. Pattangall: "Then the object of the amendment is to confer limited woman suffrage."   (Laughter.)

The question coming on the motion of Mr. Peters to reconsider the vote whereby House Amendment "B" was adopted, the motion was lost—64 in favor and 69 opposed. The bill then received its third reading.

Mr. Smith of Berwick offered Amendment "C," which was adopted.

In the Senate, March 26th, papers from the House were disposed of in concurrence, among which was An Act to divide the town of York and establish the town of Yorktown. By the House the bill passed to be engrossed as amended by Amendments B and C.

On motion of Mr. Hamilton the bill with amendments was laid upon the table.

In the Senate, March 30th, on motion of Mr. Hamilton, the bill "An Act dividing the town of York" was taken from the table, and on motion of the same Senator the Senate voted to non-concur in the adoption of Amendment "B," and on further motion the bill was passed to be engrossed.

In the House, March 31st, the bill "An Act to divide the town of York" came back from the Senate with House Amendment "B" rejected.

Mr. Additon of Leeds moved that the House recede and concur. Mr. Chase of York moved that the bill lie upon the table until "Orders of the day" was reached. The motion to lay upon the table was lost, 49 in favor and 62 negative. Thereupon Mr. Allen of Jonesboro addressed the House. He was followed by Mr. Moore of Saco and Mr. Bearce of Eddington. Mr. Marshall of Portland, in reply to Mr. Moore said: "I think I know the town of York as well as the gentleman from Saco. I know it from its mountain to its rugged coast. I know it all. I know better than the gentleman from Jonesboro. I have lived there, and I know the conditions. I know that there have been citizens of York here this winter asking and demanding that the town should be divided. They are interested. Their property is at stake. The gentleman from Saco speaks about taxing Chinese, Japanese, and that sort of people. I want to ask him whether he will give vote to a man like Francis Lynde Stetson, and a man like Thomas Nelson Page. I have here a letter from Mr. Stetson, the letter is dated January 12th, 1909, and is as follows:

" 'Edward S. Marshall, Esquire,
        " 'York Harbor, Maine.

" 'My Dear Sir:
    " 'I would state that since my erection of a house at York Harbor my judgment has been that it would be for the best interests of all parts of the town of York if the interior could be separated from the shore district, enabling each part to conduct its affairs according to local preference of each for the provision and expenditure of money for the public needs. I say this not for the benefit of the residents of York Harbor only, but for those of the western part of the town as well; for I believe there would result not only the avoidance of friction, but a better use of the public funds and the public opportunities of this attractive locality. For these reasons, as well as others, I am heartily in sympathy with the movement to divide the town of York, so that the interior part may be separate from the shore district.
            " 'Faithfully yours,
                    " 'FRANCIS L. STETSON.'

"And, Mr. Speaker, it is for 135 of the real estate owners and tax-payers there that I speak. Men who represent three-quarters of the valuation of that town, who come here and ask to be divided, and who are on the petition asking for division. It is for those people that I speak, those men who have made the town of York what it is today. Those men who have seen it grow from a little hamlet, a little fishing village, to one of the best and most popular resorts upon the coast of Maine."

Mr. Chase of York: "Mr. Speaker, the only thing I have asked for is that this amendment be retained in the bill— * * * that is all we ask, and it is a right which we demand of the House. * * * I positively deny that there has been any sectional feeling in that town. There are always certain differences where you find people of positive views, but there is no essential difference. Now, Mr. Speaker, I want to call attention to a few letters which I have here, and I will beg the pardon of the House if I overstep my time, but I want to call attention to a few out of ninety (90) or more letters I have here from citizens within the limits of the proposed town.

" 'York Harbor, Maine, March 28, 1909.
" 'Josiah Chase, Esq., House of Rep.,
"   'Augusta, Maine.
" 'My Dear Mr. Chase:—Being the oldest citizen of York Harbor, so called, and one of the largest tax-payers, I most emphatically protest against this unjust division of the town of York. * * * Oppose this unfair proposition and you will always have the good will of the citizens of the old town of York.
" 'Very truly yours,
"   'ELIAS BAKER.'

"Mr. John E. Norwood under same date wrote as follows:
" 'My dear Mr. Chase:—As one of the older citizens of

this town and one of the largest tax-payers at York Harbor, I wish to offer my most emphatic protest to any division of the town of York. Having taken all active part in the summer business here at the Harbor from its very beginning, I feel that I am able to form a fairly correct opinion in this matter. I have endeavored to give it most careful consideration from various points of view. My conclusion is that the proposed division would not only be a gross injustice to a large number of our citizens, but would result in causing serious damage to the progress of the summer business here.

" 'Yours respectfully,

" 'John E. Norwood.' "

Continuing, Mr. Chase said, "I hope the motion of the gentleman from Leeds will not prevail."

On a yea and nay vote the motion to recede and concur was carried by 69 yeas as against 58 nays.

In the Senate, April 1, passed to be enacted a bill to divide the town of York and establish the town of Gorges. And on same day the bill was passed to be enacted in the House.

The Act passed by the Legislature establishing the town of Gorges was signed by the Governor. Thereupon the opponents of the division proceeded to avail themselves of the provisions of the referendum. At the ovation given Mr. Chase on the evening of April 8th, 1909, at the Town Hall, in his remarks he said in part: "The only thing left now is the referendum. The people of the state have changed their constitution, you know, so that it is now in the hands of the people to determine whether the people of York shall have the town divided against their will or not. That is our only remedy. I hope the town will fight and beat them by the use of the referendum."

Subsequently, the York Referendum Association was formed as follows:

Executive Committee—Joseph P. Bragdon, Henry S. Bragdon, Harry H. Norton, J. Arthur Parsons, George B. Main, Charles P. Dustin, Charles E. Noble, Josiah N. Norton, E. E. E. Mitchell, A. C. Farwell, Fred H. Bowden, Edward S. Thompson, G. A. Donnell, W. L. Grant, George F. Plaisted, J. E. Barrell, George E. Blaisdell, Malcolm McIntire, Josiah Chase, F. Raymond Brewster, Fremont Varrell, Charles L. Grant, A. A. Odiorne, E. C. Hawkes, Joseph C. Bridges, Arthur E. Bragdon, Bradford S. Woodward, C. L. Bowden.

James S. Brewster was made Chairman, and George F. Plaisted, Secretary.

A Finance and Petition and Printing Committee were chosen, with Bradford S. Woodward and Joseph P. Bragdon, Chairmen. A statement of facts was formulated and printed and the work of procuring 10,000 signatures begun. That number was obtained, but the validity of some of the petitions was questioned and on request of Edward S. Marshall and eleven others the Governor gave a hearing Aug. 23d at which Mr. Marshall, John C. Stewart, Charles F. Blaisdell, Josiah Chase, Henry S. Bragdon and Charles L. Grant, all of York, were present.

At the biennial election held Sept. 12th, 1910, on the question submitted to the people as to whether the Act of the Legislature of 1909 establishing the town of Gorges should become a law, the total vote was 51,414; in favor of the Act, 19,692; opposed to the Act, 31,722.

The vote in the town of York was 90 in favor, 436 opposed.

The following is a copy of the paper sent out with the blanks for signatures for the referendum:

STATEMENT OF FACTS RELATING TO THE PROPOSED DIVISION OF THE TOWN OF YORK.

The town of York has a population of about 2800, with 760 polls, and a valuation (according to the State Assessors) of $2,745,400. It is the oldest town in the State; having celebrated in 1902 the 250th anniversary of its incorporation as a town.

The act to divide the town of York was introduced in the Senate on the 16th day of February, the day then set as the last day when such matters could be introduced except by suspension of the rules.

Up to that time the people of York generally, knew nothing about the matter except by mere rumor. The representative from York had never seen the bill and knew nothing of it, except by rumor, until it came into the House of Representatives and was laid on the table for printing, pending its reference to a committee. It appeared then as "Act to divide the town of York and establish the town of Yorktown."

It was referred to the Committee on Towns. The committee held a long and exhaustive hearing on the matter on the 11th day of March. At that hearing petitions were presented in favor of the act signed by 57 voters of the town, and remonstrances against the act signed by 382 voters of the town. A large number of the prominent citizens of the town appeared before the committee against the act, including the principal town officers, and the Chairman of the Board of County Commissioners.

As a result of that hearing seven of the committee voted "ought not to pass." One member of the committee reserved the right to make a minority report.

One week after the hearing he brought into the Senate, as a minority report, a new act on entirely different lines and with new conditions, much more offensive and humiliating to the people of York than the first bill. This new draft was entitled "An Act to divide the town of York and establish the town of Gorges." The other members were not consulted about this new act and the people of York were never given any hearing in regard to it.

This act gives to the proposed town of "Gorges" about two-thirds of the population of the town of York, two-thirds of its valuation and about 30 miles of its roads; leaving to the town of York about one-third of its population, one-third of its valuation and 110 miles of roads. It provides that the York high school building situated within the proposed new town, together with its trust fund, shall be owned jointly by both towns. It takes away from the town of York both of its grammar schools, three of the primary schools, the poor farm with its large new steam-heated buildings, the town house, the ancient jail museum, and all the ancient and current records of York up to the date of the proposed separation.

This act was substituted for the majority report in the Senate, and under suspension of the rules, it was passed to be engrossed. In the House of Representatives the representative from York offered an amendment submitting the act to the voters of York for acceptance. This was rejected. He then secured the adoption of an amendment submitting it to the voters in the proposed new town for acceptance. The Senate rejected this amendment, and the House subsequently concurred with the Senate by a majority of nine votes, and in this form it was passed to be enacted, thus denying to the people the right to determine for themselves by their ballots what is to them a most important question.

Nine out of every ten of the people of York and also of the proposed town of Gorges are bitterly opposed to this act. Out of a total of 441 voters in the proposed town, 382 are known to be opposed to it.

Shall the majority rule?

Respectfully submitted,

By EXECUTIVE COMMITTEE OF YORK REFERENDUM ASSOCIATION.

COMMEMORATION OF THE TWO HUNDRED AND FIFTIETH ANNIVERSARY

In 1902 occurred the two hundred and fiftieth anniversary of the birth of the town of York. At the annual town meeting held in March of that year it was voted to commemorate the event. An appropriation of money was made, and a committee of sixteen were appointed to carry out the vote of the town as follows: J. Perley Putnam, Joseph P. Bragdon, Harry H. Norton, Malcolm McIntire, Henry Plaisted, William T. Keene, Samuel T. Blaisdell, William O. Barrell, Josiah N. Norton, Charles H. Junkins, George F. Plaisted, J. Howard Preble, George E. Marshall, Joseph W. Simpson, Daniel Weare, John F. Plaisted. The York Historical and Improvement Society joined with the town and added Walter M. Smith, Hon. Edward O. Emerson, Rev. Frank Sewall, D. D., to the committee and also voted five hundred dollars in aid of the affair. The chairman of the Board of Selectmen, J. Perley Putnam, was made chairman of the executive committee; George F. Plaisted, general secretary; Wilson M. Walker, treasurer; Walter M. Smith was elected president of the day; J. Perley Putnam, marshal of the historical parade. The committee on program and invitations—Rev. Frank Sewall, D. D., Hon. Edward O. Emerson, Walter M. Smith.

Special committees:

Committee on Historical Parade—Frank D. Marshall, LL. B., Mrs. James T. Davidson, Mrs. F. Doubleday, Mrs. Hungerford, Miss Mary Louise Smith, Miss Theodosia Barrell, Miss Katherine E. Marshall, Miss Ruth Putnam, Miss Florence Paul, Miss Elizabeth Perkins, Mrs. George

L. Cheney, Miss Rachel K. Sewall, Miss Constance Emerson, Miss Elizabeth T. Sewall, Miss Ellen M. Dennett.

On Music—George F. Plaisted.

On Water Carnival—Freeman Sewall, Arthur E. Sewall, Burleigh Davidson, and Russell Cheney.

On Fireworks—Walter M. Smith.

On Entertainment—Joseph P. Bragdon, W. T. Keene, Hon. John C. Stewart, Wilson M. Walker, N. H. Shattuck, Samuel A. Preble, Hon. E. O. Emerson, Frank D. Marshall.

Press Committee—George F. Plaisted, Edwin D. Twombley, William J. Neal.

On Tuesday, August 5th, at sunrise, a salute of fifty guns was fired from the Palo Alto gun under direction of Edward C. Moody on Paul's Hill, and the church bells were rung.

The parade formed at York Beach and moved along Long Beach to the Harbor, thence to the Village and York Corner, and returned to the Village for the commemoration exercises.

J. Perley Putnam was marshal, with aids, W. J. Simpson, W. T. Keene, A. M. Bragdon, Frank H. Ellis, Joseph P. Bragdon, Fred G. Winn. The Marine Band of the Navy Yard at Kittery and a detachment of U. S. Marines, twelve tableaux on floats illustrating incidents and characters in the history of York from 1614 to 1816, the Kearsarge Fife and Drum Corps, a floral parade, and the attendants of the public schools.

The commemorative exercises were held on the Common in rear of the Town Hall. A platform was erected against the building, on this were assembled, the president, secretary, and visiting members of the Maine Historical Society; Justice McKenna of the Supreme Court of the United States;

Gen. Joshua L. Chamberlain, Woodbury Langdon of New York, Francis Lynde Stetson, Esq., Dr. J. B. Ayer, Boston; Hon. Edward S. Marshall, York; Jeremiah McIntire, York; John J. Loud, Weymouth, Mass.; J. Windsor Brathwaithe, Esq., Kennebunkport; A. G. Cummock, Esq., Lowell, Mass.; Hon. Thomas B. Reed, New York; William Dean Howells, New York; Thomas Nelson Page, Washington, D. C.; Samuel L. Clemens, New York; W. J. Tucker, President Dartmouth College; ex-Gov. Frank W. Rollins of New Hampshire; Charles Eustis Hubbard, Boston; Hon. Augustus F. Moulton, Portland, and others. Letters of appreciation and regretting inability to attend were received from the President, Hon. William H. Moody, Secretary of the Navy, the Governors of Maine and Massachusetts, Hon. Eugene Hale and William P. Frye, U. S. Senators from Maine; Thomas DeWitt Hyde, President of Bowdoin College; Hon. James O. Bradbury of Saco; Capt. John Dennett, U. S. R. service; Charles Ray Palmer, LL. D., New Haven, Conn.; Charles F. Adams, Boston; John Fogg, Esq., New York; William Bruce King, Esq., Washington, D. C.; James D. Smith, Esq., New York; ex-Governor Henry B. Cleaves, Portland; Major General Augustus B. Farnham, Adjutant General of Maine.

At 2.30 P. M., Hon. Edward C. Moody addressed the assembled thousands as follows:

"Ladies and Gentlemen, Fellow Citizens:—

"In the warrant calling the annual town meeting of York, held March 13th, this present year, an article appeared on the petition of six men—Wilson M. Walker, Albert M. Bragdon, A. H. Bowden, W. T. Keene, E. F. Hobson and one other—'To see if the town would vote to commemorate its 250th anniversary.' It so voted. The York Historical

Society joined hands with the town, the booming of cannon, the ringing of bells, the strains of martial music, the elaborate decorations, the passing of the splendid parade through our streets, all speak thus far in memory of the olden days. And now we shall be told of those who founded, and fostered this ancient borough.

"What was his name? I do not know his name,
I only know he heard God's voice and came,
Brought all he loved across the sea,
To live and work for God—and me;
Felled the ungracious oak;
     With rugged toil
     Dragged from the soil
The thrice gnarled roots and stubborn rock;
With plenty filled the haggard mountain side;
And when his work was done without memorial died.
No blaring trumpet sounded out his fame;
He lived, he died—I do not know his name.
No form of bronze and no memorial stones
Show me the place where lie his mouldering bones:
Only a cheerful village stands,
Built by his hardened hands;
Only one thousand homes,
     Where every day
     The cheerful play
Of love and hope and courage comes;
These are his monuments, and these alone,
There is no form of bronze: and no memorial stone.

"My friends, I am not here to weary you. It is a public honor, my personal pleasure, to present to you the President of the York Historical Society as the President of the Day, Mr. Walter M. Smith."

President Smith's Remarks

"Mr. Moody, Ladies and Gentlemen:—

"For the distinguished honor of presiding over this assemblage I am indebted, sir, to your committee. I thank you for

your kindly introduction. In making my grateful acknowl-
edgment of your courtesy, I desire to voice the sentiment
of your committee and your fellow townsmen in according
to you, sir, the inception of the movement which has culminated in this tribute to Old York."

The invocation followed by Rev. David B. Sewall, a
former pastor of the First Parish. Rev. S. C. Abbott of
the Methodist Church then read the CXV of the Psalms,
which was followed by the singing of Dr. Watts' Commemoration Hymn—"Let Children Hear the Mighty Deeds."
A letter was then read from the President of the United
States.

The President then introduced the Hon. John C. Stewart,
who delivered an eloquent address of welcome, and said in
part: "To extend to you the welcome of the citizens of
York is especially pleasing because of the presence of so
many of our non-citizen residents, whom we, as a body of
citizens, for the first time meet in common assemblage. For
many years you have been coming and going, seeing and
meeting us as we have seen and met you, without becoming
really acquainted with each other. You will I know pardon
me if I take some of my time in telling you who we are and
what we think of you. * * * And today for the citizens of York, I extend to you our most cordial and hearty
welcome. You have improved our homes, built our school-
houses, repaired our churches, given us roads equal to any
in the country towns of our state, brought the markets of
the world to our doors, established libraries for our use, and
seem constantly planning for our welfare. We appreciate
all these things. Whatever prejudice there may have been
in the past is gone. You have been our friends, we are
yours. And now to the worthy sons of a proud ancestry

who have gone out into other parts, and who have come home today to participate in these festivities, we say 'Welcome.' * * * We welcome you today to the home of your ancestors. To the strangers who are with us we give a most hearty welcome. You come from all walks of life to aid us in celebrating this day. * * * And while we make it a festal day I would recall the early struggles of our ancestors— * * * their love of freedom which led them in yonder church to draft the first Declaration of Independence ever written in America."

Then followed the address by the orator of the day, Hon. James Phinney Baxter of Portland, President of the Maine Historical Society. As might be expected, it was eloquent and scholarly, replete with historical data. The President of the Day remarked: "We have upon the platform men representative of the bench and the bar, the peers of any in the world; others renowned in art and literature; * * * The educators of our youth, the merchant, the farmer and the mechanic, * * * The soldier who has carried our flag to victory, who when called upon responded with the best that was in him." He then introduced "that veteran Christian soldier and patriot who has four times been elected Governor of Maine."

General Chamberlain gave a fine impromptu address, and in his opening said:

"Mr. President and Gracious Friends:—

"I am not one of your appointed speakers; I am one of your relics. I had the honor some time ago of giving a 'sermon' at the rededication of your historic old church here; and I dare say your committee of arrangements thought that was enough of my preaching for one generation. But now called by your courtesy to speak, even amidst these great men whose words are eagerly heard far and wide over land, and beyond the seas, some ancient blood in me, gives me the boldness to offer what I may among the testimonies of the day." In closing he said: "We desire to offer our tribute of remembrance for the strong and brave who here took the initiative in making this a world for us; for we, too, claim to have part in this inheritance of brave beginnings."

President Tucker of Dartmouth was the next speaker. In part he said: "This little settlement of York was a pawn on the chessboard of Old World politics. The game was played by wireless telegraphy. A word from the Court at Versailles, and the Indians stole down from the north on their errand of death. It was one continued move and counter-move between English and French, and it was the settler who marked the play in the fate of his wife and children."

The last public remarks made by Hon. Thomas B. Reed were from the platform on York Village Green, Aug. 5, 1902. In closing them he said: "I think that with the high example set by your illustrious ancestors, the descendants of the settlers of York should so conduct themselves as to increase the nobility and civilization of the world in which you move."

President Smith in presenting the next speaker said: "York has attracted to her borders those whom other less favored spots have failed to capture. We have made a most fortunate acquisition to our summer colony in the person and family of one of New York's most eminent counsellors. It gives me profound personal, as well as official pleasure, to introduce Francis Lynde Stetson, Esquire, of New York." Mr. Stetson said in part: "Since Gorges nine generations have stood upon the earth, but now and here we think only of such of them as have found their homes in York. How does this community differ from many others? In degree only and not at all in kind. It is a fair type of the settlements on this New England coast, and shares its characteristics. * * * Out of the present as well as from the past, in the fulness of time will develop the millennium of right that shall be the heritage alike of York, and of our beloved Union which is after all only an aggregation of Yorks. * * * At your next great feast of commemoration the sons and daughters of York shall declare that here, and in New England, life is not only true, but that it is also interesting; and that your people are as generous as just."

Thomas Nelson Page followed Mr. Stetson, and the writer is not sure that his address should not appear in full even if other matters were displaced. He said: "But York's preeminence is based on her having survived all the chances and changes of the two centuries and a half that have rolled by. * * * It is this we have assembled to celebrate. You, the native-born people of York; you the descendants of the settlers of York, and the rest of us who have come from other Yorks; but with all the blood and brawn and principles that made, and have kept this York continuously for 250 years. * * * It rests with you to preserve what your forefathers secured and handed down to you. It is on the sterling independence of our American people; on their love of liberty; their homely virtues, that the hope of liberty, and of virtue in the world rests."

Mr. Samuel L. Clemens was then introduced and spoke in his characteristic Mark Twain vein.

After the singing of "America" by the assemblage standing, Rev. Sidney K. Perkins, pastor of the First Parish Church, gave the benediction.

RECEPTION

Rev. Dr. Frank Sewall gave a reception at the close of the public exercises to the visiting members of the Maine Historical Society at Coventry Hall, the old Judge Sewall mansion. This was largely attended.

THE BEGINNING OF YORK AS A SUMMER RESORT

In 1857 Mr. and Mrs. Stephen Grant reecived at their hospitable home the first to visit York, known as "summer boarders." Mr. John Goddard of Middleborough, Mass., and a brother, Samuel Goddard of Brookline, Mass., sought and found retirement and rest from the active work of mercantile life in the seclusion of tree-shaded York Village. They were the first of succeeding thousands who have carried the fame of York as far as civilization extends. The demand for accommodation by people of that station in life who could afford to lay aside the active duties of life during the summer months was such that it soon caused Isaiah P. Moody, Esq., and Capt. George Moody to open their houses. They were followed by Capt. Samuel Young, Mrs. Charles Goodwin, and Deacon Henry D. Norwood, at the lower end of the town, as it was then called. In October, 1865, the cellar and foundation for the "Lord House" was laid by William H. Fernald, for Hon. Henry C. Lord of Cincinnati, Ohio. He was a son of ex-President Nathan Lord of Dartmouth College, and for a few years this house was the summer home of President Lord, his sons, Joseph, William H., Frank, Henry C., Nathan, and daughter, the wife of Rev. William Wright, pastor of Berkeley Street, Boston, and their various family connections. An incident may be recorded here showing somewhat the characteristics of the people, as well as of our early visitors. Ex-President Lord came to the Grant home one day for entertainment at noon; she was there entertaining a choice number of personal friends, among them were associates of Garrison, Phillips, and Whittier; among these Capt. Zimri S. Wallingford and family of Dover and Dr. Tayler and family of Andover, Mass. Dr. Lord's political views, as well as personal traits, were well known to these people, and to Mrs. Grant, and she had *no room* for him, she referred him to Mrs. Matilda Moody, where he with his son, Henry C., and family, took up summer quarters. It was in this locality that Mr. George Goodwin owned a field adjoining the Long Beach. In September, '66, Mr. Lord purchased this field, and thereon the Lord House was built. This house in 1880 became the property of Dr. Evan B. Hammond of Nashua, N. H., and was made the part of a structure known as the "Hotel Bartlett," Mr. H. E. Evans being the first manager. In 1894 it was destroyed by fire. Up to 1912 the land passed into several ownerships, but in that year it became the property of Daniel Holland, an enterprising business man, and he has erected a fine villa for the occupation of himself and interesting family.

The second cottage was built in October, 1867, at the eastern end of Long Sands, and known as the Kittery House. It was owned by ten persons—Dr. M. F. Wentworth, William H. Sanborn, Theodore Keen, Josiah W. Lewis, John C. Currier, Joshua Lewis, Henry R. Philbrick, William Mason, Charles W. Cottle, and one other whose name is not recalled. It was built by Capt. Timothy Young of Cider Hill, and cost one hundred and thirty dollars. It was arranged to be the headquarters of fishing and social parties. A partition divided the building, so that the women of the party could be by themselves when desired. Writing of this early summer home, Moses A. Safford, Esq., of Kittery writes: "Like most beginnings you perceive it was very

crude, and the parties aimed at a social, free, and easy time,
and I guess from the accounts of it as they linger fadingly
on memory's tablet, they had it.   The costumes of the early
bathers were designed and ornamented by nature herself, it
has been said."   The "Kittery House" is still standing,
having been remodeled and added to.

The first summer hotel was built by Maffit W. Bowden
in the fall of 1868, and the house was opened to the public
the 26th of June, 1869.   It stood on "Cape Neck," so called,
not far from the car barn, on the easterly side of the highway.   The house was burned in 1873.   In 1870 and '71 the
Sea Cottage at Long Sands and the Marshall House at York
Harbor were built.   Each was opened to the public in 1871,
the Sea Cottage, now Hotel Mitchell, by Charles H. Sayward and Charles A. Grant, the Marshall House by Hon.
Nathaniel G. Marshall, assisted by his sons, Edward S. and
Samuel B.   In the years following the Sea Cottage was
enlarged, and came into the hands of the present proprietor,
a nephew of Mr. Grant, Edward E. E. Mitchell.   The Marshall House is the property of Hon. Edward S. Marshall
and has been enlarged three times and will now accommodate three hundred guests.   The Goodwin House, now the
Yorkshire Inn, was a pioneer.   The Donnell House at Long
Beach, and the Thompson House, now Young's Hotel, were
the first at the Beach.   The Sea View, Long Sands, was an
early hostelry.

All these builded with faith, builded in hope, and fruition
came; they were followed by scores.   The Bakers at "Albracca," the Varrells at "Yorkshire," the "Varrell Houses,"
and John H. at "Harmon Hall," Dustin at "The Iduna,"
Henry Mitchell at "The Rockaway," the Ellises at "The
Ocean," "Union Bluffs" by Moses French, "Agamenticus,"

"Lyman Hastings," now "Arthur E. Sewall," by William H. Hogarth, "Hiawatha" by Mr. Blood, "Wahnita," H. C. Jones, "Kearsarge," R. G. Sullivan, and others; with the "Bald Head Cliff House," Theodore Weare, now Edward Weare, and the "Passaconaway Inn," on the York Cliffs Co. reservation.

To give a place, and call by name each of the villas, residences, cottages, and bungalows, that have been erected in York for the purpose of summer sojourn and those built in connection with the summer business, would require a space of many pages in this book.

At the harbor of the early builders were: Hartly Mason, Joseph E. Davis, Joseph May, William H. Lincoln, Bryan Lathrop, Thomas Nelson Page, Samuel S. Allen, Wilson L. Hawkes, W. M. Walker, H. B. Domonick, George D. Washburn, J. C. Bridges, W. S. Putnam, Willard J. Simpson, Alexander Bliss, Joseph W. Simpson, Francis A. Peters, R. J. Vinal, E. S. Marshall, John E. Norwood. On the river, W. T. Councilman, Mr. Aldis, Sidney R. Taber, Edward Sewall, Mrs. Newton Perkins, Miss Mary C. Goodrich. At Seabury, Mrs. Samuel Allen, Humphrey Nichols, George Raynes, Fred Moore (Seabury Hall). At Long Beach, Mrs. Anna F. Manvel, Washington Anderton, Abner Oakes, Freeman Ham, Charles Carter, Juliette Moody and Mrs. J. H. Burleigh, built in the last century, Hon. Edward O. Emerson in 1904. Mr. C. B. Moseley and his son at Concordville have a fine establishment, as does Mr. Worthen and Mr. Shattuck. Near "The Willows" is the residence of F. H. Ellis. A fine residence built by A. H. Bowden is now the property of his daughter, Mrs. George F. Parsons. At York Cliffs are the residences of Mr. Vermeule and Mrs. Kenny; farther on Mrs. Cannaroe, Mr. d'Este and the Misses

Pickering have villas. The result of a recent perambulation of the division line between the towns of York and Wells places the villa of the Misses Pickering in the latter town. At Dover Bluff, Gov. Charles H. Sawyer and E. R. Brown of Dover, N. H., built fine residences, which have changed hands.

The above are a few of the five hundred and fifty human dwellings built in the last half century, all in the line of the summer resort activity, which may now be said to be the real business of the town.

COTTON AND WOOLEN MILLS

THE FIRST cotton mill ever established in Maine was in the town of York.

The York Cotton Factory Company was incorporated by the Massachusetts Legislature, February 12, 1811.

The incorporators were Soloman Brooks, Alexander McIntire, Daniel Carlisle, William Chase, Daniel Brooks, William Frost, and Elihu Bragdon, all of York, and the incorporation was "for the purpose of manufacturing cotton in said town." The company was authorized "to hold and possess real estate not exceeding the value of twenty thousand dollars, and personal estate not exceeding the value of fifty thousand dollars, as may become necessary and convenient for carrying on the manufacture of cotton in the said town of York."

The company was organized early in that year with Daniel Brooks as manager and Soloman Brooks as Treasurer and Clerk. It is not quite certain who was the President of the company, but it is believed to have been Alexander McIntire.

The amount of the capital stock of the company was fixed at ten thousand dollars, divided into one hundred shares of one hundred dollars each. The whole of the capital stock was promptly taken and the company proceeded at once to erect a mill. The mill was built about one hundred yards below the outlet of Chase's Lake.

They began manufacturing goods in the autumn of that year. The first piece of cloth was woven by Miss Betsey Carlisle, who was afterward Mrs. Betsey Talpey, wife of Captain Jonathan Talpey of Cape Neddick. It was the first piece of cotton cloth ever woven in Maine.

The country people came from afar and near to see the work done. The company prospered for a number of years and at one time shares of the stock sold as high as one hundred and sixty dollars per share.

In 1815 the company built a second mill on the same stream just above the first one. Subsequently prices for goods began to go down, probably owing to the closing of the war of 1812-1815 with Great Britain, which was about that time, the mills did not pay and gradually ran down and went out of business.

A part of the foundation wall of the north side of the first mill is still standing, as is also the stone abutment of the southeasterly end of the mill dam, and when the first large main of the York Shore Water Company was laid in 1896 the workmen dug up some of the plank spiling of the old cotton factory dam.

The residence of Mr. Josiah Chase was built by that company for a boarding house, which was kept by Daniel Brooks, the manager, who boarded most of the mill help there. That house was built in the spring of 1811 when the first mill was built, and the nails used in the construction of the mill and house were wrought nails, hand forged and made on the premises.

That stream furnished the principal water power in the town. The first mill built near the outlet of the lake was a sawmill owned by Thomas Bragdon, who obtained a grant of the land from the town in 1702. In 1768 he sold a part of the mill-privilege to Josiah Chase in consideration, as the deed states, that said Chase had established a clothier's mill there. Chase raised the lake some ten or twelve feet by building a dam, the earthwork of which formed the base of and is included in the earthwork of the present dam. Chase or his son, Cotton Chase, subsequently bought the remainder of the privilege from the heirs of Thomas Bragdon.

The business of the clothier of those days consisted in finishing the cloth which was woven in the homes of the people ready to be made up into clothing. This business was carried on by Col. Josiah Chase, and by his son Cotton Chase, and his grandson, Capt. Josiah Chase, successively, from 1768 to 1845, when conditions had become changed and the business had decreased, and in that year Capt. Josiah Chase built a woolen factory where for many years he successfully manufactured various kinds of woolen goods which became widely known and had a ready sale. He carried on the business up to 1873 when he gave it up to his sons, Charles E. and John L. Chase, who enlarged the facilities and carried on the business successfully for several years, a part of the time running their mill night and day until one of the brothers died. The other subsequently leased the mill and after the lessee had operated the mill a few months it was burned down, and was never rebuilt.

In addition to the business of clothier carried on by Col. Josiah Chase, he had a sawmill and carding mill on the same stream about a quarter of a mile below his finishing mill. In that carding mill he had two machines which were said to have been brought from England, and were several hundred years old.

In this mill he took the wool brought there by the farmers and carded it into fine soft rolls about half an inch in diameter and about two feet long. These rolls were then taken home by the farmers and there spun into yarn. This work was done in the spring, and the cloth dressing mostly in the autumn and winter. The carding of rolls in that mill was carried on by Chase and his heirs from 1770 up to about 1860.

When the York Cotton Factory Company built their mill in 1811, they bought from Cotton Chase the right to take water from the lake through his gate until the water got down to the depth of four feet in the flume; he reserving all under that depth for his mill; but they could use it, of course, after it passed his mill.

From 1850 to 1860 there were nine mills on that stream between the lake and the ocean which used the water of that stream for motive power, one woolen factory, one carding mill, where wool was carded into rolls for people who brought the wool, two grist mills, four sawmills and one shingle mill. All of those mills, with the exception of one sawmill, are gone.

That lake was locally known for a great many years as Chase's Pond. That name probably became attached to it by usage, probably arising from the fact that it was controlled and the water used for manufacturing purposes by members of that family for about one hundred and twelve consecutive years.

The original name of the lake was "Lake Agamenticus," and that is the name it still bears on the charts of the U. S. Geodetic Survey, it being a rule of the government to use original names so far as they are authentically known.

The first mill building was taken down and moved to Beech Ridge and is the dwelling house of Asa McIntire and his descendants.

The second was also moved and reconstructed into a dwelling house located on the road to Portsmouth just beyond the Kittery line, and is now occupied by Newbury Haley.

WITCHCRAFT

In 1758 there was much fear that the witchcraft delusion of 1692 was to be renewed in York. Sixty years before the ancestor of the Wells Jacobs family had been executed in Salem, Mass., as a witch. Upham in his history of that crime says: "He was grey-headed and walked with two staffs." His hair was long and thin, and he was of more than ordinary stature and presented a venerable aspect. His faculties were strong, being fearless, and his speech vigorous and decided. While on trial he appealed to the court, endeavoring to bring them to a sense of fair dealing: "Pray do not accuse me, I am as clear as your worships. You must do right judgment. I am clear of the charges. I never wronged man in word or deed. I have done no harm. Burn me, or hang me, I will stand in the truth of Christ." However, he was found guilty, and executed Aug. 19, 1692.

In the month of March, 1758, a deacon of the First Congregational Church in York made the following public declaration: "A strange distemper has seized upon my sheep by which thirty, old and young, have died by apparently bleeding at the nose. Soon after all the hens and chickens were found dead with their necks twisted. A fine calf was bright and well in the evening, in the morning he was found on his back with his legs up panting until he died. Up to this time he did not suspect anything supernatural. But in April the most unaccountable things took place in the house. He took several household utensils and put them in a particular spot, just turned around and back at once, and they were all in the fire partly burnt, and while taking his meal at the table with his children who were eating porridge instantly

all the spoons were taken from their hands and were not to
be found; and afterwards, when a visitor was taking coffee
with them she was warned by him to take care of her spoon,
or it would be missing as soon as she laid it down.   She
said she would 'see to that, and put it into the coffee pot.'
She did so and shut down the lid; but on lifting it in a few
minutes the spoon was gone.   They had churned and went
for the salt but that had also disappeared."   These things
caused the good man and his family great perplexity and
worriment.   Many things in daily use were disappearing
suddenly.   At last fasting and prayer were proposed as the
only known means of driving out the unwelcome spirit.
Rev. Mr. Lyman, the minister, and many of the Parish
were much excited by these unexplained manifestations.
Finally, becoming convinced that this state of affairs was
brought about by the influence of sorcery, the people charged
it upon a bad neighhor, whom the deacon had offended.
A daughter of this neighbor, well knowing the unworthy
and in fact infamous character of her father, called upon
him and calmly reasoned with him about the matter, beseech-
ing him to cease his disturhing enchantments.   And from
this time quiet reigned in the household, and the every-
day routine of labor and rest proceeded undisturbed.   How
account for these strange doings, which are facts?

COCHRANISM

THIS DELUSION did not gain a foothold to any large extent in York, though for some weeks its devotees gathered at a barn in the vicinity of Cape Neddick Village in 1818. The principal communities were at Kennebunk, Buxton, Saco and New Gloucester. The founder of this sect, Jacob Cochrane, began his disturbing career in Fryeburg in 1816, and he succeeded in arousing wonderful interest and securing a large number of adherents in Oxford, Cumberland and York Counties. He was about thirty-five years old when he commenced his ministry. In personal appearance he was tall and robust, a handsome countenance which is said to have indicated more of sensualism than of intellect. Up to the time he conceived that he had a "call" to preach, he was engaged in the grocery business and was well patronized. He was considered by his customers as a "good fellow" but rather lazy, and his moral character was at par. That Cochrane did have wonderful hypnotic or mesmeric power is not questioned, but the use to which he put it was, and is, questionable. He soon gained a prominence he did not seek or expect. There were even among his followers some pure-minded and excellent men and women who would take no part in the practices of their leader or his "choice helpers." When it is taken into consideration that there was no pulpit, no singers' seats, but that the master and his flock joined with the sinners and scoffers on the floor, it can be easily imagined that much confusion prevailed. Speaking of this sect, the Newburyport Herald of the early part of 1819 has the following: "We have seen a pamphlet published by a Baptist minister of regular standing in New Gloucester,

Maine, giving an account of Cochrane and his deluded followers.   It appears that under the guise of religion they have committed the most indecent and abominable acts of adultery * * *   One of the leading tenets was to dissolve the ties of matrimony as suited their convenience and as promiscuous sexual intercourse was tolerated by each male being allowed to take *seven wives.*

"It seems that Cochrane, the high priest of iniquity, has had nearly half his female followers for wives in the course of his ministration which has been about two years standing."

In February, 1819, Cochrane was brought before Justice Granger at Saco, charged with gross lewdness, lascivious behavior and adultery by Mr. Ichabod Jordan.   And he was ordered to recognize in the sum of eighteen hundred dollars for his appearance before the Supreme Court at Alfred, the third Tuesday of May.   At that time he was found guilty but left the town and his bail was forfeited.   He was apprehended in November and removed to the State Prison at Charlestown.   He was in Cape Neddick for a short time in 1834.   In September, 1835, he succeeded in establishing a "Convent" at Stratham, N. H., at which some of his former York disciples were allowed a "sacred retreat" and privileged to keep the Passover.   In 1823, Mr. Samuel Junkins, a follower of Cochrane and a shining light, attempted to build up and control a new sect but did not find great encouragement.   He issued the following manifesto: "At the Baptist meeting house in York, On the Lord's Day next this House will be free for the Sons and Daughters of Zion to wait on the Lord and honor Him that hath made them free.   Also the Family of Egypt may have another opportunity to come up to Jerusalem to keep the feast in Tabernacles, or if they refuse they must not expect to have any rain of the Spirit on them. *Hypocrites,* Mongrels and Lepers are desired to withdraw. Samuel Junkins, Servant of the Church of Christ, York. York, August 1, 1823."

This proposed gathering of the children of Zion resulted in following court action:

At the October term, Court of Common Pleas, Junkins was fined twenty dollars and costs, in all forty dollars, and his wife, Olive, who was thirty-five years old, and by no means the weaker vessel, was fined five dollars and costs of thirty-four dollars, "for wilfully disturbing a meeting held at the Baptist Meeting-House in York on the Lord's Day."

THE NORRIDGEWOCK EXPEDITION

OF THE youths of 1692 who escaped death in the massacre of that year, two had reached the years of strong manhood in 1724, Captains Harmon and Moulton. They remembered the sufferings they and their parents endured at the hands of the Indians, and with others became noted Indian fighters and traveled long distances on dangerous expeditions against them. Williamson gives the following account of that against the Norridgewock Village, which had been marked for destruction: "The execution of this enterprise was committed to a detachment of 208 men who were divided into four companies and commanded by Captains Moulton. Harmon, Bourne, and Bane. (Captain Bourne was from Wells Captain Johnson Harmon was the senior officer in command.) They left Richmond fort, their place of rendezvous, on the 19th of August, 1724, and ascended the river in twelve whale boats, attended by three Mohawks. The next day they arrived at Tecomet, where they left their boats and a lieutenant and guard of 40 men; the residue of the forces on the 21st took up their march toward Norridgewock; the same evening they discovered three of the natives and fired upon them; the noted Bomazeen, one of them, was shot swimming the river, as he attempted to escape, his daughter was fatally wounded and his wife taken prisoner. From her they obtained a full account of Rale (the French Jesuit priest) and the Indians at Norridgewock which quickened their march. A little after noon on the 22nd they came in sight of the village, when it was determined to divide the detachment. Capt. Harmon led off about 60 men toward the mouth of Sandy River, imagining he saw smoke arising in that quarter, and supposing that some of the Indians might be at their corn fields. Captain Moulton formed his men into three bands nearly equal in numbers, and proceeded directly toward the village. When near it, he placed parties in ambush, on the right and left, and led forward the residue to the attack, excepting ten men left to guard the baggage. He commanded his men to reserve their fire until after that of the Indians; and then boldly advanced with so quick a step and in such profound silence, that they came within pistol shot before their approach was suspected. All the Indians were in their wigwams, when one happening to step out, looked and discovered the English close upon them. He instantly gave the warwhoop and seized his gun. The amazement of the whole village was indiscriminate and terrible. The fighting men, about 60 in all, seized their guns and fired at their assailants; but in their tremoi they overshot them, and not a man was hurt. A discharge was instantly returned which did effectual execution. The Indians fired a second volley without breaking Moulton's ranks; then flying to the water, fell upon the muzzles of the guns in ambush. Several instantly fell, some undertook to wade or swim across the river, which at this season was only sixty feet wide, and in no place more than six feet deep. A few jumped into their canoes, but forgetting to take their paddles were unable to escape; and all, especially the old men, women and children, fled in every direction. Our soldiers shot them in their flight to the woods, also upon the water; so that not more than fifty of the whole village were supposed to have landed on the opposite side of the river; while about 150 effected an escape into the thickets too far to be overtaken. The pursuers then returned to the village, where they found the Jesuit Rale, in one of the wigwams, firing upon a few

of our men who had not followed the wretched fugitives.
He had with him in the wigwam an English boy about 14
years of age, who had been a prisoner for six months.   This
boy he shot through the thigh, and afterward stabbed him
in the body, though he ultimately recovered.   Moulton had
given orders to spare the life of Rale.   But Jacques, a lieutenant, finding he was firing from the wigwam and had
wounded one of our men, stove open the door and shot him
through the head.   As an excuse for this act, Jacques alleged
that when he entered the wigwam Rale was loading his gun
and declaring he would neither give nor take quarter.
Moulton disapproved of what was done; allowing, however,
that Rale said something to provoke Jacques, yet doubt-
ing if the statement made by him was literally correct.
*   *   *   Near night after the action was over and the
village cleared of Indians, Capt. Harmon and his party
arrived; and the companies under a guard of forty men took
up a lodgment in the wigwam until morning.   When it was
light they counted, as two authors say, twenty-seven, and a
third says, thirty dead bodies, including Rale; among whom
were those of Mogg, Job, Carabesett, Wissemenent, and
Bomasun's son-in-law, all known and noted warriors.   They
also recovered three captives and four prisoners; and it was
afterward reported that they wounded fourteen Indians who
escaped.   The whole number killed and drowned was supposed to be eighty, some say more.   The plunder brought
away (most of which came to York) consisted of the plate
furniture of the altar, a few guns, blankets and kettles, and
about three barrels of powder.   After leaving the place on
their march to Teconet, Christian, one of the Mohawks,
either sent back or returning of his own accord, set fire to
the chapel and cottages, and they were all burned to ashes."

On the 27th the brave detachment arrived at Fort Richmond, without the loss of a man. It was an exploit exceedingly gratifying to the community, and considered as brilliant as any other in either of the wars since the fall of King Philip. Harmon, who was senior in command, proceeded to Boston with the scalps, and received in reward for the achievement in which Moulton had the principal agency a commission of Lieutenant-Colonel. Moulton received no distinguishing recompense, except the universal applause of the country. If, as has been said, Rale at the age of thirty-four took part in the devastation of 1692, his sin found him out when he was sixty-six. However, the version of the expedition story as told by Rev. Father de la Chasse is different. "A little army of Englishmen and their savage allies numbering *eleven hundred* men unexpectedly came to attack the village of Narransouk. * * * Father Rale, warned by the clamor and tumult of the danger that was menacing his neophytes, promptly left his house and fearlessly appeared before the enemy. He expected by his presence either to stop their first efforts, or at least to draw their attention to himself alone, and at the expense of his life procure the safety of his flock. Soon as they perceived the missionary a general shout was raised which was followed by a storm of musket shot that was poured upon him. He dropped dead at the foot of a large cross that he had erected in the midst of the village, in order to announce the public profession that was made thereon of adoring a crucified God. * * * The English did not attempt to pursue the fugitives; they were content with burning and pillaging the village; they set fire to the church after a base profanation of the sacred vessels and of the adorable body of Jesus Christ. The precipitate retreat of the enemy permitted the return of the fugitives

to the village.   Their first care was to weep over the body
of their holy missionary; they found it pierced by hundreds
of bullets, the scalp torn off, the skull broken by blows of
a hatchet, the mouth and eyes filled with mud, the bones of
the legs broken, and all the members mutilated.   *   *   *
After three devout Christians had washed and kissed many
times the honored remains of their father, they buried him
in the very place where, the day before, he had celebrated
the Holy Sacrifice of the mass—that is, in the place where
the altar had stood before the burning of the church."

ST. ASPINQUID

WITHIN THE area of the town of York there is a high hill of three summits, the highest of which is about six hundred feet above sea level. It is called Agamenticus. Upon the top of this hill, St. Aspinquid is buried. The story of his life and death is given briefly by Edward C. Moody in an address delivered on Mt. Agamenticus some years since, the reproduction of which appears in the History of St. Aspinquid Lodge, F. and A. M., and of which the following is a copy:

"In 1582 the Algonquin family of Indians was largest and most powerful on this continent. It occupied about one-half of the territory now embraced in the United States, east of the Mississippi, and contained as many warriors as the remaining families put together. Among the nations or tribes composing this great family of red men were the Narragansetts, the Pequots and Pawtuckets in New England. In a wigwam of the latter tribe in the month of May, 1588, Aspinquid was born. Very likely his early years and education were much the same as with other Indian boys, consisting chiefly of athletic exercises and such training as would enable him to endure hunger and fatigue. At the age of eighteen years he underwent his final trial; his face was blackened for the last time and he was led far into the woods, where he was left without food as long as life could be supported. He was then taken home amid the plaudits of his guardians, and after various ceremonies informed that now he was a man, that for him there was a seat at the council fire, and now he might speak for peace or for war. It may be that his physical education had been supplemented, as in some tribes was the custom, by instruction in the history of his tribe, and its institutions, the deeds of valor done by his forefathers being recounted by some old chief. However, in 1631, at the age of forty-three, in the prime of his young manhood, a change came over the spirit of his dreams; under the preaching and guidance of John Eliot, he became a warrior of the Cross, and the fierce savage, laying aside tomahawk, bow and arrow, became a devout follower of the meek and lowly Master. And thenceforth he traversed the forests, visiting the several tribes, going even to the Ottawas in Lake Huron and as one account has it, 'from the Atlantic to the California Sea,' telling them of a sure way to the happy hunting grounds, and the land of the Great Spirit beyond the river. As age grew upon him, Aspinquid became an object of great veneration to the natives. At the age of ninety-four years, in 1682, he died and his funeral was conducted with great pomp and ceremony. In honor of the deceased a great collection of many sorts of wild animals was sacrificed to the departed spirit. The following is the list as preserved, the whole number being 6,721, viz.: twenty-five bucks, sixty-nine does, ninety-nine bears, thirty-six moose, two hundred and forty wolves, eighty-two wildcats, three catamounts, nine hundred muskrats, three ermines, fifty weasels, fifty-nine woodchucks, four hundred and eighty-two foxes, thirty-two buffaloes, four hundred otters, six hundred and thirty beavers, one thousand five hundred minks, one hundred and ten ferrets, five hundred and twenty raccoons, five hundred and one fishes, thirty-eight porcupines, eight hundred and thirty-two martens, one hundred and twelve rattlesnakes.

"Many people take exception to this account, but if we take into consideration the thousands of warriors who at-

tended the burial and vied with each other in doing homage
to the departed spirit by their victims for sacrifice, and the
fact that the forests were filled with wild animals of all
kinds, the rivers with beavers, the streams and brooks with
otter, mink and muskrat, we little need to wonder; for all
these animals and reptiles were gathered in from the Atlantic
'even to the California Sea.'   On his tombstone, which might
be seen in 1780, were inscribed in the Indian language these
words:

" 'Present Useful;   Absent Wanted;
    Lived Desired;   Died Lamented.' "

THE STORY OF BOON ISLAND — HOW IT RECEIVED ITS NAME

In 1630 there were two prominent—among others—settlements on the New England coast, one at Plymouth, the other at Pemaquid. The Pilgrims at Plymouth had gained strength and their fields were waving with corn; at Pemaquid the British merchants had become prosperous. A brisk trade was opened between Plymouth and Pemaquid, shallop loads of corn being exchanged for furs and other commodities, and this continued for fifty years. On one of these coastwise voyages, the "pinky" Increase was wrecked on Boon Island rock. A portion of her hull and spars with three white men and one Indian, Asseomet, whose name has been preserved by the everlasting name of Agamenticus, known at that time as "Asseomenticus," drifted on to the island proper at the south, then without its present name. This was in April, 1682. For a month they sustained life by eating shell fish and drinking water obtained from rain water which had fallen in the depressions of the rocks. They also had flint and could strike fire. In May they observed smoke arising from the top of Mt. Agamenticus. It was the day of the funeral of "St. Aspinquid," and the smoke was that of sacrifice where 6711 victims were doing homage in death to the memory of the saint. The castaways at once proceeded to gather as large a pile of wreckage and driftwood as possible, and covering it with rock weed, soon a cloud of black smoke was ascending skyward. The warriors inland on the mountain perceived it and at once the cry arose, being interpreted, "The Great Spirit answers us," and forthwith a number of warriors hastened to the point known as the "Knubble," manned their canoes and paddled for the smoke-covered island. The castaways were taken ashore at Eastern Point, near Norwood's Grove, then and therafter giving thanks. They named the island "Boon Island," for it had proved a "boon" to them.

In an impromptu address by Rev. R. M. Sawyer, at a picnic of the First Congregational Parish at "Norwood Grove" in 1864, he referred to the incidents above related.

THE DEVIL'S INVENTION

FROM THE PEN OF G. ALEX EMERY

AT A COURT held in York, July, 1679, the following criminal case was tried. James Adams of York became affronted with one of his neighbors, Henry Simpson, and determined to avenge himself upon two of Simpson's children, whose ages were six and nine years. His contrivance and crime were as satanic as they were deliberate. In a solitary place four or five miles from the dwelling houses of the inhabitants, he built of logs, beside a ledge of perpendicular rocks, a pen or pound several feet in height with walls inclined inward from bottom to top. After he had built this he decoyed the children into the woods under the pretence of searching for birds' nests, and caused them to enter within the pound, where he left them to perish of famine. The place has since been called *"The Devil's Invention."* The children were soon missed and the alarmed inhabitants searched for them more than forty-eight hours. The boys when aware of their wretched situation made various attempts to get out and at length by digging away with their hands the surface of the earth underneath the bottom of one of the logs effected their escape. They wandered in the woods three days, being at last attracted to the seashore by the noise of the surf, where they were found.

The depraved criminal was condemned to have thirty lashes well laid on; to pay the father of the children five pounds besides fee and charges of the prison, and remain a close prisoner during the Court's pleasure or until further order. The same month he recognized before two of the Associates "Conditioned to send him within twenty-one days out of the jurisdiction."

TEA PARTY

In 1774 the citizens of York, following the example set by their friends in Boston Dec. 16, 1773, had a tea party. A lot of tea was brought to York in the schooner Sunburst under command of Capt. James Donnell. But the people would not submit to this plain insult, and it was considered as insulting to the public sentiment already existing that of determined resistance to taxation without representation.

A town meeting was immediately called, and a committee was chosen to have the tea removed from the vessel to await further developments. It was put into Capt. Grow's store. But the people were not satisfied by this way of dealing with what they considered an affront. Thereupon the following evening a number of Pickwaket Indians came into the village, broke open the store and carried off the tea, so there was no duty paid on it by the people. It did not share the fate of the Boston tea which was thrown overboard; some of the Indians being of a prudent disposition had a supper of tea for a long time, and their descendants frequently "turn tea" in York, New York, and elsewhere.

"HULL A MALEW"

The following from the pen of the late Judge Preble is herewith given:

The McIntire family were a strong, muscular, athletic race of men, perfect sons of Anak in their time. On occasion the people of Scotland Parish, as well as those from other quarters in town, came all flocking down to the central place of business and trade in York. They got up a grand "spree." The McIntire is a peaceable, well-disposed fellow if you do not chafe him too much, but beware how you start the Scotch blood. In due time the Scotland people started for home, somewhat excited by liberal potations, the fit subjects for a row. Riding on together, jostling each other, playing off their tricks accompanied by coarse jokes, they at length got into a grand "melee." And to work they went. Tradition has handed down an account of the battle, and one of the epic poets of the day celebrated this encounter in immortal verse. My memory is so imperfect that I can give entire only one stanza. It runs thus:

> "And there was Micum McIntire,
>   With his great foot and hand,
> He kicked and cuffed Sam Freathy so,
>   He could neither go nor stand."

This engagement was renewed in following years near Bass Cove and was called a "Hull a Malew," which being interpreted is—"A hell of a melee."

STORY OF SEYMOUR'S HANGING

AN AUTHENTIC TALE HANDED DOWN FROM AN EYE-WITNESS
OF THE AFFAIR

THE EXACT date at which the tragedy took place and the time when the murderer expiated the crime cannot be given. The young girl of twelve years who with her parents attended the trial heard the condemnation and sentence of death pronounced by the Court, became Mrs. Nutter, the great-grandmother of Stover Perkins, and it was she who later in gala attire witnessed the execution of John Seymour by hanging from a gibbet at the point on "Stage Neck" by which the river runs. It may be remarked incidentally that it appears to be a question undecided, whether the instrument of death was located at or near "Betty Allen's" point, or the Eastern and Southern point near Forthead. The recollections of Mrs. Irene Welch, who heard the story from Mrs. Nutter, all point in the direction of the western location. This Seymour lived near the present residence of Lorenzo Starkey at Fall Mill bridge. For some reason he had become imbued with the idea that the two-year-old child he rocked in the cradle was not his own. It may be that he had heard the song, "Rock the cradle, John, * * *." At any rate, one day in May about the year eighteen hundred, he rushed from the field to the home, seized the sleeping infant in his arms, ran to the bridge and flung the helpless child down to the ragged rocks and whirling stream below. His wife, who had followed in frenzied haste, was powerless to prevent the atrocious deed, and in turn but for flight to a neighbor's might have been a victim of the same fate as her child could Seymour have carried out his threats. Seymour's arrest by Sheriff Ichabod Goodwin of Berwick soon followed and subsequently the trial, conviction and sentence. As may well be believed, this terrible deed caused great excitement, the brutal taking of an innocent life with no justifiable cause awakened the minds of the people in all the country roundabout, and threats of early vengeance were openly and freely made.   These were not carried into effort and incarcerated in the inner dungeon of the York Gaol, John Seymour awaited his trial and the day when he should "kick the beam" at Gallows Point.   The day came with its bright August sun; and the girl of twelve in her new dress of colored linen adorned with an extra flounce for the occasion was there or this particular story would not have been told.   Hundreds of all ages and conditions were there to witness the expiation of a horrible crime.   The details of the hanging of those times need not be recounted.   The gallows or gibbet consisted of an upright with a beam extending braced from upright to beam, a narrow platform stood six or seven feet below the beam, which was reached by a ladder or flight of steps.   The rope suspended from the beam was adjusted and the victim pushed or kicked off the platform. Sometimes the rebound was such his limbs not being bound he verily "kicked the beam" amid the applause of the multitude.

COPIES OF EARLY LAND GRANTS

Grants given by the Inhabitants of the Town of York. 10: January 1652 at a Town Meeting.

1=Granted unto Thomas Crockett a parcell of ground to Plant in which Lieth betwixt the bounds of Mr. Edward Godfrey & Mr. Francis Rains, which is granted & given to him by the Town wch quantity of Land Contains the Proportion of forty Acres which is given and Confirmed to him.

2=It is ordered that Sylvester Stover is to have a parcell of Meadow, Lying at the further end of the Great marsh as we Go to Wells upon the right hand of the path, which proportion of marsh with the swamp adjoining to it, is given & Granted to Sylvester Stover & his assigns, to the Quantity of Six Acres and not above.

3=It was formerly granted unto John Daviss, the Smith and is now Confirmed by the Town of York, namely forty acres of upland is given & granted unto y^e s^d John Daviss Lying from the head of his own Marsh and so back into the Country till the whole forty acres be compleated.

4=There is likewise granted twenty acres a peice of upland adjoining & Lying next to the s^d John Daviss his upland unto John Harker and William More to run back Into the Country as the other doth.

20 Acres bounded Lib II pag 5.

THE EARLIEST AUTHENTIC RECORD IN HAND-WRITING OF THE TOWN CLERK

(See Hon. N. G. Marshall's Historical Address, 1874, Feb. 22d.)

Book A.   Page 433.   1st Record by James Plaisted, Town Clerk.

TOWN MEETINGS 1695/6

5

Att a Legall Town meeting held In york 18 march 1696

Jurors	1	Arthur Came, Thomas Donnell, Richard Hon-newell, Abraham Prebble Junr chosen Jurymen for ye year ensuing.
Const	2	Benjamin Prebble chosen Constable for the year ensuing.
Sel men	3	Mr Sam^{ll} Donnell, Mr James Plaisted, Thomas Trafton, John Brawn & Joseph Weare Chosen Select men for ye year ensuing.
Comm^{ttee}	4	Left^t Prebble to join with the Select men in Agreing with Mr Hancock for the year ensuing.
Griss mill	5	Left^t Prebble, Mr Sam^{ll} Donnell, Arthur Brag-don Senr & Joseph Weare to Indent with Capt. Pickering about erecting a good and sufficient Griest mill In York.
Fence V^r	6	William Hilton & Joseph Pray fence viewers chosen than : (?)

JAMES PLAISTED, Town Clerk.

George F. Plaisted, the Clerk at this writing, is the sixth generation from James Plaisted, Clerk in 1695-6, and has served thirteen years.   James Plaisted's is the earliest record extant.

At a Legall Town meeting held In york 20 May 1696

Surv^rs   1 Joseph Banks chosen Surveyour for the highways this year.

Pound
  Keeper   2 Joseph Carlile, pound keeper.

Town Book 3 Agreed & voted that the Town books shall be fairly & truly Transcribed & rectified; & this to be done at the Towns charge.

Rams   4 Agreed & voted that all Rams shall be kept from the youes from the last of July till the fifth of November.

JAMES PLAISTED
Town Clerk

"TOMMY DISCO"

SEAFARING MEN will, if they have reached the age of three score and ten, remember Capt. Thomas Discoll, an Irishman, who came to York in 1810. He married a daughter of Ezekial Adams of Cape Neddick. He could neither read nor write, however, James Weare, Senior, who owned the schooner Cicero, gave him command, and with a crew of one man he made the trip to Newburyport, with a cargo of thirty cords of wood. He always carried his food from home, saying that by so doing his "grub did not cost any-thing." This saying became a by-word. Finally he ran the Cicero ashore and she was a total loss. He then took the schooner Drake, owned by Capt. Theodore Donnell (grand-father of George Albra). Capt. Donnell had sailed the Drake successfully many years. Discoll had been in the Drake but two trips, when he run her on the rocks and he with the crew of two barely escaped with life. The loss of one more vessel terminated his career as a master mariner. He then followed wherry-fishing to near the close of his life. He was a member of the Baptist Church at Cape Neddick, and his nearest approach to profanity was in the occasional use of the word "damn." After such an occasion, like Peter, "he went out and wept bitterly."

WREATH ON GRAVE OF SAMUEL MOODY

DUMMER ACADEMY, CELEBRATING 150TH ANNIVERSARY, HONORS MEMORY OF INSTITUTION'S FIRST PRECEPTOR— LIFE OF NOTED EDUCATOR.

A WREATH of flowers on Samuel Moody's grave, in the old burying ground, opposite the Congregational Church, has attracted general attention this week. Through the courtesy of Edward C. Moody the Transcript is able to give a short history of the man who, more than a century ago, was one of the foremost educators in the country. Since 1795 the remains have laid in the little cemetery, the burying place of men famous throughout the colonies in their day. The name Moody is synonymous with the growth of New England, from the earliest days to the present. Scattered throughout York are many marks of the days when Master Moody was preceptor of Dummer Academy, and famous as a teacher. Now, at the 150th anniversary of the founding of the academy, the class of 1913 place upon the grave of the first preceptor of their loved school, a wreath of flowers, in token of the good he did for their school, and as mark of appreciation and respect, and to honor the memory of the man whose guiding hand started the school on its many years of success.

Edward C. Moody's article follows:

SAMUEL MOODY, ESQ.

"Peace has her victories, no less renowned than war." I have read that even in the early days of power and culture in Greece and Rome, that the people were wont to place wreaths on the last resting place of the Master Makers of Literature, Art, Philosophy and Science, and chaplets on the brow of their Pausanias and Caesars, who had borne their arms and standards to victory, and returned in triumph.   In this year of our Lord, which is the 150th from the inception and founding of Dummer Academy at Byfield, Mass., the trustees of that institution have placed on the headstone at the grave of its first preceptor a wreath.   That grave is in the old burying ground, just across from the meeting house which his grandfather founded in 1747.

I quote from the sermon delivered at his funeral, Dec. 23, 1795:

"Samuel Moody, Esq., son of that eminent man of God, the Rev. Joseph Moody, first beloved pastor of the North Church in York, and grandson of that godly and faithful man, the Rev. Samuel Moody, many years pastor of the South Church in that town, was born at York in April, 1726, and received the honors of Harvard College in the year 1746.   Designed by his friends for the ministry, he made divinity his study for some time.   When he entered the desk he made a good appearance, and was considered a popular preacher, and received an invitation to settle in the ministry, but he declined and gave up the design.   He was what has been usually termed orthodox, (i. e.) Calvinistic in senti-ment, yet Catholic, far from bigotry; considered it unprofit-able and unbecoming gospel ministers to dwell chiefly in their preaching upon the mysteries of Heaven or the atmos-phere of Hell, which are incomprehensible to all.   He was easy of access, open and frank, friendly and communicative. Composition was easy to him; no man had a greater fund of words to command, and no man seemed to possess a happier talent at arranging them properly.   *   *   *   Hav-

ing laid aside all thoughts of engaging in the arduous work
of the ministry, he devoted himself to the service of the
young and rising generation. The education of youth was
his delight, and in this sphere he long shone with distinguished lustre. * * * Being known as an inspirator of
youth, he was applied to from various points of the country.
From York he was called to take charge of a school founded
by Gov. Dummer, which the fame of Master Moody soon
filled with students, and through his influence this seminary
of learning was incorporated into an academy. Here this
learned preceptor presided with great respect and eminent
usefulness for thirty years. * * * He often reflected,
with great pleasure, that his sons (as he called his pupils)
were to be found figuring eminently in every department—
judges of courts, senators in Congress, and in the Senate
of the Commonwealth, among the most shining lights of
the bar; yea, at the heads of schools and academies, and
even the University of Cambridge was, at the time of his
death, indebted to him for their President and for the professors of Divinity, Mathematics, Philosophy and Oriental
Languages. * * * It has been frequently observed of
Mr. Moody that he spoke evil of nobody. This maxim he
inculcated upon his pupils: '*De Mortuis Absentibus nil nisi
bonum.*' This godly man was faithful in the discharge of
every trust reposed in him, and punctual to an extreme. As
a magistrate he was a terror to evil-doers. Though his plans
(in the opinion of his friends) were not always the most
judicious, he adhered to them tenaciously. In his last days,
with great zeal, he aimed to carry out a plan for establishing
a social library, and a branch of education (which we call a
high school. E. C. M.) But, alas! This godly man has
faded from among the children of men. The pious, the

learned, friendly, benevolent, generous and compassionate, industrious and faithful Moody is no more: not blotted out of being; but having bid adieu to this world has taken possession of immortal life—a life worth enjoying; the reward of a good and faithful servant.　Let us go and do likewise—like him be faithful unto death, that with him we may receive 'a crown of life, a crown of glory which will never fade away.' "

The writer is the owner of the day book and ledger of Master Moody which contains the names of many whose names I recall in the reading of the annals of New England men of one hundred years ago.　I think perhaps the trustees at Dummer may like to place it among the archives.　Anyway, I shall make them the tender.

THE LAST REVOLUTIONARY SURVIVOR

WILLIAM HUTCHINS, son of Charles and Mary Perkins Hutchins, born in York, Maine, Oct. 6, 1764, married and settled in Penobscot, Maine, then called Plantation No. 3, subsequently Penobscot in sight of Bagaduce, now Castine. His parents left York when he was about four years old.

He was the last surviving soldier of the Revolution, died May 2, 1866, aged 101 years, 6 months and 26 days. His father lived to the advanced age of 91 years. There on the same farm which his descendants now occupy, the subject of this sketch continued to reside, with the exception of a short time, during the remainder of his life. Dwelling in sight of Bagaduce, he witnessed all the events connected with the siege of that famous locality during the summer of 1779. As above stated, William Hutchins was the last survivor of the Revolution.

At the close of the war he returned to Penobscot and resided there until his death, farming, lumbering and coasting between Penobscot and Massachusetts ports, he acting in the capacity of master mariner. He was a devoted member of the Methodist Church. In 1865, when over a century old, he accepted an invitation from the representatives of the city government of Bangor to join in the celebration of the Fourth of July in that city.

A revenue cutter was detached for his conveyance to and from, and as he passed by the Penobscot River the guns of Fort Knox fired a salute of welcome. The ovation which was extended to him on the occasion exceeded that ever before given to any person in the State. Multitudes rushed to catch a glimpse of the old veteran soldier, and the sincere and grateful plaudits which constantly greeted him as surrounded by a guard of honor he was escorted through the streets of the city, constituted a marked feature of the day. His mental faculties were retained up to, and during his final sickness, which was of short duration. On Sunday, April 29, 1866, signs of dissolution became manifest, and on the following Thursday, in full consciousness of his approaching end, like a clock worn out with eating time, the wheels of weary life at last stood still. So it appears that York furnished nearly the first as also the last of that noble band of Revolutionary army soldiers that assisted this Republic to burst the bands of British tyranny, and make it possible for us to enjoy freedom from British rule.

SHIP BUILDING, SHIPPING AND SEA CAPTAINS

IT IS UNCERTAIN when the first water craft was built in York. Remick in his History of Kennebunk says: "Vessels were built in York many years before a keel was laid in Kennebunk." It seems probable that the first "coaster" built in York was constructed prior to 1670, for in that year upon the Mousam River, hailing from York, sailed the first craft of any considerable size in those waters. She carried the workmen with their tools, builder's hardware, and some of the machinery to be used in the building of Sayward's shanty, and the construction of his mills. And from that time until 1890 a large number of "deep sea" and coastwise craft have first touched the Atlantic within the sea line of York. The largest vessel built by Edward Emerson in earlier days was the "Agamenticus," in later years the "Othello" by Asahel Goodwin at Cape Neddick in 1861. The last vessels launched in York were the "Sarah Louise" by Mr. Goodwin, the "Velocipede" by Charles C. Barrell, and the "Norton" by Jotham P. Norton, these prior to 1890. A hundred years ago the shipping to and departure from the port of York was considerable as appears by the Custom House records. From Jan. 1, 1795, down to December, 1806, when Samuel Derby was collector, there were enrolled no less than fifty vessels from twenty-five to ninety feet over all, and with names suggestive, fanciful and homely. These craft were mostly owned in York, some in Kittery. The following are some of the names: Diligent, Jack, Polly, Sally, Nancy, Patty, Sea Flower, Fanny, Betsy, Lively, Ruth, Two Brothers, Friendship, Adventure, Lark, Charlotte, Lion, Blossom, Sophia, Rambler, Sunburst, Industry,

Katy, The Dove, Harriet, Olive Branch, Eagle. Among
the owners and masters of those years were Benjamin
Grover, David Baker, William Averhill, Zebulon Harmon,
Joseph Hutchins, Hannah Harmon, Jeremiah Clark, Obadiah
Donnell, George Simpson.   From 1806 to 1815 the records
are missing.   The War of 1812 was within this period.   Of
course shipping interests were at a standstill, and it was at
this time that the commerce in which the Emersons and
others were engaged received a severe blow.   But we find
that in 1815 Buckley Emerson had the sloop "Charles";
William Harmon, the "Snap"; William Seavey, the "Isa-
bella"; Samuel Lunt, the schooner "Dolphine"; Jonathan S.
Barrell, the "Polly"; Joseph Kingsbury, schooner "Ex-
change"; James Weare, "Cicero"; John Varrell, the "Return"; Samuel and Jerry Lord, the "Radius"; Geo. Moody,
the "William"; Edward Emerson, "Flying Fish"; George
Norton, the "Nemus"; Joseph Kingsbury, the "Soffronia."
There were five wharves on the northeasterly side of the
river, and that of Capt. Samuel Sewall on the south side
near the bridge with storehouses in connection therewith for
the receiving of inward and outward bound freight.   The
merchants of York were to a large extent engaged in trade
with the West Indies, and at times these wharves and ware-
houses were bustling with activity, discharging or taking in
cargoes from vessels, many of which were built and owned
in the town.   Edward Emerson had a shipyard between the
"Grow" house and the river, the site of which is now guarded
as well as the Custom House office by the Palo Alto gun.
Among others engaged in shipping on York River were
Jonathan S. Barrell, Samuel Lunt, Emerson & Lyman.   In
later years coast business flourished, and the David Crockett,
Clarinda, Eagle, Mary Remick, Susan Jane, John & Frank,

Canton, Gold Hunter, are remembered, with some of their masters—Baker, Lowe, Goodwin, Donnell, Perkins, Matthews, Hutchins, Freeman and Weare.

Among the last of the fishing schooners was the "Webster," Capt. Lowe, and the "Annie Mason," Capt. John Glenn." Among the many masters of deep sea ships are recalled the names of Thomas Clark, Charles and George Moody, George and William Putnam, John B. Fernald, Augustus Lord, Rufus Donnell, Jonathan Talpey, Joseph Swett, Timothy Winn, Frank P. and Andrew L. Emerson, and Alfred Lunt, who died at sea while in command of the ship "Anahuac." It was said in an obituary: "Capt. Lunt was a skilful and successful navigator in all waters, a rigid disciplinarian, a just and faithful agent of those he served, no man ever had a higher ideal of the order necessary to be maintained on board ship, and no man was ever able better to impress his regulations. In every position to which he was called he showed a remarkable capacity for work, and a spirit of endurance and fortitude under hardship, such as is seldom seen." He was born in York, Jan. 17, 1824.

FIRST PARISH, FIRST CHURCH OF CHRIST

As is known, the earliest form of Divine worship in Sir Gorges plantation was that of the Established Church of England, known here as the Episcopal. Under that dispensation from 1634 until 1665, expounders of the tenets of that belief labored, Mr. Thompson, in 1634-36, Mr. Burdett 1634-40, Mr. Gibson 1640-42, Mr. Hull 1642-59, Joseph Emerson 1659-62, Joseph Hull second time 1662-65, which was the time of his death. The First Congregational or the "First Church of Christ" was organized as early as 1672 by the Rev. Shubael Dummer. However, it is ascertained by parts of records that his labors in York commenced in 1662. His ordination, of which minutes have been preserved, was on December 13th, 1672. These exercises were opened with prayer by the Rev. Joseph Moody of Portsmouth. Mr. Dummer preached his own ordination sermon from the text of Scripture "Return O Lord and Visit This Vine." The charge to pastor and people was given by Rev. Mr. Philips of Rowley. Mr. Dummer was twenty-six years of age when he commenced his ministry in York, he had before been at Salisbury, now Amesbury, for two years. He married Miss Risworth, a daughter of the eminent Edward Risworth. His labor continued until January 25th, 1692, when he was shot and killed by the Indians at his door just as he was about to mount his horse to hasten to a sick and dying parishioner. Not knowing that he had passed across the river by means of the cruel work of a savage, his wife was taken into captivity with many of the settlers. In fact, the settlement was nearly destroyed. For six years following the inhabitants had but little or no preaching. On May 16th, 1698, Rev. Samuel Moody, who was born in Newbury, Jan. 4th, 1675, came to York and preached as a candidate until his ordination in December, 1700. There were at that time about twenty members of the church, but they with the rest of the people were so destitute by their losses at the hands of the French and Indians, that Mr. Moody applied to the General Court of Massachusetts, "for such an allowance for the last year, beginning May 18, 1698, as your wisdom and justice shall deem fit." That body voted him twelve pound sterling. His ministry was in the time of perils and struggle incident to war, but the Church prospered. For forty-nine years he was the religious leader of this people and his ministry was closed by his death in November, 1747.

When the parsonage was destroyed by fire in 1742 the church records were burned, no perfect account therefore of his ministry can be given. However, fragmentary records of facts are obtained from ancient diarys and letters. Mr. Moody was an able and interesting man. Speaking of him Rev. Sidney Kingman Perkins in an address delivered in the Meeting-House at the Commemorative Service held Sunday eve, Aug. 3d, 1902, says, "I have given a great deal of time to the Rev. Samuel Moody, I might easily have devoted all the time allowed me this evening to a sketch of him and his work as there is more material concerning him than any other man in the pastoral sucession here. And the work accomplished by Father Moody deserves special attention, because of its achievements and because of his wide spread fame. Samuel Moody came to a weakened and discouraged settlement and to a feeble church, when he died he left a prosperous community and a church of over three hundred members, the largest existing then in Maine. He saw power-

ful rivals during his ministry and he welcomed them.   But
he also realized that religion is something more than an emo-
tion, and he earnestly sought to develop character—strong
Christian character among his people.   His success was
great if we are to measure it simply by the change which
transformed what has been described as a largely irreligious
community, into one where it was rare to find a family where
prayer was not observed.   The appreciation in which Rev.
Samuel Moody was held summed up in the well known epi-
taph on his tombstone as he sleeps in "God's Acre" across
the way.   Here lies the body of the Rev. Samuel Moody,
A. M., the zealous, faithful and successful pastor of the First
Church of Christ in York, was born in Newbury, Jan. 4,
1765, graduated 1697, came hither May 16th, 1698, ordained
December, 1700, and died here Nov. 10, 1747.   For his further character read the 2nd Corinthians 3d chapter and first
six verses.   Before turning from the story of Mr. Moody,
it should be said that he was the ancestor of many who are
still residents of York, bearing the Moody name and of
many of other names; and also that he was the spiritual
father of a much larger number."   Mr. Perkins repeats some
of the many anecdotes of Father Moody, some of which will
find a place in this volume.

The immediate successor to Mr. Moody, and that, not for
two years, was the Rev. Isaac Lyman, who was ordained Dec.
20, 1749.   He was born in Northampton, Mass.   A graduate of Yale, a man of very different type than Mr. Moody,
but the record says "He ever sustained the character of a
faithful minister of Christ."   The great earthquake in November, 1755, was the means of awaking a revival and in 1756,
as the first forty people were received into the communion
of the Church.   Mr. Lyman's pastorate extended for two

generations, the longest of any in York, and he had the pleasure of being with a people who were united and they regarded
him it is said "with the veneration of a beloved father." Rev.
Roswell Messinger had been an associated pastor with Mr.
Lyman for the last ten years of his ministry, he was ordained
Oct. 10, 1798, and was minister for nearly fifteen years. As
a preacher he was at first popular, but his moral life was not
up to the religious standard, falling far short of that which
those who have named the name of Christ should be, and
what that of his predecessors was. After considerable trouble
he was dismissed June 13, 1813.

There was no stated preaching or pastor for about two
years. November 9th, 1815, Rev. Moses Dow, a graduate of
Dartmouth, was installed as pastor and held that relation
fourteen years. During his pastorate there was a division
which culminated in the organization of the Methodist Episcopal Church. Mr. Dow terminated his relation with the
Church, Nov. 18, 1829. He was followed by Rev. Eber
Carpenter, a graduate of Yale in the class of 1825. Mr. Carpenter was ordained Feb. 17th, 1830, and by his own request
dismissed Sept. 16th, 1835. He was a robust character, and
gained the regard of a part of his parishioners to such an
extent that a number of children were named for him. His
wife was a Lyman and his body lies in the Lyman private
burial lot in the Grant Field. Rev. John Haven, who graduated from Amherst in 1834, succeeded him, and was ordained
December 14th, 1836, dismissed in December, 1840, his wife
died here and was the first to be buried in the then "New
Cemetery." Mr. Haven's successor was Rev. John L. Ashby,
who was also a graduate of Amherst, class of 1837, he was
pastor for nearly eight years, from July, 1841, to February,
1849. Rev. William J. Newman was the next minister. He

was a graduate of Bowdoin, came to the Church in July, 1849. He was greatly loved and respected but his pastorate was brief. He died March 5th, 1850.

Rev. John Smith was settled over the Church Oct. 9th, 1850, was dismissed at his own request March 20th, 1855. He excelled as a pastor and his resignation was regretfully accepted. Rev. William A. Patten followed as "Stated Supply" in April, 1855, and remained until April, 1858. This was at a stirring time, just prior to the opening events of the Civil War. Rev. William W. Parker was ordained and began his relations as "Stated Supply" in January, 1859. He remained but one year, being succeeded by Rev. Rufus M. Sawyer, who had resigned a pastorate in Somersworth, N. H., and was "Stated Supply" from Oct. 1st, 1861, until July, 1866, covering about the years of the War of the Rebellion. There was no doubt as to his patriotism or of his devoted activity as a minister.

Rev. John Parsons from Kennebunkport became the minister from October, 1866, to May, 1869, when he was dismissed. Rev. Benjamin W. Pond commenced his ministry in May, 1870, being installed pastor, a relation he still holds. Though he left the ministry in September, 1873, and at this writing is a Principal Examiner in the Patent office and resides at 1887 Newton Street, Washington, D. C. Rev. David B. Sewall came from Fryeburg to York and commenced his ministry in December, 1873, and remained fourteen and one-half years. Rev. George M. Woodwell and Rev. M. J. Allen in turn succeeded Mr. Sewall, and they were followed by Rev. Sidney K. Perkins, and he in 1911 by Rev. Frank L. Garfield. Who were the first deacons cannot be ascertained. John Harmon was a deacon in 1731 and Joseph Holt in 1739, and in 1754, Joseph Holt, Samuel

Sewall, Abiel Goodwin and John Bradbury were elders and
Samuel Millbury, Jeremiah Bragdon, Joseph Simpson, Jr.,
and Jonathon Sayward were deacons.   In later years among
others Samuel Moody, Caleb Eastman, Henry D. Norwood,
Frank P. Emerson, Joseph Sewall, Charles C. Barrell and
John E. Staples served. The history of this Church is worth
better treatment than the writer has given it, but in the words
of Mr. Perkins I will say, "The town of York has been a
better and happier town because of the true and noble lives
that have been nurtured under the influences of its First
Church of Christ. In this connection it will not be improper
to write of the parish and of its relation to the church. In
the first settlement or early in the settlement of the country,
lands were granted and laid out in the several towns for the
support of the minister. These lands were under the control
and care of the town, until the incorporation of a parish,
when they became the property and were fully controlled by
the body corporate, organized as a parish and known as a
parish society. For the purpose of organizing a warrant to
hold a meeting was issued by William Pepperell, a justice
of the peace, on March 5th, 1731, and the first parish meeting was held March 27, 1731, at which John Harmon was
moderator, and Jeremiah Moulton was parish clerk. This
Parish Society then assumed the responsibility of raising the
compensation of the minister and the care of the parish property.   Some of its action in this direction at times is interesting. In 1732 it voted to purchase a slave for Rev. Samuel
Moody, and appointed Sam'l Came, Esq., Richard Millbury
and Joseph Holt, a committee to make such purchase and
at the same time it was voted to hire a man to live with Mr.
Moody until a slave could be purchased. In 1734 it was again
voted to hire a man or buy a slave for that year and one hun-

dred and twenty pounds ordered raised for that purpose. The assessors were instructed to buy the slave and deliver him into the hands of Mr. Moody to be employed in his service during the pleasure of the parish. In 1735 the assessors were ordered to take care of the negro until the next parish meeting. At that meeting in March, 1736, the assessors were authorized to dispose of the negro to the best advantage and thus so far as the record shows slave buying and selling was ended in the First Parish. The parsonage was burnt March 30th, 1742, and in April five hundred pounds were voted to be raised to build a new one. Samuel Sewall, John Sayward, Samuel Millbury, Benjamin Stone and Frank Farnam were appointed a committee to build the house. In this year the parish expressed their consent to the building of a bridge across the river at or near the ferry of Capt. Sewall and a committee was chosen to take subscriptions, prepare materials to build said bridge. This committee of six, headed by Capt. Nathaniel Donnell, at a subsequent meeting was enlarged to a membership of twenty-four, selections being made from all parts of the parish. In 1744 it was voted to make such repairs on the meeting-house that it might be comfortable through the winter. In 1745 Jeremiah Moulton, Esq., was elected treasurer to receive funds raised to build a new meeting-house, and Col. Nathaniel Donnell, Capt. Samuel Sewall, Joseph Swett, Samuel Millbury and Abel Moulton were appointed a committee to furnish materials. The old meeting-house was ordered to be taken down and what material was suitable to be used in the construction of the new house.

The parish voted to pay the physicians who attended Mr. Moody in his last sickness—Doctors Whitney. Sargeant and Swett—twenty-six pounds, seven shillings, and the funeral expenses of Mr. Moody, amounting to one hundred and five pounds, eighteen shillings, six pence, also forty pounds for Mrs. Moody to go into mourning. In 1760 it was voted to give Samuel Moody with the concurrence of Mr. Lyman's permission to erect a building for the instructor of youth, a lease was given him for his natural life. This Samuel Moody became the noted principal of Dummer Academy, Byfield. In 1769 singing was permitted in pews, same year, with the consent of Mr. Lyman, Moses Safford, a barber, and Eleakon Grover, a tailor, were given the right to erect buildings for their trade. They were to be of the same size, and eight feet apart. In 1797 it was voted to establish a parish fund. In 1798, Daniel Sewall, Col. Esaias Preble and Edward Emerson were chosen the first trustees. In 1810 it was voted to pay the funeral expenses of Mr. Lyman and set his gravestones. In 1837 the new burying ground so-called was located, enlarged in 1859, and again in 1870. In 1861 the vestry and the new parsonage were built. Capt. Charles Moody was awarded the contract for building the house. In 1834 it was found that the parish fund would yield an income of $250 per annum and this was used in support of the ministry.

SECOND PARISH

In 1730 a child was born to the First Parish. The Second Congregational Parish was incorporated in the northwestern part of the town know then and now as "Scotland," and in 1732 a church was organized, and Rev. Joseph Moody, yielding to the earnest solicitations of the Second Church and the desire of his father, became its pastor and was ordained Nov. 29, 1829, and herewith is placed a biographical sketch of Mr. Moody:

The life of Rev. Joseph Moody, known as "Handkerchief" Moody, has been the theme of the novelist, as in the tale of the "Veiled Parson;" of the story writer in magazines, and short stories, in periodicals, in tradition and legend, prose and poetry; and at times in authentic narrative. It is the purpose of the writer to give the facts as gleaned from the writings of Chief Justice Parsons, a contemporary, Judge William Pitt Preble, and Charles C. P. Moody, in a book published by Samuel G. Drake, No. 56 Cornhill, in 1847.

Joseph Moody, pastor of the Second Congregational church, in York, was born in the year 1700, the date of the settlement of his father as minister of the First Parish. At the age of eighteen he graduated with high honors at Harvard College, and up to the age of thirty-two years was a very active and prominent figure in civil affairs. For some years he was clerk of the town, and his work, as seen in Vol. 1 of the Records, gives evidence of the painstaking and careful scrivener. He was also Register of Deeds for the County and there, too, he left testimony as to his care and correctness.

In 1730, at the age of but thirty years, he was Judge of the County Court and a brilliant and honorable career seemed opening its path in the public service. He seemed in many respects well fitted for the work of ministry (and so his father thought). He was easy of access, open and frank, friendly and communicative. Composition was easy to him. No man had a greater fund of words to draw upon and few had a happier talent in arranging them properly and with the polish of his classical education, he could convey his ideas in language pure, and style manly and easy.

His father, Rev. Samuel Moody—"Father" Moody—was very desirous that Joseph should be a preacher of the Gospel, for with all of his other supposed qualifications he was considered a man of eminent piety. With Father Moody, to wish was to accomplish and the importunity of the father prevailed with the son.

Without delay, in 1730, the Second Parish was incorporated in that section of the town known as Scotland, from the fact that it was originally settled by the Scotch immigrants. In 1732 a church was organized and Mr. Moody, or Judge Moody, was warmly urged to become pastor. Resigning all his civil offices, "he laid his honors down," and was ordained. But the new trust proved too much for his great sensibility; and after six years he fell into a gloomy and singularly disordered state of mind, and gave up his labors. However, after this occasionally he preached a discourse in public, and often led in devotional exercises; in prayer he was ever ready and copious with that gift.

The disorder that brought to a close, in a large degree, Mr. Moody's usefulness, was of the nervous kind. He supposed that an act committed many years before had made him unfit for the sacred office he held. Ebenezer Preble, the fourth son of Abraham and Hannah, and two years the senior of Joseph Moody, was a young man of rare promise at the time

of his death, which was tragical.   He and Moody were very
intimate personal friends.   One day they went out hunting
together in the woods in pursuit of deer, and other game
that might come within range.   Having reached a thicket,
they separated for the purpose of making a circuit, so as to
start the game.   After awhile Moody heard a crackling and
saw the underbrush move, as if an animal were making its
way through them.   Instantly without thought he levelled his
gun and fired.   Hastening in triumph to the spot where he
expected to find his game, there lay his friend Preble welter-
ing in his blood, and in the agonies of death.   Moody could
never after forgive himself for his precipitancy.   The death
of Preble created a great sensation and called forth the talents of the writers of elegys in those days.   A couplet of one
of the efforts offered by them on the occasion has been preserved and runs thus:

"Oh, lamentable, lamentable!
What has become of Ebenezer Preble!"

About 1736 he lost his wife, who had always relieved him
of much of the pressure of worldly matters.   This no doubt
increased his nervous difficulty.   He ceased to preach in 1738,
and went to board with Deacon Bragdon.   He chose to eat
alone, and kept his face covered with a handkerchief, (the
side table, the property of the writer, from which he par-
took his solitary meals, is in the Old Gaol Museum), when
in company.

Deacon Bragdon, with whom he made his home, was naturally a man of hasty temper, a trait that has not become
entirely extinct in his descendants.   The Deacon had been
out one morning and had some difficulty with one of his
neighbors, a Mr. Junkins, about bad fences and breachy cat-
tle.   He made out to keep his temper fairly well while con-

versing with his neighbor; but after he left him, thinking of
some incident, "Old Adam" got up to a high pitch by the
time he got home. As soon as he entered his house, in great
excitement of spirit, he called out to Mr. Moody, "O, Mr.
Moody, you must pray for my poor neighbor up the road,
he has got terribly out of the way." "And does not Deacon
Bragdon need a few prayers, too?" replied Mr. Moody. "May
he not be some out of the way, as well as his neighbor?" "Oh!
no, no;" says Deacon Bragdon. "If I thought I was to blame
I would take my horse and ride fifty miles on end!" "Ah!
Deacon Bragdon, I beileve it would take a pretty good horse
to out ride the Devil!" This last reply of Mr. Moody calmed
the good deacon, it is supposed.

In 1745 Mr. Moody had become partially restored, and
supplied the pulpit of the First Parish in the absence of his
father, who was Chaplain of the Louisburg expedition. And
it was at this time that an extraordinary incident took place,
and may be accounted for each in his own mind. By information from Louisburg, it was found that the place was not
taken. It was suggested that a day of fasting and prayer
should be held in York. Neighboring ministers attended and
assisted. Joseph Moody offered one of the prayers that was
nearly two hours long. He went on a long time, using all
manner of argument and pleas he could think of, for the
reduction of the place, that the enterprise might be prospered; then turned in his prayer and gave thanks that it was
done, it was delivered up, it was ours. Then he went on a
long time praising God for his unmerited mercy. After the
troops returned and they and others compared notes, it was
found that the place was taken on the very day that the fast
was held and that the capitulation was closed while he was
praying! The coincident of these facts with the prayer is a
matter of history.

It appears that at the age of twenty, young Moody had a strong attachment for Mary Hirst of Boston, which was supposed to be reciprocated; but in May, 1772, she was visited by Capt. Pepperell, who was more attractive in her eyes than the humble school master, and she became the wife of Sir William Pepperell.   Moody married Miss Lucy White of Gloucester, descendant of Mayflower fame, and daughter of Rev. John White.   He left three sons: Samuel, the first preceptor of Dummer Academy in Byfield, Mass., who had no descendants, as on his tomb stone in the old burying ground reads, "he left no children for he died a bachelor"; Joseph, who had a large family; and Thomas, who also left descendants.

The death of Mr. Moody was sudden and attended by some remarkable circumstances. He had, in early life, been a great singer, but after his indisposition he laid it wholly aside, and though at times he would lay his handkerchief aside and appeared cheerful, yet he would not sing. At length, one day, which he spent alone in his chamber, he was heard to break forth into singing, to the great astonishment of the Bragdon family.   Almost the entire afternoon he was singing with great animation, the 17th hymn of 1st Book of Watts' Hymns:

> "Oh for an overcoming faith,
> To cheer my dying hours."

He did not come out of his chamber that night, and the next morning was found dead in his bed.   Such was the end of this good man, as recorded by President Allen.

On his tombstone, which has disappeared, was the following inscription:

> "Here lies interred the body
> of the Rev'ed
> Joseph Moody,

Pastor of the Second Church in York, an Excellent instance
of knowledge, learning, ingenuity, piety and usefulness, was
very serviceable as a schoolmaster, Clerk, Register, Magistrate, and afterwards as a minister.   Was uncommonly qualified and spirited to do good, and accordingly was highly
esteemed and greatly beloved.

He deceased

March 20, 1753

Aged 53 years.

Although this stone may moulder into dust

Yet Joseph Moody's name continue must."

His pastoral relation with the society was dissolved in
1741 and Rev. Samuel Chandler was ordained and remained
until 1752, when by mutual consent his pastorate terminated.
The third pastor was Rev. Samuel Lankton.   He had been
occupying various pulpits in Connecticut and had received
calls to settle but his health had become impaired and he
was hastening to regain it and when passing through York
he passed a night with Rev. Mr. Lyman of the First Parish, and through him learned of the vacancy in the Second
Parish and was urged to visit that branch of the vine and
"preach them a lecture," which he did much to the gratifica-
tion of the people, who greatly desired that he should remain
with them, and he was ordained pastor July 3rd, 1754, and
continued in that relation for more than forty years.   In
December, 1794, he died suddenly from hemorrhage of the
lungs.   He was a fine scholar, an eloquent preacher and an
earnest Christian—and a most exemplary pastor.   For three
years there was no regular occupant of the pulpit.   August
2nd, 1798, Rev. Isaac Briggs was ordained, and dismissed
July 4, 1805.   For twenty years, until Nov. 9, 1825, they
were a flock without a shepherd.   At that time Rev. Thomas
Duncan was installed pastor.   The church was very feeble

at this time and could count but eleven members. Mr. Duncan was dismissed April 28th, 1830. And again for nearly four years they were without a settled minister, until Dec. 3rd, 1834, Rev. Clement Parker was installed. After a pastorate of about four years he was dismissed, May 11, 1838. He was succeeded by Rev. Samuel Stone, Dec. 19, 1838, who remained until Jan. 1st, 1844. A year followed without a minister, when on Jan. 15th, 1845, Rev. Morris Holman was ordained. He was dismissed July 9th, 1853. From December, 1858, to May 15th, John M. C. Bartly became "Stated Supply," followed by Samuel H. Partridge, who was also excelled as a physician and was "Stated Supply" from May 22nd, 1859, to the Fall of 1868. Rev. Joseph Freeman, "Stated Supply," began his labors Aug. 1st, 1869, and continued until 1884, when he was succeeded by Rev. J. Foster in June of that year by reason of ill health. He gave up his pastorate in Sept. Rev. William Creelman followed from June, 1885, to 1888. From that time until 1890 the Church was supplied with services from students of the Bangor Theological Seminary. Rev. George M. Woodwell of the First Parish preached in 1890-91-92 and 93. Rev. Arthur L. Golder from 1894 to 1896. Rev. Andrew L. Chase from 1896 to 1899. Rev. John Wilson from July, 1900, to June, 1902. Rev. Henry Hamilton from 1903 to 1907. The present minister, Rev. Ebenezer Jenkyns, began his labors in November, 1908. William L. Donald in 1913.

The deacons are Joseph H. Moody, who has served since 1863, fifty years, and James H. Nowell, who was chosen in 1889.

The first meetinghouse stood in the field of Mr. John McIntire, near the dwelling house of Deacon Joseph H. Moody. The present house was built in 1834, and dedicated December 2nd, same year.

METHODIST

DOUBTLESS the earliest prominent Methodist to sojourn in York for a time was the Rev. George Whitefield of England and intimate friend of John and Charles Wesley; that was in 1745 and he was warmly welcomed by Rev. Samuel Moody. In later years Jesse Lee, of Virginia, came near our border to Kittery and was visited by many from York. He is described as a man "of vigorous physique, imposing presence, and great power of endurance, and weighing about two hundred and fifty pounds." In most of his journeyings two horses were required for his use alternately. Previous to 1829 were the beginnings of a Methodist Episcopal Church in York. The New England Conference had stationed in Portsmouth, N. H., a wonderful and powerful preacher possessed of charming eloquence, John Newland Maffit. Charles O. Emerson of the First Parish, a young lawyer of influence, and Jeremiah Brooks, a local merchant, upon their own motion asked Mr. Maffit to visit York, and the invitation was accepted, the first audience being responsive and enthusiastic. An appointment was made for a second meeting the following evening and the people came, filling the Court House to overflowing.

"Mr. Maffit was then thirty-four years old, a native of Dublin, Ireland, having migrated at the age of twenty-four. He was a marvelous pulpit orator, gifted in prayer, and a sweet singer, and he exercised an immense magnetic power over the large audiences that gathered to hear him."

The meetings continued and resulted in the greatest revival York ever knew. In 1829 a class or church was organized with seventy-three (73) members, by Rev. J. Spaulding and

Gershom D. Cox. On Feb. 28, 1831, under provisions of the
R. S. of Maine a society was incorporated. Seven (7) persons were chosen trustees to hold property deeded to the
Methodist church on which to erect a meeting house, chapel,
etc. A building committee was also chosen, consisting of
Soloman Brooks, Joseph S. Clark, Francis Plaisted, Jeremiah McIntire and Alexander Dennett. It required time,
patience, and not a little diplomacy to secure a suitable site
for the building, but it was finally obtained of Mrs. Mary
Lyman and her brother, Nathaniel Sargent. Of this committee Miss Ellen M. Dennett in her valuable and interesting
paper says: "A capable group of men but the "dynamo"
was Mr. Clark. Joe Clark, as he was best known, was a
man of intense purpose, never heeding discouraging circumstances, he simply must see the church built." The church
building was raised Aug. 31, 1833, and completed Oct. 1,
1834. It was under the hand of Stephen Downing of Kennebunk as master workman from plans of a meeting house
just completed at Great Falls, N. H. The church was dedicated Oct. 15, 1834. Rev. Gershom D. Cox preached the
sermon from the text found in Daniel 2 Chap., 44th verse.
Since that time the building has twice been remodeled, the
last and most extensive in 1895, during the ministry of Rev.
Mr. Wright, at which time the interior was beautified and
a bell placed in the tower. Rev. Dr. Brodbeck of Boston
delivered the sermon at the re-dedication from the text of
Scripture: "He saved others, Himself he cannot save."

A pressing need was keenly felt in the lack of a domicile
for the minister and his family, but this was to be remedied.
In 1846 Rev. Isaac Lord, who had been assigned to this part
of the vineyard, said to a good but incredulous brother,
"We must have a parsonage," who replied softly in an aside,

"Let's see you get it." But the little parsonage was built, the plans were drawn and much of the work done by Mr. Lord, who was a practical mechanic and had often used his skill in building and repairing churches, chapels and parsonages in other places during fifty-one (51) years of active service without a leave of absence. Among the forty-eight worthy men who from its inception to the present have served their day and generation well in this church, and among the pleasant memories is that of William H. Strout, who was in York in '59 and '60. His appointment had been urgently requested. Of him Miss Dennett says: "The people knew him; he had begun as a lawyer, but his natural traits and purposes in life were such as to lead him toward the ministry. A man of fine qualities, intellectual and moral, and sure of some degree of success in whatever he might undertake. He was allied to York further by ties of family. Mr. Strout was afterward transferred to an Illinois Conference feeling that it would be for the advantage of his four young sons, and his hopes were realized in living to see them develop as young men of marked character and ability."

Of the occupants of the pews Miss Dennett gives interesting sketches. "The Lords, John and Jerry, of Cape Neck (The Willows) and their wives walked across Long Beach to and from meeting. Mr. Jerry Lord in social meetings was wont to relate his experience; his feelings as he reviewed the scene came to a kind of rapture as he went on. In those straight-backed pews sat the heads of families; from the harbor almost exclusively seafaring men, Capt. Joseph and Edward Lowe, Capt. George and James Donnell, Capt. Kingsbury and his wife Hannah Grow; three talented sisters of Capt. Kingsbury, Mrs. Emerson, Mrs. Crane, and Mrs. Moulton, had gone forth from this place to fill worthy ones in Boston, Taunton and Vineland."

Mary Ann Derby was graceful and refined, a delightful Sabbath school teacher, and whose religious life was almost an ecstasy.

A very active member of the society from its inception was Jeremiah Brooks, Esquire, being one of Mr. Maffit's first converts. The early records are in his handwriting and are easily read. Mr. Brooks was very fond of music, vocal and instrumental, especially the violin, but he at once laid it aside as being an unholy instrument.

Several hundreds of persons have been members of this church and many have gone over the river, and we trust "met their pilot when they crossed the bar."

The following is a list of the ministers of the society. In the last part of the year 1829 Rev. John Atkins of Kittery supplied; the first actual pastor was Mr. Cox.

1830	G. F. Cox	1856-57	John M. Woodbury
1831	M. Hill	1858-59	William H. Strout
1832	A. P. Hillman	1860	C. Philbrick
1833-34	P. C. Richmond	1861-62	Nathan D. Center
1835	Francis Masseure	1863	F. C. Ayer
1836	W. H. Pillsbury	1864-65-66	John Collins
1837	H. M. Macomber	1867	Orange W. Scott
1838	T. Rawson	1868	W. C. Stevens
1839-40	H. M. Blake	1869-70	E. K. Colby
1841-42	A. Hotchkiss	1871	Daniel Halloran
1843	F. Yates	1872-73-74	Ruel H. Kimball
1844	J. W. Atkins	1875-76-77	James H. Trask
1845	J. Weston	1878	Joseph Hawkes
1846-47	Isaac Lord	1879	Daniel B. Randall
1848	John Rice	1880-81	I. H. Stevens
1849	A. Hatch	1882-83-84	Geo. C. Andrews
1850	John Mitchell	1885-86	J. A. Corey
1851	John Moore	1887 to '92	G. D. Holmes
1852-53	F. C. Ayer	1893-94	William P. Lord
1854-55	L. B. Knight	1895	James Wright

1896 to '99..Wm. S. Bovard 1904......James H. Bounds
1900........C. C. Whidden 1905-6-7.....Insley A. Bean
1901........O. S. Pillsbury 1908-9......Albert J. Croft
1901-2-3...Dudley C. Abbott 1910........Arthur J. Price
                            1913......Alvin C. Goddard

These forty-eight men of different gifts and characteristics have served as pastors, and "one star differeth from another in glory."

METHODIST SOCIETY AT SCOTLAND

This society was formed in 1830 and Rev. George Webber was sent by the Conference to preach in that section. A meeting house was built in 1833. However, since 1866 the society grew weak and finally disbanded. The following list comprised the names of the settled ministers: 1842, T. M. Hall; 1848, A. R. Lunt; 1859-60, Benjamin Lufkin; 1861, J. R. Smith; 1862-63, George W. Barbour; 1864-65, O. M. Cousins; 1866, J. W. Savage.

METHODIST SOCIETY AT CAPE NEDDICK

Was formed consisting of Moses Brewster, John Norton, Oliver Preble, Richard Talpey, George Phillips, Jonathan Talpey, Obadiah Stover, Samuel Welch, George Norton, Henry Talpey, Timothy Ramsdell, and Hannah Clark. They withdrew from the First Parish in 1822, but there is no record that they were organized as a church, or had existence for any great length of time. A part of them joined the Baptist Society.

SAINT GEORGE'S (EPISCOPAL)

THE MONEY was raised for the church in the 80's by the Right Reverend Benjamin H. Paddock, Bishop of Massachusetts, the Right Reverend Alexander Burgess, Bishop of Quincy, Illinois, and several summer visitors at Norwood Farm and cottagers at York Harbor. John C. Ropes and Dr. Charles B. Tower were trustees in charge of the church for many years.

Mr. E. B. Blaisdell was the builder.

The church was consecrated by the Right Reverend Alexander Burgess. This is stated in the Diocesan Journal of the Diocese of Maine by Bishop Neely in one of his addresses. For several years services have been held every Sunday in St. George's during the months in which Trinity Church has been closed.

The date of consecration was in August, 1886, the church building having been completed in the spring of that year.

TRINITY CHURCH (EPISCOPAL)

THE LOT for the church was purchased in 1904. Mr. Henry J. Handenburgh prepared plans for the church in 1907. The contract was given to Mr. E. E. Goodwin and the first services were held in the church in August, 1909. The lot and church have been paid for and there is no debt.

The committee in charge during the building of the church were: Thomas Nelson Page, H. Blanchard Dominick, Francis Lynde Stetson, William H. Lincoln, E. H. Siter, Elihu Chauncey.

At this writing Trinity Church has not been consecrated.

SAINT PETER'S BY THE SEA (EPISCOPAL)

IT WAS said to the Master nearly nineteen hundred years ago of one:

"For he loveth our nation, and he hath built us a synagogue."

A change of a few words, and the sentiment would yet remain, and could with eminent propriety be used in speaking of Mr. and Mrs. George M. Conarroe of Philadelphia, Penn. For they loved York and Ogunquit and founded Saint Peter's by the Sea in 1898. It was consecrated July 12, 1898, Bishop officiating, Rt. Rev. Henry Adams Neely, D. D., Diocese of Maine.

NON-SECTARIAN

AT Clay Hill a neat and commodious building for religious purposes was erected previous to 1901. The active promoters of the good work among others were Frank C. Bridges, Josiah N. Norton, Leon S. Moulton, Jeremiah Moulton, Mr. and Mrs. R. F. Chalk. It was intended to be a non-sectarian religious place of assemblage within the walls of which the truth might be proclaimed, "no matter whether it was found on heathen or Christian ground." When conditions warrant services are held.

CHAPEL AT AGAMENTICUS

PREVIOUS to the year 1900, by the labors of Rev. Harmon Goodwin, aided by John F. Plaisted, Alvah Trafton and others, and supplemented by generous outside contributions, a chapel was built in the Agamenticus District and religious services have been conducted from time to time as circumstances seemed to demand.

UNION CONGREGATIONAL SOCIETY AND CHURCH, YORK BEACH

THE "Union" Church was founded in 1895.

"The Ladies' Aid" to assist in the work of establishing a religious society and building a church edifice was formed Dec. 3, 1894. This arrangement continued until several wished to join the church upon confession of faith, and then it was seen that there was not anything to join (or perhaps everything) for the Union Church was everything. So in process of time Articles of Faith were drawn up and a church body was established retaining the name of Union Church.

February 1, 1910, Charles L. Bowden, Reuben B. Morgan, Frank E. Parsons, J. B. Paul, W. C. Hildreth, F. H. Ellis, I. B. Camp, John S. Young, W. N. Gough, Austin McKowen, Frank W. Armstrong, H. L. Shattuck, N. C. Simonds, Harry A. Platts, Edward Shattuck and M. Q. Adams petitioned John C. Stewart, a notary public, to take the action required by the law to incorporate a religious society under the name of Union Congregational Church, which was done under notarial seal Feb. 2, 1910, and it is now a part of the Maine Congregational body.

Armenius H. Bowden donated land and the society purchased land adjoining sufficient on which to erect a commodious and tasteful "meeting house."

The first Sunday School at the Beach was formed, July, 1886, by Romie M. Ellis at her home at Union Bluff, York Beach.

BAPTIST

THE First Baptist Church of Cape Neddick was formed Aug. 20, 1829, with a membership of twelve persons, five males and seven females. It was organized by Rev. Oliver Barron. The inception of the movement originated with a few members of the Baptist Church at South Berwick, who had resided at Cape Neddick for years. As far back as 1780 Elder Nathaniel Lord preached a sermon at the house of Jeremiah Weare. However, the opposition to the introduction of Baptist sentiments was so strong that further effort to inculcate their doctrine was discontinued for more than twenty years. After that time elapsed Elder William Batchelder deilvered an address in David Webber's orchard, which received great attention and about fifty souls were converted, some of whom joined the church in South Berwick. During this time up to 1829 they were favored with preaching at intervals by several ministers who came to them as opportunity granted. Among these were Elder Andrew Sherburne and Joshua Chase. The meeting house was built in 1823 by the combined efforts of Baptists and Methodists. When it was completed the question of owner-ship and the supplying of a minister brought about an un-pleasant struggle. It appears that the Baptists maintained their contention and in May, 1829, Rev. Mr. Barron com-menced preaching. He continued as pastor for about three years. In May, 1830, the church with a membership of twenty-four joined the York Association, and was repre-sented at that meeting by Rev. Mr. Barron, Deacon Cotton Chase, and Daniel Norton. Rev. John Hainer preached part of the time in 1832 and Josiah Ames occasionally in

1833. Jan. 9, 1834, Rev. Clark Sibly became pastor and remained three years, then Noah Hooper, Jr., a student, supplied for several weeks. Rev. Daniel McMaster preached nearly a year and was followed in April, 1838, by Rev. Gideon Cook, who resigned in 1841. It was during Mr. Cook's ministry that the church was deprived of a large portion of its membership. Twenty-five members were dismissed to organize a church in Wells. Rev. Isaac Merrill followed Mr. Cook, July 4, 1841. In 1842, in spite of the reduction in membership under ministration of L. L. Tripp the twenty-five who were dismissed the church had at this time increased to sixty-six. Rev. Mr. Cook returned Nov. 9, 1843, and was dismissed March 4, 1847. July 4, 1847, Rev. B. Pease began his ministry and remained until Oct. 2, 1851. Rev. S. F. Kendall followed Aug. 29, 1852, and was dismissed July 2, 1854. Elder John Hubbard began his ministry in December, 1854. Rev. A. E. Edwards became pastor Oct. 28, 1858, and continued to April 4, 1861; being followed in January, 1862, by B. F. Lawrence, who was ordained May 22, 1863, and resigned January 8, 1865. Rev. C. P. Bartlett received a call April 16, 1866, which was accepted May 6. He resigned April 28, 1866. From that date until 1870 Rev. J. M. Mace was pastor. In 1871 Rev. J. A. Tooker supplied. Preaching was by supplies from 1871 to 1873, when Rev. William Beavens was pastor to 1875, followed by Rev. Henry Stetson, 1875 to 1879; Rev. Gilbert Robbins, 1879 to 1886; Rev. H. B. Marshall, 1886 to 1888; Rev. C. H. Eveleth, 1889 to 1891; Rev. P. T. Gallaher, 1892 to 1894; Rev. William Fletcher, 1894 to 1902; Rev. William Reid, 1902 to 1906; Rev. H. A. Platts, 1906 to 1908; Rev. J. S. Osborne, 1909 to 1912. Rev. F. H. Gardner became the present pastor, May, 1912. Among the deacons of this church have been Cotton Chase, Samuel Webber, Jonathan Talpey, and Oliver Norton. Since 1880 the meeting house has been remodeled, and a new parsonage house and church vestry built.

CHRISTIAN

THE York Christian Church was organized May 13, 1808, under the auspices of Elder Elias Smith at Tenney Orchard, in the dwelling house of John Terry. Twenty-six persons constituted the membership. Peter Young was ordained first pastor in September, 1808. Sept. 4, 1809, Moses Safford began his labors as a preacher. He was followed by Mark Fernald, May 24, 1819.

On June 29, 1829, Elder Peter Young was again called to the flock. In December, 1836, Elder Robinson came, remaining for one year, and on January 10, 1839, Rev. Abner Hall was ordained pastor. He was succeeded by Stephen R. Bickford in October, 1842.

From May, 1846, to May, 1849, Elder Thomas Bartlett occupied the pulpit. After an absence of about a year, in May, 1850, he resumed his pastorate until October, 1851.

In the years 1852 and 1853 Rev. P. L. Beverly supplied, and on May 4, 1853, Rev. Charles E. Goodwin began his long pastorate which ended in May, 1874.

Elder Hezekiah Short followed, from June 5, 1874, until May, 1881; Elder James A. Phillips, May, 1881, to March, 1884; Rev. J. W. Card, May, 1884, to March 31, 1885; Rev. B. S. Maben, June, 1885, to June, 1887; Rev. W. B. Flanders, September, 1887, to Jan. 31, 1891; Rev. C. V. Parsons, April, 1891, to December, 1893; Rev. W. G. Voliva, March, 1894, to March, 1895; Rev. T. G. Moses, May, 1895, to May, 1900; Rev. John A. Goss, July, 1900, to July, 1908; Rev. C. J. Yeomans, September, 1908, to April, 1910; Rev. C. V. Parsons, from October, 1910, to the present time of writing, Feb. 1, 1913.

The building now used by Allen C. Moulton as a manufactory for the sawing and dressing of all kinds of lumber is the original meeting house of the society and was located at the junction of the Portland and Cider Hill roads. On the completion of the new edifice it was used by the High School until the High School building was occupied. The construction of the new meeting house was begun in 1891 and completed and furnished May 1, 1893; dedicated May 13th that year. The sermon was preached by Rev. E. A. Hainer. In 1910 extensive repairs and changes were made in the interior.

William Gardner Moulton at the time of his death, Dec. 13, 1906, had been a member of the church seventy-eight years, and served as deacon for forty-three years. The present deacons are William P. Titcomb, chosen in 1888, and J. Albion Littlefield in 1907. Elder Peter Young in his autobiography gives an interesting account of the early days of the society which is given herewith:

"I was born in York, in the County of York, District of Maine, on the 29th of April, in the year of our Lord 1784. My parents' names were Rowland and Mary Young; they belonged to the Congregational Society in that place, and brought up their children in that order.

"About the last of February, A. D. 1805, I took leave of my friends in York, for a little season, to travel in the country, to sound salvation to my fellowmen.

"I rode to Berwick and Sanford, tarried about a week, preaching Jesus, sometimes in one town, and sometimes in the other. From thence, in process of time, I arrived at Alton, N. H., and there it pleased the dear Lord, to lead me out of Calvinistic bondage into the glorious liberty of the gospel of Christ.

"While at Alton I went to bed and dreamed that I was at York, and that somebody had a flock of sheep that had no shepherd, and they desired me to take them and feed them and take care of them; and I thought I did it; and I awoke and behold it was a dream.   Nevertheless I thought it was my duty to visit York.   In February, 1808, by the desire of the brethren, I hired a house and sent to Alton and moved some of our effects here and set up housekeeping.

"In April the brethren were very much engaged and we enjoyed a refreshing time in the presence of the Lord.

"In May we thought it our duty to consider ourselves a church of Christ, and on the thirtieth day of May, Elder Elias Smith came here and preached.   Two related the reason of their hope in Christ, and after baptism in Little River the brethren met and agreed to lay aside all party names, by which professors of religion have been and are now called, and to name the name of Christ only which is CHRISTIAN; having no creed, platforms or articles of faith but the New Testament; and to endeavor to walk according to that and the teaching of the spirit.

"There were about twenty-four of us there in Tenny's Orchard, who made this agreement; and the Lord has, I trust, made additions to us since, of such as shall be saved, so that now there are nearly thirty, who stand together as a church of Christ."

THE CHRISTIAN CHURCH

THE Christian Church of York and Kittery was organized June 9th, 1866. It was about this time that the Rev. Joel Wilson of Kittery began labor among the people of Beech Ridge and vicinity, holding religious services, with preaching in the schoolhouse. As the result a church society of twenty-seven members was gathered. A neat and commodious meeting house was built in the months of November and December, 1866, and early in 1867, at a cost of $3,500. It was dedicated Feb. 21, 1867. A bell was given the society by the Hon. Ichabod Washburn of Worcester, Mass., and hung in position Oct. 26, 1867.

The first deacon was Henry Grover. In 1873, Rev. Mr. Wilson was succeeded by Rev. Joseph H. Graves. In 1874 Mr. Wilson returned to the pastorate, being succeeded by Elder George Moore Payne in 1876, who was followed in 1878 by Joseph Whitney. In 1879 ministerial labor was conducted by Edwin D. Wells of Portsmouth for three years, and from 1882 until 1885 Elder Payne labored, and was followed by William P. Iseral of Portsmouth for two years, when Rev. John H. Mugridge—who served until 1891— succeeded. Rev. James R. Phillips was pastor from the last named date to 1895, being succeeded by Rev. George H. Kent; Rev. Eben S. Greenleaf of Lynn followed Mr. Kent in 1899. In 1904 Mr. Kent returned, remaining until 1907, since when the house has been closed to preaching services.

At frequent occasions Sabbath school exercises have been held. The meeting-house is being maintained in good condition. And there is opportunity for some shepherd without a flock. (The Beech Ridge church has again been opened for services, with Rev. Mr. Eldredge in charge.)

ROMAN CATHOLIC

At York Beach the first Mass was the last two Sundays of August, 1895, in Clement's Hall, which is now known as the Algonquin. The next two seasons the services were at the Myrtle Cottage, the summer home of Mr. Bernard O'Donnell, of Brooklyn, N. Y. In 1898 Mr. Elisha Brown, who was president of a bank in Dover, N. H., and not a Catholic, invited the Catholics to have Mass said in his cottage at Dover Bluffs. The Myrtle Cottage again served as the chapel for the years 1899 and 1900, the last Mass being said August 5, 1900, at which more than 175 persons assisted. It was now evident that some other arrangement must be made to accommodate the Catholics coming to York Beach for the summer months as they had outgrown all the places offered to them.

As several Catholics had contributed to the erection of the Union Church, it was thought that this building could be had, but no arrangements could be made with those in charge of the church.

A committee consisting of the late Hon. John M. Mitchell, a Justice of the Superior Court of New Hampshire, Mr. Roger G. Sullivan of Manchester, N. H., with Mr. Bernard O'Donnell of New York as Treasurer, with the permission of the Church authorities of the Diocese of Portland assumed all the burden of erecting a church at York Beach. A lot of land was bought on Church St. and the beautiful "Church of the Star of the Sea" was erected on it and opened for service, the first Mass being said in it by the Rev. James P. Gorman, pastor of South Berwick, July 7, 1901. The number of Catholics continued to increase so that it was necessary to have two Masses on Sundays, and even with this double service it was soon apparent that the church building could not accommodate the great number coming for the two Masses. It was then decided to enlarge the church. A transept was built and the seating capacity of the church increased to nearly eight hundred by the installation of pews, and even now with the two Masses and the increased seating room there are Sundays when even standing room is difficult to be had. The church is practically out of debt.

Mass was said for the first time at York Harbor up stairs in Mason's Bath House in 1895; afterward in the Library. Some objection was made to having the services in the Library, and as no other suitable place could be found they were discontinued for a couple of years. When Mass was again said it was in the dance hall of the Albracca and continued there until the erection of the Church of the Immaculate Conception on Woodbridge Road in 1903. The first Mass was said by the pastor, Rev. James P. Gorman, who had the general supervision of the building of the church. The congregations here have so increased that it has been necessary to have two Masses every Sunday from June to the last of September. Though many improvements have been made to this church it is now out of debt.

Mass was said for the first time in the winter at the home of Mr. James P. Eaton in 1911, and services are held there now each winter.

A rectory was completed and furnished in 1913. Rev. Denis J. O'Brien succeeded Rev. Mr. Gorman and is the present beloved pastor.

PHYSICIANS AND SURGEONS

AMONG THE earliest of whom there is record were Doctors Bulman, Joseph Swett, Sargent, Whitney, Job Lyman and Josiah Gilman. The Day Book of Dr. Gilman, by the thoughtfulness of the late Dr. Wilson L. Hawkes, has been preserved and is now, by the kindness of Mrs. Hawkes, in the Old Gaol Museum. He appears to have had a wide and long-continued practice from late in the eighteenth century down to 1840. The entries are of interest. Under date of August, 1803, is a charge against Micum McIntire, "visit to him $1.00, six portions for his son $.25." Samuel Emery, Wells, "visit and medicine $3.00." His fee for visits in the village was 25 cents. In parturition cases, $3.00 for male child and $2.00 for female. From 1803 to 1813, a decade, his professional calls numbered 17,200. Somebody has written on the last page of the book, "Lyman Gilman is a bad boy."

In the last century were Dr. Jeremiah S. Putman, a native of Danvers, Mass.; Caleb Eastman, from Conway, N. H., and many years a Deacon of the First Church and Treasurer of the First Parish; Charles Trafton; Christopher P. Gerrish, who was born in Lebanon, Maine, came to York from Great Falls (Somersworth) in 1857; Jasper J. Hazen, born in Cabot, Vt., served in the Union Army, began practice of medicine in York in 1867; Wilson L. Hawkes, born in Windham, Maine, in 1848, commenced practice in Portsmouth, N. H., came to York in November, 1872; John Conant Stewart, born in Vermont, 1850, commenced practice of medicine in York, 1877, later read law with Moses A. Safford and admitted to the Bar in 1895; Frank W.

Smith, born in Gray, Maine, in 1859, entered practice in 1884 at West Buxton, came to York in 1889; Edward Chase Cook, born in Vassalboro, 1869, located at York Village in 1895; Charles H. Harmon, now in New Sweden, came to York in 1907.

Doctors Bulman, Sargent, Gilman, Lyman, Putnam, Gerrish, Hawkes, Hazen, Cook and Stewart all lived on Main Street between the Town Hall and York Corner.

YORK COUNTRY CLUB

ON THE 15th day of September, 1900, the York Country Club was incorporated with the following as officers of the organization:

President, Charles Eustis Hubbard of Boston.

Vice President, Frederick H. Tappan, Boston.

Secretary, Frederick H. Tappan.

Treasurer—Charles W. Fox, Philadelphia.

Clerk of Corporation, Frank D. Marshall, Portland.

Directors and Trustees, Arthur T. Aldis, B. Ogden Chisholm, James T. Davidson, Charles E. Hubbard, Elihu Chauncey, Joseph E. Davis, Thomas Nelson Page, Frederick H. Tappan, Charles W. Fox.

The farm of Jeremiah McIntire, nearly all of the E. A. Bragdon real estate, and two-thirds or more of the estate of the late Nathaniel G. Marshall, owned by Samuel W. Junkins, approximating one hundred and fifty acres, was purchased, and a club house erected thereon near Sewall's Bridge. The house was opened in the early summer of 1901 with these persons as members: Arthur T. Aldis, Owen F. Aldis, L. Bolton Bangs, M. D., John Cadwalader, Elihu Chauncey, George L. Cheney, Knight D. Cheney. B. Ogden Chisholm, Joseph E. Davis, George B. Dexter. H. B. Dominick, Edward O. Emerson, Julian d'Este, Charles W. Fox, M. D., Charles E. Hubbard, W. L. Hawkes, M. D., J. D. J. Kelly, Barbour Lathrop, Bryan Lathrop, William H Lincoln, Thatcher Loring, Frank D. Marshall, W. R. Mercer, Jr., Thomas Nelson Page, John W. Pepper, F. A. Peters, Henry Sampson, Walter M. Smith, Wilson M. Walker.

In addition to the eighteen-hole golf course the club has twelve single tennis courts, fine croquet grounds, a large garage, and caddy house.

William Wilson is the superintendent of the Club and a professional golf player of fine attainment.

From its inception the Club House has been under the personal care of Charles E. Noble, as Steward. Mrs. Noble has charge of the cuisine, and as a writer has said, "A visit to the York Country Club is incomplete without a dinner at the Club served by Mrs. Noble. Her exquisite taste and genius for arranging menus have placed her in the class with Sherry and Delmonico." Much of the elaborate furnishing of the house has been made by the gifts of Mrs. Goodrich, Mrs. Davis, Mrs. Fox, Mrs. Henry S. Grove, Mrs. Chisholm, Mrs. Hubbard, Mrs. Denny, Mrs. S. E. Price, Mrs. Bryan Lathrop, and others.

A lease of the William O. Bragdon property has been taken for twenty years, giving more areage for needed additions as they arise.

Thanks are rendered to Misses Adaline Marshall, Rita Putnam and Miss McMullan for their aid.

As the last word the writer will say, that there is but little in the pages of this "Handbook," that may not be found elsewhere, and it is difficult at times to avoid similarity of expression. Plagiarism is often charged to eminent writers. I have endeavored as far as possible to name the authority for some statements of facts; in others my own. "All of which I saw; part of which I was."

Edward C. Moody.

INDEX

----, Dustin 176 John 201 John H 176

ABBOTT, Dudley C 235 S C 169

ADAM, Old 227

ADAMS, Charles F 167 Ex-president 103 Ezekial 206 James 198 John 103 John Q 78 Joseph 59 M J 78 M Q 238 Mr 103 Philip 28 Richard 70 S Judson 76 Stephen 116

ADDITON, Mr 157

AGRICOLA, Emperor 26

ALBRA, George 206

ALCOCK, Job 30 52 105-106 John 28 Joseph 28 Samuel 28

ALDIS, Arthur T 117 250 Mr 177 Owen F 250

ALLEN, 54 M J 220 Mr 155 157 Mrs Samuel 177 Mrs Samuel Seabury 118 Pres 228 S W 148 Samuel S 177 Seabury W 117 Seabury Wells 132

AMES, Josiah 239

ANDERTON, Washington 177

ANDREWS, Geo C 234

ANDROS, Edmund 35

ANGIER, Sampson 28

ARMSTRONG, D N 127 Frank W 238

ASHBY, John L 219

ATKINS, J W 234 John 234

AUSTIN, Ezekiel 74 G Frank 90

AVERHILL, William 214

AVERHILLS, 40

AYER, F C 234 J B 167

BAILEY, Col 70 John 69 71

BAKER, 40 176 215 David 214 Edward W 105 108 Elias 159 Jotham 70 Rufus 72

BALL, Samuel 86

BANE, 40 Capt 188

BANGS, L Bolton 250

BANKS, 40 Charles 78 Charles H 74 E H 149 Edward H 105 108 Gen 76 George 78 John 114 116 John I 132

BANKS (Cont.)
Joseph 205 Mr 109 Mrs
John 114 Richard 28 Ross
78 W G 78
BARBOUR, George W 235
BARRELL, 40 Charles C 95
104 213 221 Charles
Colburn 93 J E 161 John E
149 Jonathan S 72 214
Nathaniel 104 Theodosia
165 William O 165
BARRON, Oliver 239 Rev Mr
239
BARTLETT, C P 240 Thomas
242
BARTLY, John M C 230
BARTNETT, Bartholmew 22
BATCHELDER, William 239
BAXTER, 81 153 James
Phinney 170
BEAL, Capt 59 John 71
Matthias 70 Theodore 116
BEAN, Insley A 235 Johnathan
83
BEANTON, George 28
BEARCE, 150 Mr 157
BEAVENS, William 240
BEDEL, John 71
BELKNAP, 24 Dr 20
BELLINGHAM, Richard 32
BERRY, George W 74 Joseph
72
BEVERLY, P L 242
BICKFORD, Stephen R 242
BIRD, George E 133
BISHOP, Louis F 117
BISSELL, Mr 111

BLAISDELL, 40 Bradford W
74 76 Capt 71 Charles F
132 161 E B 133 135 138
149 236 Edward B 93 115-
116 135 138-139 Elvira 76
George E 76 161 Joseph 74
76 Mr 133 Nicholas 71
Samuel T 165 William 74
BLAKE, H M 234
BLIASDELL, George 74
BLISS, 140 Alexander 177
BLOOD, Mr 177
BLOOME, Solomon 71
BOND, Nicholas 28
BONIGHTON, Richard 19-20
BOSTON, Isaiah 75 Joseph 60
Shubael 60
BOUNDS, James H 235
BOURNE, Capt 188 Judge 43
47
BOVARD, Wm S 235
BOWDEN, 40 A H 167 177
Armenius H 238 C A 75 C
L 161 Charles L 238 Fred
H 161 George 104-105
George G 108 Henry 75
Maffit W 176
BOYNTON, 153
BRACY, 40
BRADBURY, 40 Abigail 101
Bion 101 Cotton 101
Dorothy 101 James O 148
150 167 Jeremiah 101 105-
106 108 John 65 67 104
106 221 Joseph 104 Mary
Langdon 101 Messr 102 Mr
87 102 149 Thomas 101

BRAGDON, 40 228 A B 105 A
M 166 Abigail 101 Albert
M 117 120 167 Arthur 22
28 38 Arthur E 104 132
149 161 Arthur Jr 37
Arthur Sr 126 204 Charles
74 132 Daniel 65 70 101
104-105 Deacon 226-227 E
A 250 Edward A 105 108
Elihu 101 104 179 Henry S
133-134 136-138 149 161 J
P 137 James 101 James A
104 114 Jeremiah 221
Joseph 104-106 114 Joseph
Jr 104 Joseph P 122 131
133-134 136 138 147 149
161 165-166 Josiah 70 104
Josiah D 104 114 Mary 101
Messr 102 Mr 121 Samuel
Jr 54 Thomas 65 104 180-
181 William O 251
BRATHWAITHE, J Windsor
167
BRAWN, John 204
BREWER, Col 71
BREWSTER, 40 F Raymond
161 J S 74 James S 72 75
77-78 161 Moses 72 235
William H 75
BRIDGES, 40 Frank C 237 J C
177 Joseph C 161 Stephen
71
BRIGGS, Isaac 229
BRODBECK, Rev Dr 232
BROOKS, Col 70 Daniel 179-
180 Jeremiah 105 108 231
234 Mr 234

BROOKS (Cont.)
Soloman 179 232 Solomon
104 106
BROWN, E R 178 Elisha 246
BULMAN, Alexander 61
Doctor 61 Dr 248-249
BURBANK, Capt 71 Silas 70
BURDETT, George 21 Mr 216
BURDETTE, 45 George 43-44
BURGESS, Alexander 236
BURLEIGH, Mr 156 Mrs J H
177
BURRAGE, Dr 59
CADWALADER, John 250
CAME, 40 Arthur 204 Charles
104 Frank 74 Mary 101
Saml 221 Samuel 104-106
Small 126
CAMP, I B 238
CANNAROE, Mrs 177
CARD, J W 242 William B 147
CARLILE, Joseph 205
CARLISLE, Betsey 179 Daniel
179
CARPENTER, Eber 219 Mr
219
CARR, Moses 85-86
CARTER, Charles 177
CARTISLE, John 71
CASWELL, George 78
CELLARS, John 71
CENTER, Nathan D 234
Wilbur 74
CHADBOURNE, Alice 52
CHALK, Mrs R F 237 R F 237
CHAMBERLAIN, General 170
Joshua L 93 167

CHAMPERNOON, Francis 19-20
CHANDLER, Samuel 229
CHAPMAN, Charles H 74 Eben 91 Ebenezer 72
CHARLES, I King Of England 16 25 King Of England 15 21 29 Prince Of ? 16
CHASE, 40 Andrew L 230 Charles E 181 Cotton 104 181-182 239 241 John L 125 181 Joshua 239 Josiah 74-75 78 104 104 122 125 159 161 180-181 Mr 147-148 153-155 157 159-160 William 179 William H 116
CHAUNCEY, Elihu 236 250
CHENEY, George L 250 Knight D 250 Mrs George L 165-166 Russell 166
CHISHOLM, B Ogden 250 Mrs 251
CLARK, C O 105 Dorothy 101 Hannah 235 Jere 104 Jeremiah 214 Joe 232 Joseph S 232 Mr 232 Samuel 104 Thomas 215
CLARKE, Jeremiah 105 108 Thomas 88 Thos 84
CLAYTON, 21 35-36
CLEAVES, B F 148 Henry B 167
CLEMENS, Samuel L 167 172
CLEMENT, John 60
COCHIE, Joseph 74 Thomas 74
COCHRANE, 186 Jacob 185

CODAGON, Richard 28
COLBY, E K 234
COLCORD, 150
COLLINS, John 234
CONARROE, George M 237 Mrs George M 237
CONSTANTINE, The Great 26
CONWAY, William 71
CONY, David 103
COOK, 135 Dr 249 E C 132 Edward C 117 128 130 Edward Chase 249 Gideon 240 Mr 240 Rev Mr 240
COREY, J A 234
CORNISH, J 139
COTTLE, Charles W 175
COUCH, Will 70
COUNCILMAN, W T 177
COUSINS, O M 235
COX, G F 234 Gershom D 232 Mr 234 Myron F 124
CRANE, Mrs 233
CREELMAN, William 230
CROCKETT, Thomas 203
CROFT, Albert J 235
CROMWELL, 28-29 Oliver 25 William A 109
CUMMOCK, A G 167
CURRIER, 40 G W 144 George W 105 108 116 John C 175
CURTIS, Thomas 28
D'ESTE, Julian 250 Mr 177
DAHLGREN, Lieut 75
DANFORTH, Mr 34 Pres 30 35 Thomas 30 33 35
DARBY, Capt 70 Mary 70

DARBY (Cont.)
Samuel 69-70
DAVIDSON, Burleigh 166
Elizabeth B 120 James T
120 128-130 250 John 71
Mrs James T 165
DAVIS, John 28 30 33-34 John
2nd 28 Joseph E 177 250
Mrs 251 Nicholas 28
DAVISS, John 203
DELACHASSE, Rev Father
191
DENNETT, Alexander 104 232
Ellen M 166 232 John 74-
78 120 167 Mark 105 108
Miss 233
DENNY, Mrs 251
DERBY, Mary Ann 234
Samuel 104-105 108 213
DEWEY, George 75
DEXTER, George B 250
DICKSON, William 28
DISCO, Tommy 206
DISCOLL, Thomas 206
DIXON, John F 75
DOMINICK, H B 250 H
Blanchard 236
DOMONICK, H B 177
DONALD, William L 230
DONIEL, Saml 27
DONIGAN, 153
DONNELL, 40 73 150 215
Alice 52 Capt 206 Frances
51 G A 161 George 233
Hannah 52 Henry 28 51 72
James 60 70 199 233
Jonathan 70

DONNELL (Cont.)
Nathaniel 51-52 54 60 222
Obadiah 214 Rufus 74-75
77 215 Samll 204 Samuel
38 51-52 104-106 Theodore
206 Thomas 28 28 54 204
Timothy 71
DOTSON, Sergeant 60
DOUBLEDAY, Mrs F 165
DOW, Henry 75-76 Moses 219
Mr 219
DOWNING, Stephen 232
DRAKE, Samuel G 224
DRURY, John M 77
DUDLEY, 35 John 74 Joseph
34
DUMMER, Gov 209 Mr 216
Shubael 34 37 49 216
DUNCAN, Mr 230 Thomas 229
DUSTIN, Charles P 161
EASTMAN, Caleb 221 248
EATON, 153 James P 247
EDGE, Robert 28
EDWARDS, A E 240
EFFINGHAM, Will 45
ELDREDGE, Rev Mr 245
ELIOT, John 194
ELLINGHAM, William 28
ELLIS, 176 F H 177 238 Frank
H 148 166 Romie M 238
EMERSON, 40 A L 78 Abigail
114 Andrew L 74-75 77
215 Buckley 214 Charles O
91 104 231 Constance 166
E O 166 Edward 56 213-
214 223 Edward O 122 165
177 250

EMERSON (Cont.)
Frank P 95 215 221 Frank
Phillips 93 Joseph 51 62
216 Mary 51 Mrs 233
EMERY, 153 G Alex 198
Samuel 248
EMMONS, Willis T 132
EVANS, 111 H E 175 Henry E
110 115
EVELETH, C H 240
EVERETT, Andrew 28
FACUNDUS, Abraham 71
FARNAM, Frank 222
FARNHAM, Augustus B 167
FARRAGUT, 77
FARWELL, A C 149 161
Isaiah 110 Mr 110
FELLOWS, Oscar E 148 150
FERDINANDO, Sir 20-23 27
29-30 44
FERNALD, John B 92 95 215
Mark 242 William H 174
FERNANDO, Sir 25
FFROST, Jno 81
FITZGERALD, David 52-53
74 77 King David 52-53
Patrick 52-53
FLANDERS, W B 242
FLETCHER, William 240
FOGG, John 167
FOLSOM, Harold M 24
FORSAITH, Sarah A 43
Thomas 43
FOSS, 111
FOSTER, Enoch 134 J 230
FOX, Charles W 250 Mrs 251
FREATHER, William 28

FREATHY, Sam 200
FREEMAN, 40 215 George M
104 John 70 John Jr 70
John W 74 78 John Wesley
75 Joseph 230 Mr 126
Nathaniel 126
FRENCH, Moses 176
FROST, Charles 34 William
179
FRYE, William P 167
FURBISH, Timothy 116
GALE, Hugh 28
GALLAHER, P T 240
GARDE, Roger 22
GARDNER, F H 240
GARFIELD, Frank L 220
GARRISON, 175
GATCHELL, Zachariah 70
GAYL, Hugh 45
GEORGE, Ii King Of Great
Britain 58 Josiah 60 The
Third King Of England 64
GERRISH, Christopher P 248
Dr 249
GIBSON, John 70 Mr 24 216
Richard 24
GILMAN, Dr 248-249 Josiah
248 Lyman 248
GLENN, John 215
GODDARD, Alvin C 235 John
174 Samuel 174
GODFREY, 26 Edward 19-22
25 28 32 203 Mr 25
GOLDER, Arthur L 230
GOMSEY, William 28
GOOCH, John 28 44 Ruth 44
GOODALE, C A 149

GOODMAN, Sharon 13
GOODRICH, Mary C 177 Mrs 251
GOODWIN, 40 215 Abiel 86-87 221 Asahel 213 Charles A 74 Charles E 242 E E 236 Francis 72 George 175 Harmon 237 Ichabod 202 Ivory L 74 Mr 213 Mrs Charles 174
GOOLD, Nathan 70
GORGES, 23 25-26 29 32 45 Ferdinando 7-8 12 15-19 31 Fernando 30 Gov 20-21 Thomas 19-20 22 44 Thos 16 William 18
GORMAN, James P 246-247 Rev Mr 247
GOSS, John A 242
GOUGH, W N 238
GOWELL, 153
GOWEN, A W 135 Angevine E 138
GRANGER, Justice 186
GRANT, 40 Charles A 114 120 176 Charles L 74 77 149 161 John P 74 77 110 Joseph 28 69 Lowell S 132 Mr 176 Mrs 175 Mrs Stephen 174 Peter 71 Stephen 174 W L 161 William 110 William H 116
GRAVES, Joseph H 245
GREELEY, Horace 124
GREENLEAF, Eben S 245 John 87-88
GRISCOM, 28

GROVE, Mrs Henry S 251
GROVER, Benjamin 214 Eleakon 223 Henry 115-116 245
GROW, 40 Capt 199 Edward 65 69 104 Hannah 233
HAINER, E A 243 John 239
HAINS, Samuel 69
HALE, Col 87 Edward E 17 Eugene 167
HALEY, George F 148 Newbury 182
HALL, Abner 242 T M 235
HALLORAN, Daniel 234
HAM, Freeman 177
HAMILTON, 153 Alexander 108 Benjamin F 144 Henry 230 Mr 157 Senator 147 151
HAMLIN, 150
HAMMOND, Dr 112 Evan B 111 175
HANCOCK, John 67 Mr 204
HANDENBURGH, Henry J 236
HANNIBAL, 99
HARKER, John 203
HARMON, 40 191 Benjamin 59 Capt 59-61 188 190 Charles H 249 Hannah 214 John 39 59 220-221 Johnson 60 104 188 William 214 Zebulon 214
HARRIS, Daniel B 104
HASEY, Benjamin 42
HASTINGS, 153 Lyman 177
HATCH, A 234

HATCH (Cont.)
John L 77 Philip 28
HAVEN, John 91 219 Mr 219
HAWKES, Dr 249 E C 161
Edward C 124 Joseph 234
Mrs 248 W L 250 Wilson L
92 117 125 177 248
HAYS, James 60
HAZEN, Dr 249 Jasper J 78
117 248
HEATH, Gen 70
HETHERS, Robert 28
HILDRETH, Charles 78 W C
238 Will C 149
HILL, 153 John T 75 Joseph
74 M 234
HILLMAN, A P 234
HILTON, Eliakin 69 William
28 204
HIRST, Mary 228
HOBSON, E F 167 Edwin A
132 Ernest F 122
HOGARTH, W H 132 147 149
William H 148 177
HOLLAND, Daniel 175
HOLMAN, Morris 230
HOLMES, G D 234
HOLT, Joseph 41 54 65 220-
221
HONNEWELL, Richard 204
HOOKE, Francis 33-34
William 19-20
HOOKER, John 28
HOOPER, Charles H 74 Noah
Jr 240 William 74
HOTCHKISS, A 234
HOWARD, William R 125

HOWELLS, William Dean 167
HOWES, 153
HUBBARD, Charles E 250
Charles Eustis 167 250
John 240 Mrs 251 T 84 87
HULL, Joseph 216 Mr 216
HUNGERFORD, Mrs 165
HUSSEY, Henry C 147
HUTCHINS, 40 215 Charles
211 Charles I 105 George H
75 Joseph 214 Mary 211
William 211
HUTCHINSON, 135
HYDE, Thomas Dewitt 167
INDIAN, Aspinquid 193
Asseomet 196 Bomasun
190 Bomazeen 188 Job 190
Mogg 190 Wissemenent
190
INGRAHAM, Col 50 Lydia 41
IRVING, 153
ISERAL, William P 245
JACKSON, Michael 70 Pres 42
JACOBS, Wells 183
JACQUES, 190
JAMES, Ii King Of England 34
King Of ? 17
JEFFERSON, Mr 67-68
Thomas 64 68
JENKYNS, Ebenezer 230
JOCELYN, Henry 20 Thomas
19
JOHNSON, Edward 22 28 32
James 47
JONES, Frank 111 H C 177 Mr
111-112
JORDAN, Dominicus 24

JORDAN (Cont.)
Ichabod 186 Jedidiah 24
Jeremiah 24 John 24 Olive
101 Robert 24 Samuel 24
Sarah 24
JOSELIN, Henry 19
JUNKINS, 40 Andrew W 109
Charles 104 114 Charles H
132 165 Charles W 129-
130 Chas H 123 J Howard
149 John 78 Joseph P 91
105 108 Luther 105 108 Mr
111 226 Olive 187 Robert
28 Samuel 106 186-187
Samuel W 104 111 122 132
140 148 250 Washington
92 94 105
KEEN, Hampden C 74
Theodore 175
KEENE, Frank 78 Hampden C
78 John D 78 W T 166-167
Will T 78 William T 165
KELLOGG, 153 Senator 150
KELLY, J D J 250
KENDALL, S F 240
KENNY, Mrs 177
KENT, George H 245 Mr 245
KIMBALL, Ruel H 234
KING, Gov 101 William 103
William Bruce 167
KINGSBURY, 40 Capt 233
Hannah 233 John 60 65
Joseph 214
KNIGHT, L B 234 Robert 28
KNOWLTON, 153
KOMURA, Baron 117
LANGDON, Elizabeth 56

LANGDON (Cont.)
Paul 91 Woodbury 167
LANKTON, Samuel 229
LATHROP, Barbour 250 Bryan
117 177 250 Mrs Bryan 251
LAWRENCE, B F 240
LEAVITT, 60
LEE, Eugene 78 James 231
LEOPOLD, L D 60
LEWIS, 28 Joshua 175 Josiah
W 175
LINCOLN, Benj 87 William H
177 236 250
LITTLEFIELD, J Albion 243
Joseph E 74
LOONEY, 153 Deputy
Collector 107
LORD, 40 Augustus 215 Dr
175 Frank 174 George W
75 Henry C 174-175 Isaac
232 234 Jerry 214 233 John
233 Joseph 174 Mr 175 233
Nathan 174 Nathaniel 239
Pres 174 Samuel 214
William H 174 William P
234
LORING, Thatcher 250
LOUD, John J 167
LOUIS, Xiv King Of France 58
Xv King Of France 58
LOWE, 153 Capt 215 Edward
233 John M 74 78 John
Moore 76 Joseph 108 233
LUCAS, Benjamin 72
LUFKIN, Benjamin 235
LUNT, 40 A R 235 Alfred 215
Capt 215 Horace 75-76 78

LUNT (Cont.)
   Samuel 56 214 Skipper 72
LYMAN, 214 Abigail 55
   Doctor 56 Isaac 55-56 104
   218 Job 55 248 Mary 232
   Moses 55 105 Mr 218-219
   223 Rev Mr 184 229
MABEN, B S 242
MACE, J M 240
MACOMBER, 153 H M 234
MADISON, Pres 42
MAFFIT, John Newland 231
   Mr 231 234
MAIN, George B 161
MANSON, Joseph W 75
   William H 75
MANVEL, Anna F 177
MARSHALL, Adaline T 109
   Adaline Talpey 107 E S
   150 177 Edward S 92-93 95
   104 106 110-111 119-120
   122 124 128-130 148 155
   158 161 167 176 Frank D
   27 31 37 60 72 88 120 122
   135 165-166 250 Fred W
   119 George E 105 108-109
   122 165 H B 240 Katherine
   E 165 Mr 21 25-26 30 32
   98 111-112 153-157 161 N
   G 27 67 204 Nathaniel G
   21 32 36 98 105-106 108
   176 250 Samuel B 176
MASON, Hartley W 125 Hartly
   177 John 17 William 175
MASSEURE, Francis 234
MATHEWS, 40
MATTHEWS, 215

MAY, Joseph 177
MCCULLUM, Albert G 78
MCDONALD, James 69
MCICNTIRE, Messr 102
MCINTIRE, 28 40 Alex 55
   Alexander 54-55 104-106
   108 179 Asa 104 182
   Daniel H 75 78 Edgar 55
   Edgar A 54 105 Jere L 78
   Jeremiah 55 97 147 167
   232 250 Jeremiah L 75
   John 55 230 Major General
   99 Malcolm 42 149 161
   165 Micom 39 Micum 54
   200 248 Micum 1st 54-55
   Micum 2nd 54 Micum 3rd
   54 Thornton 75 William
   104 106
MCKENNA, Justice 166
MCKIE, Sergeant 77
MCKOWEN, Austin 238
MCLUCAS, 40 Joshua 70
MCMASTER, Daniel 240
MERCER, W R Jr 250
MERRILL, 111 150 Isaac 240
MERROW, Almon H 114
MESSENGER, Rev Mr 73
MESSINGER, Roswell 219
MILLBURY, Richard 104 126
   221 Samuel 54 221-222
MILLIKEN, 153
MINOTT, 153
MITCHEL, Henry 176
MITCHELL, E E E 138 161
   Edward E E 138 176
   Horace 47 John 234 John M
   246 Lemuel 114-115

MONSON, David 60
MOODY, 26 40 226 Caleb 48
    Charles 72 91 215 223
    Charles C P 224 E C 129
    Edward C 25 92-93 95 98
    105-106 112 116 135 166-
    167 193 207 Father 31 50-
    51 62 217-218 225 Geo
    214 George 174 215
    Handkerchief 224 Hannah
    51 Isaiah P 127 174 Joseph
    50-51 62 105 208 216 224-
    225 227-229 Joseph H 230
    Judge 225 Juliette 177 Lucy
    51 228 Lydia 31 42 Mary
    51 Master 127 207 209-210
    Matilda 175 Mr 39 50-51
    62-63 90 168 209 217-218
    221-225 227-228 Mrs 223
    Samuel 31 38 42 48 51 62
    105 127 207-208 217-218
    221 223 225 228 231
    Thomas 228 William 48
    William H 167
MOORE, 40 Edward 69 Fred
    177 George 72 John 234 Mr
    157 William 28
MORE, William 203
MOREY, 153
MORGAN, Reuben B 238
MOSELEY, C B 177
MOSES, T G 242
MOULTON, 40 190-191 Abel
    222 Abigail 55 Albert 75
    78 Allen C 105 243
    Augustus F 167 Capt 69
    188-189 Daniel 65 67 105

MOULTON (Cont.)
    Danl 87 Jeremiah 37 56 59
    61 104-106 221-222 237
    Jeremiah Jr 106 Johnson 68
    106 Johnson B 116 Joseph
    126 Jotham 106 Leon S 237
    Mrs 233 William Gardner
    243 Willis G 132
MUGRIDGE, John H 245
MULLEN, 153
NASON, Shubael 71
NEAL, William J 166
NEELY, Bishop 236 Henry
    Adams 237
NEWMAN, William J 219
NICHOLS, H T 148 Humphrey
    177
NILES, Mr 87
NOBLE, Charles F 78 161 251
    Mrs 251
NORTON, 40 Addison G 116
    Daniel 239 Francis 18
    George 116 214 235 H H
    134 Harry H 131 133 136-
    138 149 161 165 Henry 28
    32 79 106 John 235 Josiah
    116 Josiah N 161 165 237
    Jotham P 213 Oliver 241
NORWOOD, Henry D 174 221
    John E 125 159-160 177
NOWELL, 40 Abraham 105
    James H 230 Peter 104
NUTTER, Mrs 201
O'BRIEN, Denis J 247
O'DONNELL, Bernard 246
OAKES, Abner 177
ODIORNE, A A 161

OFT, Mr 42
OSBORNE, J 87 J S 240
OSGOOD, 153
PADDOCK, Benjamin H 236
PAGE, Mrs Thomas Nelson 117 Thomas Nelson 117 158 167 172 177 236 250
PALMER, Charles Ray 167
PARKER, Clement 230 George 28-29 John 28 Mary 56 William W 220
PARSONS, 40 C V 242 Frank E 238 J Arthur 149 161 John 220 Joseph 69 Josiah 70 Mrs George F 177
PARTRIDGE, Samuel H 230
PATCH, Daniel 75
PATTANGALL, Mr 156
PATTEN, William A 220
PATY, Thomas 47
PAUL, Florence 165 J B 238 Samuel F 147 149
PAYNE, 40 Elder 245 George M 104 George Moore 245 Samuel E 104
PEARCE, Stephen 86
PEASE, B 240
PEEL, William 77
PEIRCE, Stephen 80-83 85
PENDEXTER, Lewis W 132
PENDLETON, B 33 Brian 34
PEPPER, John W 250
PEPPEREL, Gen 62 Mrs 61
PEPPERELL, Capt 228 Col 58-59 Gen 52 61 William 58-59 221 228 William Sr 38

PERKINGS, John 70 Spencer 69
PERKINS, 215 Elizabeth 165 Mary 211 Mr 218 221 Mrs Newton 117 177 Sidney K 172 220 Sidney Kingman 217 Stover 201
PETERS, F A 250 Francis A 147 177 Mr 156-157
PHILBRICK, C 234 H D 78 107 109 149 Henry R 175 Herbert D 105 108 130
PHILIP, King Of ? 191
PHILIPS, John 71 Rev Mr 216
PHILLIPS, 175 E B 110 George 235 James A 242 James R 245 Mr 110
PICKERIN, John 38
PICKERING, Capt 204 Misses 177-178
PIERCE, 28 John 54 Mr 54
PILLSBURY, O S 235 W H 234
PLAISTED, 40 87 Charles W 132 Francis 232 G F 136 George F 105 123 132-133 161 165-166 204 Henry 165 James 105 204-205 John F 114 165 237 Jos 83 Joseph 80-85 88 104 116 Mr 123 Sheriff 86
PLATTS, H A 240 Harry A 238
PLUMBERY, Oliver 71
POND, Benjamin W 220
POOLE, Solomon 75
PORTER, Billy 70

POTTER, Dr 111 F E 111
POWELL, William 75
PRAY, Joseph 204
PREBBLE, Abraham Jr 204
Benjamin 204
PREBLE, 40 Abra M 126
Abraham 28-32 41 70 104-
105 225 Abraham Jr 31 106
Abraham M 38 Charles D
75 Charles Donnell 76 Col
42 Daniel 69-70 Ebenezer
225-226 Edward 43 Esaias
41 223 Esais 104 George F
78 Hannah 41 52 225 J
Howard 165 John 52 Judge
42-43 200 Judith 41 Lieut
31 Lydia 31 41-42 Nancy
Gale 43 Oliver 235 S A 149
Samuel 41 Samuel A 166
Sarah 41 Sarah A 43
Stephen 27 William 70
William P 43 William Pitt
42 224 Zebulon 60
PREPLE, Abra M 126
PRESCOTT, Col 70
PRIBBLE, Abraham 71
PRICE, Arthur J 235 Mrs S E
251
PRINCE, Ceaser 71
PUDDINGTON, George 22 44
Mary 44
PUTMAN, Jeremiah S 248
PUTNAM, 40 Dr 109 249 Gen
70 George 215 George W S
104 J Perley 122 131 133-
138 165-166 Jeremiah S
105 108 Ruth 165

PUTNAM (Cont.)
W S 149 177 William 215
RAINS, Francis 203
RALE, 188-190 Father 191
RAMSDELL, Charles H 75 78
Joshua 60 Paul R 75
Timothy 235
RANDALL, Daniel B 234
RAWSON, T 234
RAYNES, 40 Francis 29 60
George 177
READING, Frances 51
Thomas 51
REDDING, William H 75
REED, Thomas B 167 171
REID, William 240
REMICK, 213
REYNOLDS, 153
RICE, John 234
RICHMOND, P C 234
RISWORTH, 40 Edward 28-34
104 216 Miss 216 Susan 31
ROBBINS, Gilbert 240
ROBINSON, Elder 242 George
M 116
RODGERS, Ezekiel 104
ROGERS, John 22 William 29
ROLLINS, Frank W 167
RONALDO, Capt 77
Commander 77
ROPES, John C 236
ROWE, Moses 75
RUTLEGE, Archibald 71
SAFFORD, Moses 223 242
Moses A 175 248
SAMPSON, Henry 250
SANBORN, William H 175

SARGEANT, Dr 222
SARGENT, Charles 70 Daniel
  70 Dr 248-249 Nathaniel
  232
SAVAGE, 25 J W 235 Thomas
  104-105
SAWYER, Abraham 71
  Charles H 178 R M 197
  Rufus M 17 49 220
SAYWARD, 213 Charles E 47
  Charles H 116 176 Henry
  45 70 John 222 Jonathan
  59-60 104 Jonathon 221
  Joseph 39 Mary 48
SAYWORD, 46 Henry 45 47
SCAMMON, 69 James 70
SCHOFIELD, O B 78
SCOTT, Orange W 234
SCOTTAN, Joshua 33
SCREVINE, William 104
SEAVEY, William 214
SEWALL, 40 Arthur E 166
  177 Capt 60 222 Daniel
  106 223 David 56 97 104-
  106 David B 169 220 E A
  78 Edward 177 Elizabeth
  56 Elizabeth T 166 Frank
  56 165 173 Freeman 166
  Hannah 51 Henry 70 J Alba
  77 John 51 Joseph 221
  Joseph A 75 Judge 173
  Major 54 Mary 56 Mr 220
  Nicholas 90 Rachel K 166
  Samuel 53 214 220-222
SEYMOUR, 89 John 201-202
SHATTUCK, Edward 238 H L
  238 Mr 177 N H 166

SHATTUCK (Cont.)
  Nathaniel B 130
SHAW, 153
SHEA, Edward 78
SHERBURNE, Andrew 239
SHIRLEY, Gov 58 W 88
  William 82 84
SHORT, Hezekiah 242
SIBLY, Clark 240
SILLOWAY, 93
SIMONDS, N C 238
SIMPSON, 40 D Webster 75
  Daniel W 75 George 214
  George H 132 George M
  120 147 George O 75
  Henry 22 83 198 Ivory 72 J
  P 111 114 J W 134 150
  Jeremiah P 111 120 125
  Joseph 64 104-106 Joseph
  Jr 221 Joseph W 104 106
  120 133-138 148 165 177
  W J 166 Willard J 177
SITER, E H 117 236
SMILEY, G E M 127
SMITH, 153 Capt 17 Elias 242
  244 Frank W 117 248-249
  J R 235 James D 167 John
  16 220 Mary Louise 165 Mr
  154 157 Pres 168 171
  Walter M 122 165-166 168
  250
SNOW, 135
SPAULDING, J 231
STACY, William 72
STAPLES, 111 153 John E 92
  95 104 110 221
STARKEY, Lorenzo 201

START, Edward 29
STEPHENSON, Ensign 77
STETSON, Francis L 158
    Francis Lynde 122 158 167
    171 236 Henry 240 Mr 158
    171-172
STEVENS, Daniel A 77 I H
    234 W C 234
STEWART, Charles 75 78 Dr
    148 249 J C 148 150 John
    C 106 110-111 122 128-
    130 134-135 137-138 143
    161 166 169 238 John
    Conant 248
STONE, Benjamin 222 John 65
    Samuel 230
STORER, Mary Langdon 101
    Olive 101 Seth 101
    Sylvester 29
STOVER, Hiram D 75 Obadiah
    235 Sylvester 203
STROUT, Mr 233 William H
    233-234
SULLIVAN, R G 177 Roger G
    246
SUTTON, John 71
SWEET, John 61
SWETT, 40 Dr 222 Edward 69
    Gardner 116 John 104
    Joseph 215 222 248
    William H 104
SYLVESTER, Edward J 77
SYMONDS, 135
TABER, Sidney R 177
TAFT, Pres 107
TAKAHIRA, Count 117
TALPEY, 40 Appleton H 72

TALPEY (Cont.)
    Betsey 179 Henry 235
    Jonathan 72 179 215 235
    241 R F 149 Richard 235
    Richard F 104
TAPP, Mary 29
TAPPAN, Frederick H 250
TAYLER, Dr 175
TERRY, John 242
THERRIAULT, 153 Mr 150
    152 Patrick 148
THOMPSON, 40 Capt 99
    Edward S 161 John S 55
    Joseph 72 Mr 216 Rev Mr
    25
TITCOMB, William P 116 243
TODD, John F 116 147
TOLMAN, Capt 102
TOOKER, J A 240
TOWER, Charles B 236
TRAFTON, 40 Alvah 116 237
    Benjamin 70 Charles 248
    Thomas 204
TRASK, James H 234
TREVETT, Richard 105 108
TRIPP, L L 240
TUCKER, Joseph 43 104-105
    108 Nancy Gale 43 Pres
    171 W J 167
TUPPER, Col 71
TURISDEN, John Jr 29
TURPREY, Moses 104
TWOMBLEY, Edwin D 166
TWOMBLY, E D 78 Edwin D
    124
UPHAM, 183
VARNEY, 150

VARRELL, 40 176 Fremont 104 161 Harmon 75 78 John 214 John H 78 125
VERMEULE, Mr 177
VINAL, R J 177
VINES, Capt 17 Richard 19-20
VOLIVA, W G 242
VOSES, Col 71
WALKER, 153 Albert B 75 Albert R 75 Charles W 75-77 Clarissa 76 John H 75-76 Richard 76 W M 177 Wilson M 75-76 78 92 95 114 120 165-167 250
WALLINGFORD, Zimri S 175
WALTON, Elizabeth 85-86 Geo 86 George 85 Saml 82-83 86-88 Samll 82-83 Samuel 80-81 84-85
WARREN, 153 James 116
WASHBURN, George D 177 Ichabod 245
WASHINGTON, 64 71 Pres 108
WATTS, Dr 169
WEARE, 40 215 Charles 133 Charles E 134-138 Chas E 136 Daniel 165 Edward 177 James 214 James Sr 206 Jeremiah 69 239 John F 75-76 Joseph 204 Joseph Jr 104 Peter 29 104 Theodore 177
WEBB, Lindley M 125
WEBBER, 40 Daniel 69 David 239 George 235 Joseph 60 Nathaniel 104 Paul 70

WEBBER (Cont.) Samuel 104 108 241
WELCH, Charles 75 E A 147 Ellen M 136 Irene 201 John F 75 Luther D 75 Samuel 235
WELLS, Edwin D 245
WENSTOME, Edward 29
WENTWORTH, M F 175 Mark F 76
WESLEY, Charles 231 John 231
WEST, George F 119
WESTON, J 234
WHEELER, 153
WHEELWRIGHT, Capt 71 Daniel 70 S 34 Susan 31 Thomas 29
WHIDDEN, C C 235
WHITE, John 228 Lucy 228
WHITEFIELD, George 231
WHITNEY, Dr 222 248 Joseph 245
WHITTIER, 175
WHITTLE, Thomas A 116
WIDEY, Judge 102
WIGGLESWORTH, Col 71
WILCOX, David 101-102 108
WILLIAM, Sir 63
WILLIAMSON, 20-22 188 James 70
WILSON, Charles H 78 Joel 105 108 245 John 230 Mr 245 Rev Mr 245 Theodore 104 William 251
WINCOTT, John 33
WINN, Fred G 166 Joseph 75

WINN (Cont.)
  Timothy 215
WINTER, Sarah 24
WITTE, Count 117
WOODBURY, John M 234
WOODWARD, Bradford S 105
  115-116 147 149 161
  George 116 John E 78
  Joseph 116 William H 75
WOODWELL, George M 220
  230
WORTHEN, Mr 177
WRIGHT, James 234 Rev Mr
  232 William 174

WYER, Peter 29
WYMAN, 153
YATES, F 234
YEOMANS, C J 242
YOUNG, 40 C H 149 Charles
  H 132-138 Chas H 136
  Daniel 60 Ebenezer 71
  Edward E 116 John 69 John
  S 238 Joseph 126 Mary 243
  Mr 134 Nathaniel 70 Peter
  242-243 Rowland 29 243
  Samuel 174 Samuel P 92
  105 Stephen 69 Timothy
  175